By Christopher Dow

Fiction
Effigy
> Book I: Stroud
> Book II: Oakdale

The Books of Bob
> Devil of a Time
> Jumping Jehovah

The Clay Guthrie Mysteries
> The Dead Detective
> Landscape with Beast
> The Texas Troll Unlimited
> Darkness Insatiable

Roadkill
The Werewolf and Tide, and Other Compulsions

Nonfiction
Lord of the Loincloth (nonfiction novel)
Book of Curiosities: Adventures in the Paranormal
Occasional Pilgrimage: Essays on Film, Literature, and Other Matters
Living the Story: The Meandering Adventures of an Unknown Writer
> Vol. I: Growing Up Takes a Long Time
> Vol. II: Growing Old Takes Longer

Martial Arts
The Wellspring: An Inquiry into the Nature of Chi
Circling the Square: Observations on the Dynamics of Tai Chi Chuan
Elements of Power: Essays on the Art and Practice of Tai Chi Chuan
Alchemy of Breath: An Introduction to Chi Kung
Leaves on the Wind: A Survey of Martial Arts Literature (Vol. I–VI)

Poetry
City of Dreams
The Trip Out
Texas White Line Fever
Networks
A Dilapidation of Machinery
Puzzle Pieces: Selected Poems

Editor
The Abby Stone: The Poetry of Bartholo Dias
The Best of Phosphene
The Best of Dialog

I0638805

Occasional Pilgrimage

Occasional Pilgrimage

Essays on Film, Literature, and Other Matters

Christopher Dow

Phosphene Publishing Company
Temple, Texas

Occasional Pilgrimage: Essays on Film, Literature, and other Matters
© 2021 by Christopher Dow
ISBN 13: 978-1-7369307-0-0

Published by
Phosphene Publishing Company
Temple, Texas, U.S.A.
phosphenepublishing.com

Versions of the following articles have appeared elsewhere:

"Down the Bayou" originally appeared in *Texas Journey*, Nov.–Dec. 1998.

"Out of the Blue" originally appeared in the fall 1995 issue of *Sallyport: The Magazine of Rice University*.

"Private Snafu's Hidden War: A Historical Survey and Analytical Perspective" originally appeared in *Bright Lights Film Journal*, Issue 42 (www.brightlightsfilm.com).

"The Ultimate Chicken" originally appeared in *Phosphene* (Vol. I, #2, 1978) and is reprinted in *The Best of Phosphene*.

For
Ditto Davis

Contents

Part III: Other Matters

Occasional Pilgrimage

About the Cover

OCCASIONALLY I DABBLE WITH VISUAL art, but not much—
I simply haven't had the time or energy during the past few
decades. Art takes both and so does writing, and I chose
writing. As an artist, my forte is collage, but I also enjoy
painting. I like paint. I like smearing it and daubing it and
blending it and experimenting with it. I like its smell. During
my "artistic career," I've actually sold a few pieces, paintings
as well as collage, and if you want to buy one, I have more
for sale, so get in touch.

But my purpose here isn't to operate an ersatz art gallery.
Instead, I want to tell you about the painting pictured on the
cover and what happened to it. It's called, appropriately
enough, *Wildfire*, and it's 20" x 24", enamel on masonite. I
painted it in 1981, and there is a good chance that the person who now possesses it thinks it's worth a lot more than it
really is.

In 1984, a colleague and I started a video production
company, and that kind of enterprise is about as time- and
energy-consuming as you can get. Although we often oper-
ated on shoestring budgets, we managed to eke out a sketchy
living for five years before I returned to my first love, publishing. Those five years spanned a time during which our
home city of Houston was in the throes of a crash in the oil
industry, and times were tough. In the midst of that local-

ized depression, I would have gladly sold more of my art than I actually did.

After about two years, my partner and I joined forces with another small-time video producer. Or should I say, studio owner. My partner and I were creative but had very little equipment, and this fellow had lots of equipment and a studio, but no creativity. It was a good match, at least at first, but I won't go into the details of how our little enterprise eventually disintegrated. Suffice it to say that soon after my original partner and I moved our operation to the studio, we realized that it needed a bit of sprucing up. He suggested that I bring in some of my artwork to hang on the walls. I liked the idea. Even if I wasn't selling it, at least people would see it. Among the four pieces I hung was *Wildfire*.

The studio actually consisted of two studio spaces—one larger and one smaller, each with its own glass-fronted control room. We occupied the larger space and rented out the smaller space to a small production company that produced local programming. We were on good terms with the people who ran this other production company, and we occasionally hired their personnel as crew on shoots that required more than the five people we had in our own company, and we worked on some of their projects, as well. But even if we liked and trusted them, you never could tell what sort of client might walk through their door—or our door, either, for that matter. Low-rent video draws all kinds of oddballs, fly-by-nighters, and sleazoids as well as the honest and upright. Incidentally, we were cheated by lawyers more often than by any other type of client, and the cheapest client we ever had was one of the wealthiest doctors in a city full of wealthy doctors.

One of our clients was a pretty famous car dealer who owned a dozen or more dealerships, mostly in Texas and California. I won't name names, but he wore a big cowboy hat and had a dog in most of his commercials. We didn't do his major commercials—those for new cars. We were the second string, and we shot the used car commercials. He ran a different one each week, and we'd shoot two, back-to-back, in one afternoon every two weeks. Or rather, I shot them because I managed to master the funky panning technique required.

This was the way these commercials worked: On the morning of the appointed day, the lot's car jockeys would line up the ten used cars the company planned to feature in the first of the two commercials. This row was located in the back lot, with the dealership building in the background. The cars, even the cheap ones, always looked so nice and neat and shiny sitting in their row. That's because they'd just been washed and waxed. What television viewers didn't see, however, was that about half of them had to be pushed into position, and the dealership had a tire repairman on hand to replace flats that wouldn't remain inflated long enough to shoot the footage.

These cars were lined up in a particular order that corresponded to descriptions on a prerecorded voice-over audio tape that the car dealer, who lived in California, would send to the manager of the Houston dealership. The descriptions went something like, "Look at these great deals! Here's a 1981 Chevy Nova with factory air, only $2,999. And how about this 1979 Dodge Dart, fully loaded, only $3,199! Or this Ford Pinto...," and so on until all the cars had been described. To reinforce the great deal, the price of each car was laid out in large red numerals on its windshield. The big, bright lettering helped mask any crack in the windshield glass.

My task was to synchronize the camera with the prerecorded spiel, and although I mastered it, it wasn't easy at first. The dealership manager would bring up a nice late-model used pickup truck with a sliding rear window from the lot, and I'd load my camera on its tripod in the bed. Then, the manager would slowly drive the pickup along the lane in front of the line of used cars, playing the taped spiel through the open sliding window, and I'd have to quickly but smoothly pan from car to car as we passed them, keeping each in frame just long enough for its description to play before quickly but smoothly jumping to the next. All this while trying to keep the tripod—and myself—from jerking, tilting, or tipping out of the bed as the pickup rolled over irregularities in the pavement.

We'd usually do three takes, and then I'd sit around and wait for half an hour or so while lot jockeys moved the first line of cars and replaced them with a second. Then, with a second audio tape playing, we'd do it all over. When we were done, I'd give the video tapes to the manager, who sent them to the dealer owner in California, who had the editing and postproduction done there. Then, for the next couple of weeks, I'd see my nifty camerawork on TV, and soon after that, a check would come in the mail.

One day while I was off on one of these shoots, a group of visitors came to the studio to participate in a shoot by the production company that rented the smaller studio space. While the visitors were there, one of them, a middle-aged woman, commented that she liked *Wildfire* and asked if it was for sale. One of my colleagues stupidly quipped that it was by a famous artist and was worth $10,000. That price was apparently too high for the woman's budget, and that seemed that. When I returned from the car lot, long after the visitors had left the studio and passed into anonymity, my colleagues told me about the encounter.

They thought it was funny, but as you can imagine, I was somewhat pissed. If my colleague hadn't been so quick to joke but had gotten the woman's name, I may have been able to sell *Wildfire* to her for a few hundred much-needed bucks. As it was, all I had was the vague satisfaction that someone had been interested enough in one of my pieces to inquire about its price, but praise doesn't pay the bills.

The next morning, I was feeling a little more mellow about the affair. After all, praise isn't entirely worthless, and validation is encouragement that future sales might be in the offing as well as the notion that my art—at least this piece—was admired by someone. As I passed *Wildfire* in the hall, I looked at it a little more lovingly and thought, yeah, it's not so bad. Little did I know that would be the last time I ever laid eyes on it.

Several busy days passed during which we spent most of the time on location shoots, and I wasn't seeing much of anything besides video images and the roads between locations. When I finally had time to notice that anything was different about the studio, I saw that the wall where *Wildfire* had been hanging was bare.

My painting had been stolen.

Generally, when people are robbed, they become upset. That's the way I've felt two of the three times I've been burglarized. The third time, I had insurance, and got all new stuff while the burglars got a bunch of old crap, so I didn't feel so bad that time. But the theft of *Wildfire* was different. It made me feel good. It made me laugh. I liked the painting, but I like even more the idea that someone out there stole it thinking it was painted by a famous artist and is worth $10,000. I hope they have it in a nice, expensive frame hanging in a prominent location in their home. I hope they brag about its value to their friends, or at least feel smug that they are big-time art thieves.

So, if you happen to see *Wildfire* in someone's home or business, please don't let on that the current owner is deceived. I'd hate to see my tiny moment of fame shrivel as suddenly as a dotcom stock. I want them to continue thinking that a Christopher Dow original is valuable. And if you're reading this and you're the person who stole *Wildfire*, don't worry that your investment in guilt was completely wasted. Instead, tell everyone you know to check out my website. If enough people read this and buy some of my books, then maybe *Wildfire* will gain sufficient fame that it actually will be worth $10,000. And if that ever happens, I'll be glad to legally sign it over to you, and we can both laugh about how you got an artistic bargain and I sold a lot of books and other art.

Part I
Film

The Oklahoma Kid Meets Frankenstein

IN MY CHILDHOOD IN OKLAHOMA, I was on my way to becoming the Oklahoma Kid—an Oklahoma cowboy with red clay on his boots and eyes the color of dust on the horizon. I loved the red clay and the dust storms and the flat rivers and the wide sky. I had a Mattel Fanner 50 in a real leather holster and a brand-new black cowboy hat.

The color was no random choice, but I wasn't trying to play the bad guy. James Garner, who portrayed one of my favorite TV characters, Bret Maverick, on the TV series *Maverick*, wore a black hat. It so happened that Garner's brother was the principal of my elementary school. One year, on the annual Wild West Day, all the Mavericks came to school dressed in costume. I got to touch Bret's gun. Not only that, my first-grade teacher was the niece of Gene Autry.

Living in Oklahoma with all those Western influences, it seemed like my cowboy future was assured, but fate intervened. My friends and I went to see a Saturday morning matinee featuring *The Revenge of Frankenstein* in a double-feature with *Night of the Demon*, a nifty supernatural thriller marred by uninspired producers. *The Revenge of Frankenstein* was the second of Hammer Production's Frankenstein movies, and as with the first, Peter Cushing played the baron. It was a kiddy matinee, but I came out a lot older than I went in. I was so completely captivated that I accidentally left my brand-new cowboy hat in the theater and never saw it again.

My sorrow at its loss was surprisingly brief. The range rider's laconic life may have been punctuated by exciting gunfire, but it paled next to Baron Frankenstein's maniacal drive to create life anew amidst all those bubbling vats and sparking machines. Maybe I was just feeling the beginnings of the creative drive in myself. Little did I know what a personally maddening journey it would be—and how provincial villagers love to chase after creators, torches in their hands and charges of blasphemy on their lips.

But Peter Cushing didn't care. His portrayal was convincing and incredibly intense as he single-mindedly kept trying to make that one being that wasn't a shambling parody of humanity—that one creation that might possess a soul. He was even willing to die to see his obsession come to fruition. Unrealized by me at the time, it was a parable of artistic endeavor.

So I guess it's all Peter Cushing's fault that I am who I am today—that I left the Oklahoma Kid back there in the red dust to follow Frankenstein's dream.

Human Bounty
Blade Runner and the Essence of Humanity

IN A WORLD WHERE HUMANITY is increasingly divided by barriers constructed of racial, ethnic, religious, cultural, social, and economic differences, the essential qualities that define humanness are called into question. Shakespeare often used the word "kind" to indicate the inner linkages that unite people—linkages that include race and ethnicity, socio-cultural background, mutual support and respect, and love. The concept of "kind" conferred affinity, equality, and justice upon similar sorts of people. In *Blade Runner* (1982)[1], director Ridley Scott and screenwriters Hampton Fancher and David Peoples take this idea a step farther as they explore the essential qualities not just of "kind," but of "humankind."

Rick Deckard (Harrison Ford) is a "blade runner," a government assassin whose job is to kill androids, called Replicants, who have escaped from forced labor or warfare in off-Earth colonies and come to live in secret among humans on Earth. Replicants are not machines with superficial layers of apparent humanness that cover a metal, robotic frame, à la a Terminator. Instead, they are physiologically indistinguishable from humans. Only an expert—a blade runner—using sophisticated psychological tests is able to tell if an individual is a Replicant.

Even with all their apparent humanness, Replicants are not considered human. Replicants, being manufactured, are superior to humans in certain aspects—primarily strength and agility—and their intelligence reflects the entire spectrum of human intelligence, from low to high. So perhaps there is a fear factor at play here: humans fearing they will be replaced by Replicants in a silent, internal, and implacable invasion. But despite their sophisticated physical abilities, Replicants also have extremely limited life spans due to unsolvable factors in the manufacturing process that cause their bodies to shut down after about seven years.

Because they are stuck in psychological preadolescence, Replicants exhibit an extremely unsophisticated emotional development that is constantly at odds with their adult physiology and intelligence and the brutal and violent adult jobs they were designed and built to do, either as laborers in dangerous situations, as soldiers, or as sex objects. They are, essentially, child laborers and soldiers. Their arrested development ensures a certain moral primitivism, and they can be violently murderous in the same way that a three-year-old child can throw a temper tantrum. Witness the overreaction of Leon (Brion James) in the opening scene, where he shoots a blade runner who simply asks him about his relationship with his mother. Thus, Replicants are the perfect devices to represent the dichotomy that resides within humanity itself—that of cold, mechanistic rationality set against emotional bestiality.

Portrayal of Replicants as creatures at once sub- and superhuman yet walking in the guise of humans links them to the very real problems of racial and cultural hatred and prejudice. Right up front, Deckard's cop boss, Bryant (M. Emmet Walsh), calls the Replicants "skinjobs," a pejorative term that Deckard points out is like calling a black man a "nigger." The metaphor is further reinforced by the fact that Replicants are slaves used for forced labor in off-world colonies, just as African slaves were used for forced labor in the American colonies, far removed from their homelands. Replicants become, in disguise, all oppressed minorities who have been subjugated and who have struggled for justice and recognition of their essential humanity. This is ironically set off by Roy's appearance and character. Even the Aryan Superman can be downtrodden and his dreams squashed by hatred and bigotry. However, the pejorative also points to the superficiality of all such pejoratives because Replicants are not simply "skinjobs," but are indistinguishable from humans through and through. If Replicants are skinjobs, then, ultimately, so too are humans born of woman.

Deckard, hunter and killer of Replicants, represents the cultural, political, and economic forces that seek to dominate and destroy elements within society that are perceived as being different from a prescribed cultural, ethnic, and behavioral norm. Or rather, Deckard is the tool of those forces. And like any tool, he is forced to come into intimate contact with the workpiece—in this case, to directly interface with and understand the "other" in order to find its weaknesses and use them to destroy it. But in understanding the "other" and tracking it down, Deckard little realizes that he will ultimately come to identify with it on a visceral level, leading him to become "divergent"—something other than the norm or even the "other." Something that might find its genesis in both is beyond either.

On top of that—or perhaps because of it—Deckard is not a self-assured assassin. In his early scenes, he is brooding and depressed, at once bound by a system he hates and unable to escape it. Although his thoughts have not yet fully gelled, he has begun to question the morality of killing Replicants. His doubts balance on one single pivot: the Replicants are so indistinguishable from true humans that only an expert like himself can tell the difference, often using intuition more than hard scientific data.

The test to determine if one is a Replicant or not is, ultimately, subjective. "What reading would you get if you tested a human?" Tyrell asks Deckard. There is no final, solid, and indisputable parameter, such as an established weight or measurement, that can determine if the results of the test are valid or merely an opinion or assumption on the part of the blade runner. Hence, there is no way to pragmatically determine how many people have been mistaken for Replicants and murdered as a consequence. Or how many Replicants have gone free to to potentially menace society. "Have you ever retired someone by mistake?" Rachel asks Deckard, and it is a question he cannot answer. Or rather, it is a question he can answer as he begins to realize that everyone he's killed might have been a mistake and that he has become a dehumanized machine programmed as a tool of slaughter and thus has no moral high ground from which to eliminate his targets. He is nothing but a government-paid serial killer, and his targets appear to be as innocently human and desiring of freedom as he is.

Deckard is not allowed to simply brood on his crimes against humanity, however, but is forced to face them. Four Replicants are walking the streets. If Deckard refuses to hunt them, Bryant threatens that Deckard will be treated like "little people," or, further dehumanized and put into the category of slave—or even Replicant. Deckard gets a description of the Replicants. They are Roy (Rutger Hauer), a sophisticated military combat model; Pris (Daryl Hannah), a pleasure model; Zora (Joanna Cassidy), another combat model; and Leon, a worker unit.

During the course of his investigation, Deckard learns that the newer, more sophisticated models of Replicants have implanted memories that are indistinguishable from genuine memories of real experiences and that are so consummate that they even can confer artistic ability, such as playing a musical instrument. These memories can be so thoroughly integrated within the personality that a sophisticated Replicant may not be aware that it is not actually human. Deckard discovers this fact when he accurately deduces that Rachel (Sean Young), purported to be the niece of Replicant inventor Eldon Tyrell (Joe Turkel), is really a Replicant, though she is unaware of it.

Through his investigation, Deckard learns that crucial characteristics stand in the way of simplistic categorization of Replicants as coldly mechanistic or bestial, and thus inhuman. First, their range of intelligence is equal to that of humans. Batty is intelligent enough to discuss details of android manufacture with Tyrell, despite the fact that he is, in reality, only about seven years old, and during that short life, he also served as a warrior fighting off-world. Leon's intelligence is much more basic, but whatever a Replicants' individual levels of intelligence, they all have the power of reason to help balance the coldly mechanistic with the bestial, just as do humans. Second, Deckard discovers that even an unsophisticated worker unit like Leon can develop emotions and feel the power of loyalty. Deckard can't help but realize that the Replicants are infused with a moral imperative that he, himself, lacks. They might kill, but it is in the name of freedom, whereas, Deckard kills simply to aid oppression.

Replicants, formerly defined through their contrast to humans, suddenly take on very human qualities. These qualities are defined through Deckard, the film's major representative of humanity. Deckard's human qualities should contrast sharply with the inhumanity of the Replicants, but the more that Deckard interacts on a personal level with the Replicants, the more the differences lose focus. He discovers that any quality that defines humans also defines Replicants, and vice versa.

It is true that the androids regularly kill those they meet who are not their "kind," but Deckard does no less, killing every android he comes in contact with But if both Deckard and the Replicants have negative emotions that emerge as murderous intolerance, both have positive emotions as well. Deckard and Rachel fall in love despite their "racial" differences, and their developing emotional attachment is mirrored by the emerging love between Roy and Pris. The kissing of the two couples underscores the parallel emotional desires and needs within both humans and Replicants—and between the two "species," as well.

Another aspect that further conjoins humans and Replicants is that both groups have a sense of personal history.

Personal history is initially ascribed to humans, who have real families with genuine historical backgrounds, evidenced by Deckard's collection of family photographs. But false as their recollections might be, the Replicants also have indelible memories of family reinforced by photographs. Family photos are important to both Leon and Rachel, and even coldly calculating Roy acknowledges their importance after Leon loses his collection. Interestingly, although Deckard presumably has a real family, there is no sense that he has any more continuity beyond himself than do the Replicants. His personal history is programmed by his photos no less than the Replicants' memories have been programmed into them. In fact, Deckard is even more personally isolated than are the Replicants. They have each other—have bonded with each other as a family—but Deckard has no one who even pretends to care for him. He is alone and lonely.

It is clear that the Replicants also have both genuine personal memories and genetic continuity. Roy tells Deckard, "I've seen things you people wouldn't believe." His personal memories are as unique, meaningful, and ineffable as those of any human, and further, his family history is as unique as those of humans, and even includes a genetic inheritance. Chew, the eye-maker (James Hong) tells Roy and Leon that he designed their eyes. Even more poignantly, the genetic designer, J. F. Sebastian (William Sanderson) proudly tells Roy, "There's a little bit of me in you." The Replicants are not machines, but have direct genetic continuity from all parts of humanity, and Roy has just visited two of his uncles before going to see his father, Tyrell, to learn more of his family background—including his family's genetic predispositions for certain diseases.

Human excellence in art and philosophy also are matched by the androids. Deckard, as human artist, plays the piano, but Rachel also plays and does it more beautifully than he. This, alone, demonstrates her essential humanity. Philosophically, the androids show an identity corresponding to human. Deckard's brooding considerations on the morality of killing Replicants is matched by even the lowest-level of the androids, Leon. This emerges when Leon delivers a philosophical diatribe on how living in fear heightens the sense of self and the joys and beauty of living, while at the same time giving a practical demonstration by beating up Deckard and trying to kill him.

Human Deckard feels pain and fear, first in his encounter with Leon, then later when he battles Roy in the deserted apartment building. But his fear already has been echoed by Zora's desperation as she flees from him through the crowded streets, by Pris's caution as Deckard hunts her amid a forest of human and humanoid figures, by Leon's diatribe on the subject, and by Roy's very similar statements during the final battle. Deckard's human pain also finds its counterpart during the final battle in Roy's own obvious physical, mental, emotional, and spiritual suffering. And the fear is further mirrored in Rachel's angst and sorrow when she discovers she is a Replicant. She kills Leon not to save Deckard out of either principle or love. It's too soon for those. Instead, she does it because she is afraid that she is a Replicant, and Deckard is the only one who can tell her the truth. Having believed that she was Tyrell's niece, she is a little like the the belle of a Southern ball who has just discovered she is a quadroon.

But the essence of humanity rests in overcoming fear and showing both compassion and personal evolution. Zora demonstrates these qualities when she does not kill Deckard after she knocks him out, though, as a combat model, she could easily have finished him off and probably should have as a merely practical consideration. She obviously wanted to, but her growing human compassion held her back. And she shows personal evolution when she trades in the profession of soldier, or public killer, for that of erotic dancer, or public lover. This change indicates that Replicants, just as humans, have a predilection for personal behavior that runs deeper than societal expectations or training. Rachel falling in love with Deckard only underscores the idea that love is the force that can unify the opposites in humankind, just as it unifies man and woman.

Both Deckard and Roy show extraordinary courage in the face of fear: Roy in his quest to confront his creator, and Deckard in his desperate climb up the face of the building during the climax. Deckard's climb testifies not only to his courage, but to his intense will to live, as do Zora's panicked flight and the furious hammering of Pris's feet on the floor as she lies prematurely dying, letting out the entire energy of her unlived life in one frenzied spasm. But even more telling is that Roy demonstrates honor equal to the best in humans when he saves Deckard's life even after Deckard has made repeated attempts to kill him and has murdered all his comrades, including his budding love, Pris. This is the ultimate expression of the will to live, demonstrated through Roy's desire to preserve the integrity of his immortal soul. That soul, new-found and symbolized by the dove Roy clutches to his breast, flies into the blue heavens above the polluted clouds of the city as Roy dies, indicating that his soul is, indeed, as pure and immortal as that of any human. Perhaps more pure than most because he lived a principled life.

Reinforcing the theme of human equality almost from the start is the mounting evidence that Deckard is, himself, a Replicant. Over the decades since the film's initial release, much argument has been made on both sides of this issue. Initially, I was of the opinion that Deckard was indeed a Replicant, and there is strong evidence backing up this conclusion. Plus, it was an interesting twist to contemplate. Even during the film's initial release, when cuts eliminated some of the evidence supporting this assumption, it was clear that Deckard could very likely be a Replicant. Like them, he performs the dirtiest work of society by serving as an assassin. He is isolated, and the only sense of any family he might have comes from the few photos on his piano, all of which are so old as to be meaningless on a personal level. Are they present simply to amplify and reinforce implanted memories?

Further, even after Roy mangles Deckard's hand, Deckard continues his desperate attempt to complete his mission. And he does so despite the seeming impossibility that he could ever succeed and the distinct possibility that Roy will kill him first. His climb up the side of the building in the rain is not simply desperate. It shows the kind of superhuman tenacity, determination, courage, and strength that Roy has exhibited all along. And then, Roy rescues Deckard and lifts him onto the roof. This is a singular act for Roy, who has killed every human he has come into direct contact with. Does he not let Deckard fall to his death or kill him outright because he has gained compassion, or is it because he recognizes that Deckard is in reality a Replicant—one of his own "kind?"

And, of course, there is the origami unicorn left by Ganz (James Edward Olmos) on the steps of Deckard's apartment, a clear sign he is aware of Deckard's unicorn dream, which would be possible only if he knew it had been implanted in Deckard's memory. Also unmistakable is that Deckard's eyes exhibit the same golden sheen as the eyes of the Replicants. Finally, capping everything off, is the idea that only blade runners can distinguish Replicants from humans. Like the old saying goes: It takes one to know one.

A lot also has been made in this regard of the so-called "fifth Replicant." When Bryant first assigns Deckard to the case, he says there are five skinjobs running around, but during the course of the story, Deckard encounters only four, and the fifth one is completely ignored. Many commenters believe this is proof positive that Deckard is that fifth Replicant. But according to the filmmakers, this is an artifact from a working copy of the script, in which there were originally five Replicants. One of those characters was dropped from the script, but by then, the scene with Bryant instructing Deckard to go after five replicants, instead of four, had already been filmed and was not reshot due to time and financial constraints. But let's say that the presence of the fifth

Replicant remains. Is it truly Deckard, or is you? Or maybe it's me, and I don't even known it.

More recently, I've backed off the Deckard-as-Replicant hypothesis, not because it isn't valid or possible, but because it doesn't matter. The whole point is to conflate Deckard, who we initially take to be human, with the Replicants, who we initially take to be inhuman, mix them up, shake them out, and show that they are the same in all points. Human is human, whatever its source.

In the final analysis, those who are human are those who—like Replicant recognizing Replicant—recognize the humanity in others. Both Deckard and Roy realize this truth at the conclusion of their battle, and though Roy dies, Deckard retains this knowledge when he returns to his apartment to rescue Rachel. They escape, carrying with them an acceptance of their mutual humanity that had been sparked by their love and fanned into flame through Deckard's repeated encounters with his own humanity in the faces of "others." Their future is uncertain, but they are no longer bounded by artificial constraints on what it means to be human.

Kung Fu's Number Two

WHEN TRAILERS FOR THE MOVIE *Kill Bill, Part 1* began appearing, they promised slam-bam martial arts action, with Uma Thurman facing off against Lucy Liu and other villains over a scything of razor-edged blades and equally sharp repartee. They also promised a healthy dose of humor—not just in the snappy dialog but in the film's pastiche of stylistic trends that low-budget action adventure films have exhibited over the past forty years. But those aspects aren't what intrigued me—it was one single flashed image among the trailer's riot of quick cuts that caught my attention.

It was the craggy, care-worn face of an older man who has seen the bottom as well as the top but whose eyes retain a sense of pride, power, and, yes, purpose. It was the face of David Carradine. As I saw the image come and go in the blink of an eye, I was struck by the appropriateness of Carradine's appearance in a film by Quentin Tarantino, who is known for paying homage to past action and crime films in his own work. *Reservoir Dogs* is steeped in the subgenre of the noir heist film, and *Pulp Fiction* is as much a paean to the crime drama as it is a breakthrough of stylistic and storytelling conventions. And his third film, *Jackie Brown*, featured Pam Grier, whose work in low-budget crime and action films spans several decades, and revitalized the career of Robert Forster, whose solid work was one of the highlights of genre films like *Alligator*.

Like Grier, especially, Carradine has done so much of this sort of stuff over the years that he has virtually become an icon, even ignoring his several turns as various incarnations of Kwai Chang Caine. But of course, it is his portrayal of the displaced Shaolin monk traversing the post-Civil War American West on a quest for family and spiritual absolution that most defines Carradine.

In *Kill Bill*, Carradine plays Bill, the boss of a group of assassins who, in a fit of personal pique, shoots one of his own—Thurman—and leaves her for dead. Bill is as bad as Kwai Chang is good, but Carradine is experienced at playing various levels of the human spectrum, and no matter how he is cast, he deserves a role in a Tarantino film that is a tribute to and extension of martial arts and action movies.

Until the 1960s, martial arts as a cinematic action device was virtually unknown in the West. Mr. Moto (Peter Lorre) of the pre-World War II Mr. Moto film series, uses jujitsu on his enemies, but aside from that, the few brief mentions of martial arts in mainstream film came principally after the war, when GIs returning from Japan brought back a smattering of karate. The perfect example is *Bad Day at Black Rock*, in which one-armed veteran Spencer Tracey uses karate to defeat Ernest Borgnine.

Those instances were rare, though, and early martial arts movies were the province of the Eastern—Chinese and Japanese action films that were those countries' equivalents to the American Western. Samurai movies predominated in Japan, and they were generally of higher artistic quality than the plethora of Hong Kong chop-socky flicks churned out by the likes of the Shaw Brothers Studios and Golden Harvest Productions, which portrayed kung fu as a mayhem of flying fists and feet fueled by hot heads and turgid emotions.

Camp spy movies and television shows of the 1960s helped bring martial arts to the fore in the West as Derek Flint (James Coburn) of *Our Man Flint* and *In Like Flint*, Illya Kuryakin (David McCallum) of *The Man From U.N.C.L.E.* series, and Emma Peel (Diana Rigg) of *The*

Avengers series chopped and kicked their enemies into submission. And then Bruce Lee exploded into the public consciousness as the Green Hornet's sidekick, Kato, who did more than just sidekick.

Bruce Lee is undoubtedly cinema's most important martial arts star because he made martial arts combat in movies an international phenomenon. And he accomplished that because, first, he really knew his stuff. No one who watched him move on screen could doubt that he truly was very dangerous. Lee also had a powerful screen presence, and even better, he could bring some measure of depth to his portrayal of a character. His untimely demise may leave us wondering if his acting abilities would have eventually approached his physical expertise, but even at his worst, he was a better actor than most of his predecessors and successors, no matter how skillful they might be as martial artists. And last, which is arguably more important than his demonstration of expert fighting technique, Lee transmitted aspects of the self-realization and self-perfection that are inherent in the martial arts and all too often ignored in films featuring martial arts combat.

When the *Kung Fu* television series premiered, few viewers, if any, could have known that the character of Kwai Chang Caine was, to all practical purposes, created with Bruce Lee in mind or that he had been passed over for the role because he was "too Oriental" in appearance. The producers chose David Carradine because he had enough of an Asian cast to his features to pass for half-Chinese, half-Anglo, and because he had enough physical grace to fake the fight scenes. Even so, it was obvious to any viewer of the *Kung Fu* pilot who had seen Bruce Lee in action that Carradine knew about as much martial arts as David McCallum or Diana Rigg. I except James Coburn, who was, in real life, one of Bruce Lee's students.

Since the days of *Kung Fu*, scores of martial arts actors have made their marks. Many of them have been extremely expert in a physical sense, and their fighting skills are exciting and deserve to be highlighted. Often, however, the brightness of these stars' martial expertise has left Carradine in shadow, and many viewers, as well as observers in the martial arts community, have unfairly disparaged his abilities. Despite this, I would argue that Carradine is, historically, cinema's second-most important martial arts star, and interestingly, the reasons are exactly opposite those that made Bruce Lee number one.

While Lee's martial arts mastery made him stand out, Carradine in the *Kung Fu* pilot was unquestionably a dancer going through the moves. He was an amateur pretending. But as the series progressed, an interesting thing happened. Carradine actually began to gain real skill. Perhaps that skill never reached the level of someone like Lee, who had trained for a lifetime, but by the time the series ended, it was obvious that Carradine really had learned something. And that something showed in many of his subsequent films, both good and bad, where he demonstrated that the moves he once mimicked had become genuine.

For Western viewers, this was a revelation. While it seemed impossible to many of us that we could ever attain the level of a Bruce Lee, we saw that Carradine, with instruction and hard work, had truly learned something useful, worthwhile, and real. Essentially, we were witnessing firsthand the process of an apprentice being instructed in the martial arts, and in doing so, we understood that we, too, could learn. If Lee was the opening of the door, Carradine was the nudge across the threshold. It's no coincidence that Western interest in kung fu and other martial arts blossomed in the wake of *Kung Fu*. If an amateur like Carradine could gain a degree of proficiency, then so could we.

But there was another truth that we learned by watching the growing proliferation of martial arts combat in the movies during the next couple of decades—you can train a reasonably fit actor to perform martial arts sequences with some believability, but training a martial artist to act is another matter entirely. A few martial artists, such as Jet Li and

Michelle Yeoh, are decent actors as well as high-level martial artists, but just as often these days, we see actors performing the moves, and we prefer them because they can credibly portray characters. In *Kill Bill*, Tarantino has Uma Thurman and Lucy Liu kicking ass, but if you believe that in real life they are expert blade masters, I've got 40 acres in West Texas that you might be interested in buying. Likewise, Tom Cruise in *Mission Impossible 2* was convincing in the fight scenes, and so was Matt Damon in the *Bourne* films. And of course, the *Matrix* series shows that intense training for the actors coupled with camera and editing techniques and special effects can make for exciting, if not always realistic, martial arts combat.

For all his martial ability, Lee was never more than an adequate actor. Given time—and the roles of more diverse characters—he might have matured as a thespian, but time was something he didn't have, and he used what he did have to become a great martial artist. Carradine, on the other hand, came from an acting family, was trained as an actor, and had made more than a dozen appearances in film and TV before the *Kung Fu* pilot aired in 1972.

Since then, in nearly 150 roles, he has portrayed an incredible variety of characters. This isn't to say that he hasn't done an awful job on occasion or that he hasn't been in some terrible movies. Both are true, but only to be expected considering the sheer volume of his work. We all have bad days along with the good, and if Carradine has suffered the former with the likes of Fred Olen Ray and Mats Helge, he also has worked for outstanding directors such as Martin Scorsese, Robert Altman, Hal Ashby, Ingmar Bergman, and Walter Hill. Can we imagine Chuck Norris, Steven Seagal, or Jean Claude Van Damme (ignoring the accent) adequately portraying Woody Guthrie in *Bound for Glory*? Or the tormented Vietnam veteran in Carradine's own *Americana*? Would any of them have the pure panache to play Pearl in *Sonny Boy*?

The point is that, being an actor, Carradine set a standard with Kwai Chang Caine that probably no other martial arts star has managed to equal in terms of character. Bruce Lee may have been dynamic and intense, but he also was aloof, and his tremendous skills elevated him above the rest of us. Carradine's Caine, on the other hand, is a character with skill as great as Lee's real skill, but in him, it is secondary to his earthy intellect, kindness, humility, and personal warmth. He is such a spiritual and questioning soul that the other characters are amazed that his apparent naïveté and modesty mask a profound philosophy and formidable physical prowess. Instead of rising above us, Caine lifted us up to a higher level. Even his enemies often benefited from their interaction with him.

Carradine invested Caine with a sense of humanity and kinship that I don't think Lee could have managed. Had Lee played the part, he could have kicked ass and taught the lesson, and we would have been impressed and we would have learned, but we would not have felt the emotional attachment to him that we felt for Carradine's Caine. And it was precisely through that emotional attachment that the spiritual aspects of the martial arts were finally portrayed onscreen, showing how the philosophy behind the techniques can apply not simply to combat but to daily life. So, if Lee represents the realization and perfection of self through the martial arts, Carradine is the understanding of the ways martial arts teaches that self to function harmoniously within society and culture. Lee shone the international spotlight on martial arts and brought them into our consciousness; Carradine brought the martial arts not just into our living rooms but into our hearts.

One final sidelight is pertinent here, and that has to do with techniques used to film martial arts sequences. The old Hong Kong chop-socky movies generally were content to film fights with relatively static camera angles, varying only from medium shots to close-ups. Bruce Lee's best complete film, *Enter the Dragon*, raised the level of martial arts cinematic technique to that of the basic Hollywood action-adventure of its day, with a greater sophistication in camera angle and movement. But it was with *Kung Fu* that we really saw the genesis of the next level of camera and editing technique for fight sequences, particularly in the use of creative camera angles and slow motion.

It is likely that the use of slow motion in *Kung Fu* was the result of several factors. Most obvious is that two major Hollywood directors—Arthur Penn and Sam Peckinpah—had pioneered the use of slow motion in violent action sequences with dramatic effect, and when something is successful in film, some minor rendition of it is sure to show up on television. And having appeared there, it quickly re-enters the realm of film to become an established phrase of our visual language.

On a more practical level, I suspect that, at least in the beginning, slow motion also helped gloss over Carradine's weaknesses as a martial artist, making him look faster, more accurate, and more powerful than he really was. We can't imagine directors slowing down Bruce Lee, for example, when his blazing speed, accuracy, and power begged for real-time display. But if the slow motion was there to mask Carradine's initial lack of abilities, it was a serendipitous circumstance. Using slow motion for the fights in *Kung Fu* had the artistic effect of suspending viewers in the timeless space created by Caine's training, lending them a sense of oneness not simply with the character and his extraordinary abilities but with his inner calm even while in the midst of battle.

Today, we see slow motion in fighting sequences all the time, as well as the diversity of camera angle and movement for martial arts fighting that were pioneered in part by *Kung Fu*. The slo-mo martial arts acrobatics of Neo and his compatriots and enemies in the Matrix series, for example, owe a direct debt to the *Kung Fu* series. And those techniques have led to even greater variety, such as the herky-jerky acceleration and deceleration of camera speed now frequently used to impart a more visceral involvement with the pace and intensity of a fight à la the *Bourne* films.

So, with that much cinematic history embodied in Carradine, how could Quentin Tarantino not feature him in *Kill Bill*? Once the second part was released, my initial hope that Carradine's latest moment in the sun might be a little more substantial than his all-too-brief appearance in the trailer has been rewarded. In his scenes, he breathes obligatorily into a flute but all the while delivers a performance that is not simply nuanced but fresh and believable. As always, Carradine is the actor first and the martial artist second, and that fact not only focuses the spotlight on his contributions to action films but highlights the influence he has had on countless people who practice the martial arts in real life.

Out of the Blue

THE EVENING STARTED INNOCENTLY ENOUGH in the Media Center at Rice University in Houston. But now, here we were, on the outskirts of town, at the Big H Speedway, where hurtling steel and engine thunder split the air with the thrill of spinout and victory.

We weren't here to watch the race, though. We were here to watch Dennis Hopper blow himself up.

As the half-dozen school busses we rode in pulled to a stop in a vacant area on the periphery of the speedway, the final race of the night was winding down. Some pretty ugly vehicles lurched and slid around that dinky oval track. The raw clay surface was packed to the density of stone and slicked by grease and damp night air, and the cars looked like go-carts on steroids instead of something you'd see at Le Mans.

While the drivers clashed and jostled for final position, the announcer's amplified voice, nasal and filled with bored indulgence, hung limply in the oily air. "Stick around after the race, folks," he intoned. "Watch a famous Hollywood film personality perform the Russian Dynamite Death Chair Act. That's right, folks, he'll sit in a chair with six sticks of dynamite and light the fuse. Will the flagman please come out and flag him as he comes down?"

It was April 1983, and Hopper had come to the Media Center to screen his movie *Out of the Blue* (1980) and deliver a lecture. The film, a classic of nihilism, portrayed the ultimate dysfunctional family. The father, played by Hopper, is an ex-biker turned truck driver who crashes into a school bus, killing all the children aboard, and the mother is a junkie. And there is a subtext of incest. No wonder their daughter, a seminal punker in a huge leather jacket, finds it difficult to cope. The film's culmination was death in an exploding school bus. It wasn't a bad film, but it was grim.

Hopper's "lecture" wasn't particularly grim, but it certainly was dysfunctional. He was too drunk and stoned to stand in front of us, so he stayed in the projection booth and rambled on over the PA system for twenty or thirty bizarre minutes. I couldn't tell you what he talked about; I'm not sure he really talked about anything. The one thing that did register, however, was that he wanted to blow himself up in the parking lot of Rice Stadium.

As it turned out, Houston fire marshals wouldn't let him set off the explosion in the city, so Hopper had to take us outside the city limits where he would be allowed to detonate in peace.

That's Dennis Hopper for you—always pushed to the limits.

Someone rented enough school busses to haul the whole crowd and sent us off to the Big H, on Houston's north side, to watch the explosion. The motif of explosions and school busses remained consistent enough between film and reality that some of us may even have felt a touch of paranoia as we boarded.

At Big H, we waited, and at last Hopper stepped onto the track. He'd been with us all evening, yet it was the first time most of us had seen him.

He seems taller in real life.

Behind him a stunt coordinator and accomplices set up the Russian Dynamite Death Chair. It looked like just a big cardboard box covered with aluminum foil, but six sticks of dynamite make one heck of a whoopee cushion. At last it was ready, and Hopper and his stunt coordinator approached. The coordinator talked to Hopper, gestured to the chair, talked some more, then moved off.

Way off.

Hopper crouched on the chair. The police pressed the rapt crowd back. Hopper lit a match, and the breezy air went silent with expectation.

The wind blew out the match.

He lit another, and it, too, went out. And another.

It didn't take much imagination to hear him cursing the damp, brisk air and cruddy matches. He struck the whole pack all at once.

That did the trick. The sparked fuse sizzled for a moment then abruptly blossomed into a brilliant flash. We were all slapped by an invisible hand, yelled at thunderously.

Dennis Hopper, at one with the shock wave, spasmed headlong in a halo of fire. For a single, timeless instant he looked like Wile E. Coyote, frazzled and splayed by his own petard.

Then billowing smoke hid the scene.

We all rushed forward, past the police, into the expanding cloud of smoke, excited, apprehensive, and no less expectant than we'd been before the blast. Were we looking for Hopper or pieces we could take home as souvenirs?

Later Hopper would say blowing himself up was one of the craziest things he'd ever done and that it was weeks before he could hear again. At the moment, though, none of that mattered. He had been through the thunder, the light, and the heat, and he was still in one piece.

And when he staggered out of that cloud of smoke, his eyes were glazed with the thrill of spinout and victory.

Private Snafu's Hidden War
A Historical Survey and Analytical Perspective

PROPAGANDA, THE METHODICAL SWAYING OF public opinion toward certain attitudes, opinions, or procedures, is probably as old as public speaking. The concept was refined in 1622 by Pope Gregory XV, who convened the Congregation for the Propagation of the Faith, a group of cardinals in charge of foreign missions. Gregory's contribution to propaganda, aside from the word itself, was to add to the idea of persuasion the condition that the persuasion should be of large groups of people beyond the purview of immediate authority—possible only since the invention of mechanized printing a century and a half before Gregory's time.

The early twentieth-century development of electronic mass communication further extended the scope and immediacy of propaganda. By the end of World War I, radio and film had been refined to a high degree, and the beginning of World War II saw the rise of nationalist film propaganda with Leni Riefenstahl's pro-Nazi production, *Triumph of the Will*. The United States was not far behind, producing the film series, *Why We Fight*. But when the United States Army began showing a series of cartoons featuring a bumbling infantryman named Private Snafu, it proved that indoctrination could be fun as well as functional.

Private Snafu was named after the popular military acronym: Situation Normal, All Fouled (or Fucked) Up. "Warner

Bros. cartoon studio produced twenty-six 'Private Snafu' cartoons for the U.S. Army Signal Corps"[1] between 1943 and 1945. "They were used as part of the *Army–Navy Screen Magazine*, a film series shown at military bases around the world."[2] The settings of the cartoons reflected this global presence of the U.S. fighting man, and Snafu finds himself in Europe, the South Pacific, and Africa as well as the United States. Snafu, himself, personifies the universal nature of the U.S. fighting forces by portraying the everyman soldier. Snafu is the little guy, the common army grunt caught up in a global conflict that is beyond his understanding and, seemingly, beyond his power to cope with. As the narrator of "Coming Snafu," the first *Snafu* cartoon, says, "He is a patriotic, conscientious guy."

But Snafu is much more, or less, than that. Although he is described as "conscientious," he is, in fact, "the worst soldier in the army, the one who does everything wrong."[3] Snafu's plebeian nature, powerlessness, and mediocrity are all symbolized by his homeliness and his diminutive stature. Snafu is only half as tall as all the other characters, women included, with the exception of Japanese characters, who are occasionally even shorter than Snafu. But despite his shortness and mediocrity, Snafu was a big idea with a substantial history.

Private Snafu's earliest genesis can be found in U.S. government studies of the propaganda potential of comic strips and film.

> On June 13, 1942, an executive order signed by President Roosevelt established the Office of War Information [(OWI)] ... [whose mandate was to] formulate and carry out, through the use of press, radio, motion pictures and other facilities the development of an informed and intelligent understanding, at home and abroad, of the status and progress of the war effort and of the war policies, activities, and aims of the government.[4]

One of the earliest OWI studies examined comic strips. "The appeal of comic strips as potential instruments for propaganda was a function of their popularity with readers."[5] In the end, however, OWI abandoned attempts to use comic strips for propaganda purposes. The strips inclined toward hackneyed portrayals of patriotic ideals and overly stereotyped characterizations of the enemy as stupid and incompetent, and these depictions tended to lull viewers into complacency rather than prompting them toward greater effort on behalf of the war.[6]

More importantly, however,

> comic strips in newspapers and magazines did not lend themselves to control or manipulation…. Actual government production of comics did not appear to be an answer, either…. OWI ultimately decided to leave comics alone for the remainder of the war, ironically after demonstrating the considerable power of the cartoon images and their undeniable hold on the American public.[7]

OWI's attempts to use comic strips as propaganda ceased in November 1942, but other branches of the government had not lost interest.

> Within the American Army, acceptance of social science research techniques and heavy reliance on media technology suggests that generals can sometimes be True Believers…. Military enthusiasm for social science research and media technology relates to the concept of Social Engineering, an outgrowth of behavioral psychology arguing that human behavior can be manipulated towards socially desirable goals.[8]

The Army's Information and Education Division was headed by Brigadier General Frederick H. Osborn, a noncareer officer who, before the war, had been an active social science researcher and an important member of the Social

Science Research Council. Osborn's interest in using film as a means to educate and indoctrinate helped turn General George C. Marshall, army chief of staff, into "a zealous proponent of educational film."[9]

Although OWI had found itself unable to adequately control and manipulate comic strips in magazines and newspapers and incapable of producing its own, the United States Army was in a different position. It could produce its own vehicles of propaganda—films—the content of which could be fully controlled, and it could then disseminate these vehicles to a captive audience of servicemen. The main thrust of the army's effort was to produce the *Why We Fight* film series under the direct supervision of Frank Capra. This series "became mandatory viewing for all military personnel in 1942."[10] Official U.S. film propaganda was under way.

The *Why We Fight* series was a sort of overview of the seriousness of the war and the importance of sincere efforts to win it. *Why We Fight*, however, was primarily indoctrination, and General Marshall expressed his "intense dissatisfaction with existing methods of troop indoctrination," which generally consisted of lectures.[11] Part of the problem was that lectures were not on a large enough scale, and although the film series may have dramatically boosted the numbers of the lecture audience, it was still missing one vital element—the element of instruction.

The massive scale of the war demanded a proportionally larger scale of instruction, for the army needed an efficient and economical way to train the enormous number of raw recruits flooding through basic training camps. "The uses and maintenance of new and intricate weapons and equipment presented an awesome problem. The nation was faced with the need to convert hundreds of thousands of civilians into military specialists."[12] Thus, Marshall and others displayed a growing interest in using film in more specific and intensive ways by combining indoctrination and instruction into a single, concerted effort. But despite the overarching presence of the *Why We Fight* films, there was a void of instructional materials and methods.

Into that void stepped Eric Knight, who had provided important input into the *Why We Fight* scripts. He "argued that 'positive assertion of your beliefs and aims' was more effective than 'refutation of enemy assertions.'"[13] To this idea of education, Knight added an important element—animation. "Knight had long been interested in animation. He was assigned to work at the Disney Studio in July 1942, to work out the extraordinary animated inserts for the first four [*Why We Fight*] films."[14] Knight wedded the use of film for indoctrination and education to the idea of using animation to provide specific instructional material. *Private Snafu* was only a few marching steps away.

Those steps were taken by several one-shot cartoons that graphically demonstrated proper and improper military behavior. One of these was "Flat-Hatting," by John Hubley.

> "Flat-Hatting"....was a huge success. Flat-hatting was air force slang for the custom of putting a plane into a screaming dive at some innocuous target, animal, architectural, or civilian, sometimes with fatal results.... Hubley's picture showed, in a series of very funny gags, just how stupid and useless this form of braggadocio really was.... It totally demolished the image of flat-hatting as an admirable feat of derring-do.[15]

Films like Hubley's proved the ability of cartoons to positively affect behavior through a combination of graphic representation and humor. The *Private Snafu* series quickly emerged to take up the banner in a more consistent, controlled, and continuous manner.

The first *Private Snafu* cartoon, "Coming Snafu," appeared in June 1943. Despite Disney's involvement in the *Why We Fight* films and Hubley's success with "Flat-Hatting," their contributions to *Private Snafu* were nil. Instead, Warner Bros. and Leon Schlesinger contracted to produce the entire series. They were among the last cartoons produced by Schlesinger before he sold out to Warner in July 1944.[16] According to animator/director Chuck Jones, the films were produced "on a cost-plus basis."[17] Twenty-six *Private Snafu* cartoons were made between June 1943 and October 1945, including two that remained unreleased by the end of the war. One of these, "Coming Home," remained on the shelf due to its depiction of a super bomb that was to be used against Japan. This reference to the top-secret atomic bomb was a little too informational to pass army censorship.

The choice of Warner Bros. to produce the Snafu series undoubtedly was influenced by several factors. First, Warner directors, animators, and writers, whose stable of characters included Bugs Bunny, Daffy Duck, Tweetie Pie, Porky Pig, and Elmer Fudd, had already demonstrated a superlative knack for investing their animated characters with real personality. This was an important consideration since, without proper (or improper!) personality, Snafu would not have the intended effect. Secondly, the Warner staff had clearly displayed in their civilian fare the ability to combine unpretentious humor and surface narrative with adult-oriented double-entendres and subtexts. Such a combination is ideal for propaganda films intending to deliver hidden messages as well as more obvious ones. Simply put, Warner Bros. made the best cartoons around, and they were cartoons with all the right characteristics. But there was another, perhaps more significant point in Warner's favor. The studio had been the first American studio to jump zealously into war propaganda, and it had done so at its own expense well before anti-Nazi and anti-Japanese sentiment became a Hollywood bandwagon.

As early as 1938, Warner Bros. had sent a script titled *Storm Over America* to the Breen Office, then the federal watchdog of Hollywood modesty and appropriateness. The script "pulled no punches in identifying Nazi Germany as a threat to American security."[18] More anti-Nazi films by

Warner Bros. followed, but Warner's ideas were not shared by other studios. "Warner Brothers' boldness spread apprehension among other studios. The foreign department of Paramount thought Warner was making a grave mistake."[19] Among Warner's foremost critics was Senator Gerald Nye of North Dakota, who decried the pro-interventionist stance depicted in Warner productions. But "Harry Warner, whom Nye had accused of producing more propaganda films than any other, proudly announced his opposition to Hitler. Nazism was 'an evil force,' he said, and 'the world struggle for freedom was in its final stage.'"[20]

The combination of Warner Bros.'s staunch anti-Nazi sentiment, its prior independent efforts to sway public opinion toward support of the war, and the excellence of its cartoon department's productions made it the ideal studio to produce the *Snafu* series. For two years, Private Snafu was as much a member of the Warner family as were Bugs, Daffy, Elmer, and the rest of the gang.

The *Private Snafu* cartoons were Warner Bros. products in every respect. "Each cartoon is approximately three minutes long and in black-and-white. The cartoons utilized all of Warner's cartoon directors and voice artists [Mel Blanc as Snafu and Robert C. Bruce as the narrator] and Carl Stalling's music."[21] They were "written by [Theodore] Geisel, a cartoonist already famous in civilian life under the nom de plume of 'Dr. Seuss,' and Phil Eastman, who later wrote most of the *Magoo* pictures at UPA."[22] W. Munro Leaf, who wrote *Ferdinand the Bull*, also had a hand in at least one episode. The series had the two-fold purpose of instructing and indoctrinating enlisted men serving in the army, and each installment presented specific instructional material in a surface story, under which lay the indoctrination subtext.

In a sense, the *Snafu* cartoons are modern military fables, presenting a character who makes behavioral decisions and lives or dies as a result of his actions, leaving a practical moral as denouement. In each cartoon, "Snafu would commit a blunder or infraction, then learn the consequences of such errors."[23] The instructional material was always presented in simple, straightforward terms so that the message could be understood by any soldier, whatever his level of education. Commenting on the effectiveness of the films as teaching tools, Mel Blanc says,

> One picture was an aerial gunnery picture with Snafu telling what to do. He would always tell them wrong, and they would correct him. I remember there were three guys who had never taken any lessons in aerial gunnery but just saw this picture three or four times. They went up in a plane and they scored three 'positives' and one 'possible' on their first flight, just from looking at the cartoon pictures. So that shows you how important the cartoons were.[24]

As Blanc's statement indicates, the primary instructional function of the cartoons was, to some extent, successful. But the cartoons went beyond instructional specifics to encompass a plethora of aspects of military life and the war. For example, in "Fighting Tools," Snafu has the most advanced and powerful weapons and equipment the military world has ever seen, yet he constantly mistreats them, and his lack of maintenance has turned them into junk. In the end he is blown up by a German who, though initially frightened by Snafu's arsenal, is contemptuous of Snafu's lax care of it. Thus the cartoon demonstrates the importance of equipment and weapon maintenance.

Personal health and hygiene are the concern of "Private Snafu vs. Malaria Mike." Mike is a mosquito who guzzles malaria out of a hip-flask, and Snafu is the foolish soldier who ignores all military instruction on prevention of malaria and winds up with his head mounted as a trophy on Mike's wall. Self-defense was an equally important topic. "Gas" showed the vital necessity of maintaining defensive equipment like gas masks, and "Booby Traps" demonstrated that alertness for dangers far more subtle than bullets but equally deadly could mean the difference between living and dying.

Some of the instructional messages had more to do with proper attitude than with equipment or behavior. For example, in "The Goldbrick," Snafu constantly pursues easy but incorrect methods of training, and when he arrives at the scene of real combat, his slackness results in his death. "Infantry Blues" is another good example of instilling proper attitude. In this film, Snafu is a dogface slogging through rough terrain, and he fantasizes that the other branches of the military have an easier, better, and safer time of it than does the infantry: Tank corpsmen get to ride in style, navy personnel are aboard what amount to cruise ships, and air force pilots fly above the fray. Presto, here comes the Technical Fairy First Class to grant Snafu his wish. In quick succession, Snafu experiences the unpleasant aspects of being a tankman, a sailor, and a pilot, and he discovers firsthand the dangers they face. When he finally returns to his infantry persona, Snafu is content with his place in the war effort.

It is when they emphasize attitude that the *Snafu* cartoons begin to drift from instruction into indoctrination, and the drift is most pronounced in the several *Snafu* cartoons that feature the "loose lips sink ships" syndrome. This syndrome can take an obvious form, as in "Spies," an admonitory tale warning against carelessly blurting military secrets, or it can take a more inverted form, as in "Rumors," which decries disreputable gossip. The former shows how misused information directly aids the enemy, and the latter demonstrates how misinformation demoralizes and damages U.S. troops. Both demonstrate that information improperly used is detrimental to the war effort.

"Snafuperman" takes the idea of information in yet a third direction. Snafu, changed into Snafuperman by the Technical Fairy First Class, does his best to use his super powers to wreak havoc on the Germans, but he only succeeds in blundering in where, given greater tactical insight and military knowledge, he should fear to tread. Instead of aiding the

Allied war effort, he does it great harm. The message is that physical might and superiority without information or knowledge of how to properly use and direct that might is as harmful as misused information or misinformation. The emphasis on information contained in these entries becomes a subtle reminder to heed the hidden messages of these cartoons as closely as the surface instructional material.

Indoctrination continues to play a more important role than does instruction when the *Snafu* cartoons depict the enemy. The enemy is fearsome, dangerous, brutal, sly, and ubiquitous. This cautionary portrayal is a direct descendant of OWI's belief that popular propaganda should not minimize the dangers posed by the enemy by portraying the enemy simply "as 'evil, stupid and abnormal.'"[25] OWI had urged that the Germans and Japanese be considered formidable foes, and the *Snafu* cartoons treated them as such. In "Spies," enemy agents are everywhere—in stores, at newsstands, in restaurants, and even in the boudoir. The German soldier who confronts Snafu in "Fighting Tools" is a huge, beefy brute at least four times bigger than Snafu. Worse, he is very determined to kill Snafu. The fearsome quality of the war in the South Pacific is vividly shown in "The Goldbrick," and "A Lecture on Camouflage" demonstrates the cleverness of enemy soldiers as they hide in trees, bushes, and rocks.

But OWI did not understand that comic strips, and by extension cartoons, must rely on stereotypes, and that the exigencies of war and propaganda demand that stereotypes be utilized and that the enemy be portrayed negatively in ways aside from the direct threats he represents. So, although the enemy in the *Snafu* cartoons is dangerous, his danger arises from insidious cleverness rather than from real intelligence, from his bullying size rather than from real courage.

The Germans, even the spies, although big, also are uniformly fat and somewhat dull-witted. The Japanese are always runty and a little simple-minded. The assertion in "Fighting Tools" that the U.S. has the most sophisticated and powerful weaponry is tacitly acknowledged by the German soldier. Since American know-how built these weapons, the German soldier's admission concerning their superiority further grants to the U.S. serviceman an intellectual as well as physical superiority. The enemy is, thus, inferior to the "know-how, can-do" American, and he is inferior in other important ways. The craven cowering of that same German when he is faced by the much smaller Snafu, even when both are armed, indicates that the enemy has a fatal, internal weakness that debilitates him despite his apparently impressive physical might. The enemy is internally weak, denoting in him moral failing and spiritual inferiority.

Even these stereotypes contain a message. Because the enemy is inferior, he can be defeated as long as the American soldier retains the proper attitudes and behaviors. The dangers to the GI are deadly—bullets, bombs, gas, tanks, and so on, all delivered by an enemy driven by determined aggression—but deadliest of all are unpreparedness and lack of common sense. Intelligence and superior moral ground are as indispensable as brawn or the desire to fight and win.

Another important indoctrinational element of the *Snafu* cartoons is that they promote confidence in the chain of command. Officers do not often appear in *Snafu* cartoons, but the chain of command is amply represented by the only other recurring character aside from Snafu: the Technical Fairy First Class. The Technical Fairy is a rugged and tough-looking brute—if one doesn't take into account his somewhat dainty wings! He has broad shoulders, a slender waist, and a jutting square jaw, and he exudes the competent confidence of the seasoned warrior.

The Technical Fairy's rank—sergeant—is important, for as a noncommissioned officer he has risen to his position from the ranks of the enlisted men, the raw recruits—Snafu's own lowly position. Noncom officers are less intimidating to servicemen of low rank than are commissioned officers, and they are personally closer to the troops, both important devices to gain the trust of the common service-man. Furthermore, although he is tough and rugged, the Technical Fairy is never overbearing or brutal, even though he does wield the power of the entire chain of command symbolized through his ability to grant reality to Snafu's daydreams. As if embodying all officers, the Technical Fairy has the power to let Snafu do or be anything. With a flick of his wand, the Technical Fairy changes Snafu's branch of the service ("The Infantry Blues"), increases his awareness ("The Home Front") and personal power ("Snafuperman"), and even grants promotion in rank ("Gripes").

Not only does the Technical Fairy wield the power of the chain of command, he promotes confidence in superior officers and the chain of command in an important way, for the Technical Fairy is the epitome of wisdom. If Snafu has a self-serving fantasy or a problem that inhibits proper military functioning, the Technical Fairy demonstrates by personal, direct, and immediate example why and how Snafu's wrong thinking and attitude are dangerous and self-defeating. The Technical Fairy is always right, and he always has good, practical reasons to support his position.

Equally significant, he is ready and willing to impart his knowledge for Snafu's benefit. And his knowledge does more than help Snafu to function efficiently. In a sense, the Technical Fairy promotes the "sarge" as the soldier's fairy godfather, his guardian angel whose advice and wisdom are important not only for victory but for personal survival. Further, the Technical Fairy's competency and knowledge extend by inference to officers of higher rank on the chain of command. No wonder Snafu shakes with mute fear in "Snafuperman," despite his superhuman strength and invulnerability, when he encounters an American general. If the Technical Fairy, even at his nominally low rank, is so competent and knowing, a general must approach the omnipotent and omniscient.

The surface levels of the *Private Snafu* cartoons are always simple enough to understand—keep your weapon clean, don't blab military secrets, maintain personal hygiene, perform your duties correctly and with care—making them ideal training tools. The *Snafu* information and morals could be understood by every soldier, no matter what his educational level. But for the films to be effective, they first had to attract the attention of the serviceman and then had to present the material in such a way that the serviceman would accept the recommendations of the cartoons and act upon them. Army brass

> soon found that any picture that tried to "sell" the army audience with a suave, unctuous approach was quickly rejected. Any hint of talking down to the troops with high-flown hyperbole was promptly greeted with catcalls and Bronx cheers. In some instances, especially in the war zones, rocks were thrown at the screens.[26]

As the producers of military instructional films quickly learned, attention and acceptance cannot be begged or even blatantly demanded. But animators had long practiced the art of willing attention and acceptance, and the writers and directors of the *Private Snafu* cartoons followed John Hubley's lead in using a variety of more subtle means to beguile their viewers into compliance.

Probably the most obvious means the filmmakers used to gain attention and acceptance was the entertainment value of the cartoons. The cartoons were funny, and humor is an effective way to gain the attention and relaxed confidence of an audience by opening them up, without intimidation or restraint, to new and shared experience. The single most important humorous device in the *Snafu* series is Snafu himself. Snafu is a diminutive, weak, lazy, careless, ugly bumpkin. He also is an amusingly inept soldier. Even his name indicates the bawdy, irreverent tone which these cartoons take.

But the humor of Snafu's character hides a useful message. Snafu is not only the worst soldier in the army, he is a blatant fool. In at least three numbers—"Coming Home,"

"Spies," and "Fighting Tools"—Snafu is literally depicted as a "horse's ass." Snafu is an excellent teaching tool because no viewer would consider himself as stupid as Snafu and so would not want to commit the kinds of blunders that Snafu makes, for doing so would define him as being equally stupid in his own eyes and in the eyes of his fellow soldiers. No one would want to pull a Snafu. Thus, Snafu is a cautionary reminder not to be the one who fouled up, because such behavior could bring not only disaster but public ridicule and censure.

Other humorous devices include Geisel, Eastman, and Leaf's funny dialogue. The scripts, often written in comical verse, are rife with gags and provide plenty of inherent opportunities for humor. Equally important, Snafu's voice invokes a subliminal relationship to all incompetent, somewhat pitiful blunderers by sounding just like Porky Pig. These are the only two voice characterizations done by Mel Blanc that sounded alike. "I thought, Porky's voice will be kind of crazy for Snafu because he's a little sad character," Blanc commented. "And that's the reason I did Snafu practically the same way I did Porky."[27]

Beyond these relatively typical cartoon attention-getting devices, the Snafu series delved into areas that cartoons for the general public could not. The adult, all-male composition of the audience allowed the animators to utilize material that would have been considered risqué, or even taboo, for general release.

> Because it was important to establish an honest rapport with the soldiers, the SNAFU [sic] films went far beyond traditional Hollywood propriety in the use of four-letter words, broad sexual imagery, and mild scatological humor. [28]

The relative mildness of the profanity by today's standards—words like hell and damn—did not detract from its risqué quality at the time. After all, general audiences had gasped in shock only four years earlier at Rhett Butler's "damn" in *Gone With the Wind.*

Nudity was another naughty subject of humor. Certainly there was a lot of cheesecake in the *Snafu* series, but Snafu himself was often, quite literally, the butt of the nude joke. In "Fighting Tools," Snafu winds up naked as a German prisoner of war—not simply a dangerous situation but a humiliating one as well. The scatological humor is even bolder in "Private Snafu vs. Malaria Mike." While Snafu is skinny dipping, the camera zooms in on his bare buttocks until they fill three quarters of the screen. There they remain for a prolonged scene as Mike lands, peers at these gigantic hemispheres of the type of flesh unknown on any mainstream movie screen, and dryly comments, "Why, it's Snafu. I never forget a face." Then Mike pokes and pinches one cheek, sending out huge jiggling ripples, before launching himself into the air to dive bomb this brave new world.

Female anatomy and sexual innuendo are, perhaps the most powerful and consistent motifs in the Private Snafu series. Interest in sex and women was a natural device to put the GI audience at ease and gain its attention, considering that the audience was composed of young males with high testosterone levels who were deprived of female company for long periods of time and who were facing the terrors of combat and possible death. Except for Snafu's mother, all the women are young, buxom babes who wear scanty, clinging clothing or, in a subtle shot or two, like the one of the women in the harem in "Booby Traps," absolutely nothing at all.

This portrait of all women as highly developed and desirable physical specimens might be completely unrealistic and, from a latter-day perspective, sexist, but the portrait was probably extremely flattering to the egos of young soldiers who thought these luscious babes wanted nothing more than to entertain and bed them. After all, pinups, whatever the source, tend toward idealized form, and eventual concerns of propriety and sexism were probably of little importance to the army, to the filmmakers, or to the hundreds of thousands of horny, lonely, and frightened young servicemen hungry for female companionship.

The behavioral portrait of women fares little better than the physical portrait but is, again, in keeping with the desires of the audience and the tenor of the times. In "Coming Home," the "good" girls back in the U.S. spend most of their time smooching with soldiers under bushes, in cars, hanging out of windows, and just about everywhere else conceivable. Snafu's jitterbugging girlfriend even swings the lucky private beneath her skirts. Subliminally, these views promise every soldier that a loving and enthusiastic beauty was just waiting to lift her skirts for him when he returned home from the war—a sure-fire unconscious stimulus for the soldiers to fight harder so they can end the war as quickly as possible and attain their sexual rewards.

This stimulus–response is directly displayed in "A Lecture on Camouflage" when, at the end of the picture, the Technical Fairy's expert knowledge and actions afford him the privilege of cradling a buxom and very topless mermaid in each arm. The Technical Fairy, beaming broadly, says, "So gentlemen, remember. If you want to fool 'em, you gotta get into the picture." It becomes problematic if the "they" he refers to are the enemy or women, for the implication is that proper performance of duty is what women look for in a man and that beautiful women are the reward for services well performed.

But the avoidance of public ridicule and censure and the promise of sexual rewards are only parts of the psychological picture of the *Private Snafu* series. Equally important is that Snafu is a lone character. It seems that most of his personal contacts are with the officers who give him orders and the enemy he fights, both of whom cause consternation and hardship. He is swamped with duties, overwhelmed by his small stature, and in constant danger of losing his life. Snafu not only represents the abstract everyman soldier but the concrete reality of every individual soldier watching the films, for his smallness and confused and overwhelmed outlook access the personal loneliness and fear haunting each of them.

Because of this, the *Private Snafu* series had to be non-threatening and sympathetic to the fears, desires, and problems of enlisted men. Some of this emerges, as has been discussed, in the Technical Fairy and his nonthreatening, godfatherly relationship to Snafu, but other elements contribute to demonstrating a sympathetic kinship with the soldier in order to put him at ease and achieve a commiserate resonance with him.

Foremost among these elements is the semi-realistic ambiance of the cartoons. When weapons and other military equipment are displayed, they are depicted in a realistic fashion. "Fighting Tools" even opens with a visual catalogue of infantry weapons, all drawn in photo-realistic detail. But the realism of the cartoons extends beyond the physical details into the difficulties the servicemen faced daily. Such problems were never minor for them but were pervasive facts of life.

The boredom and dirtiness of unpleasant duties, such as KP, are dealt with in numbers like "Gripes," where Snafu learns that these duties have a purpose in maintaining discipline as well as enabling the military machine to function on a practical level. The pain and rigors of basic training are depicted in "The Goldbrick," where Snafu learns that the hardships imposed on him during training have the twin purposes of winning the war and keeping him alive. "Private Snafu vs. Malaria Mike," "A Lecture on Camouflage," and "Gas" contain a similar message plus a demonstration that the need to follow orders predicates personal survival.

And underlying almost every *Snafu* cartoon is an injunction for alertness and exactness of personal behavior, without which the war will be lost and Snafu killed. These themes come across most strongly in "Spies," "Coming Snafu," "Rumors," and "Snafuperman." In "Spies" and "Coming Home," Snafu's lack of alertness and exactness results in mass destruction of American forces, and in "Rumors" they destroy not only Snafu's personal will to fight, but the internal cohesion of the army itself. "Snafuperman" demonstrates that even superhuman powers are ineffective without awareness, training, and intelligence.

But the most important point here, at least with respect to gaining the confidence of the GI viewer, is that Snafu, just like any soldier, is always uncomfortable and overburdened with dirty, boring, exhausting, exacting, and fearful work. The sympathetic resonance that the common soldier had to feel for Snafu would lead that soldier into a mutual bond with Snafu—a bond that would encourage the soldier to accept and act on the behaviors that Snafu comes to accept and that keep him alive and to shun the behaviors that result in Snafu's death. And here, with the subject of death, the psychology of the Snafu series takes a turn into grimmer territory.

Since combat and death were constant threats to the soldier, they serve an important function in the *Snafu* series. Death in these cartoons is unlike death in any other cartoon of the time. In all other cartoons, at least until the pseudo-realistic cartoon adventures and artistic animations pioneered in the 1960s, death was simply not a fact of cartoon life. Elmer Fudd or Daffy Duck or any other civilian cartoon character can get shot or smashed or blown up ad infinitum and still find instantaneous resurrection. Snafu, on the other hand, does not find resurrection so readily. He may reappear alive in the next installment, or, rarely, his death occurs in a dream from which he awakes. Most often, however, if Snafu dies in a cartoon, he stays dead in that cartoon.

And die he does, with great frequency. Out of the first thirteen *Snafu* cartoons, Snafu dies at the end of six. In one more he ends up as a German prisoner of war, in another in a military jail, and in yet another as an inmate in a psycho ward. In each case, Snafu is killed or imprisoned due to faulty behavior. Thus, to promote positive military attitude and action, these cartoons use a psychology whose message is clear—either Snafu understands that the promoted behavior is truly appropriate and acts accordingly, or Snafu dies or undergoes unpleasant, humiliating, and possibly permanent confinement. The rapport between Snafu and the average GI would not have to be as strong as it probably was for this reality to be frighteningly clear to the soldier.

An important adjunct to this grim reality of death also functions psychologically in these cartoons in the depiction of carnal desires, which include the desires for sex, alcohol, tobacco, and recreation. As noted before, sex is a major motif in the *Snafu* series. The surface message of "Coming Home" is that when you get home after a successful war there will be a sexy, buxom babe waiting for you with open arms. And for even more immediate gratification, it is strongly hinted that the soldier who knows and performs his duty will be rewarded with the sexual favors of women, just as the Technical Fairy is rewarded with his brace of nubile mermaids in "A Lecture on Camouflage." In "Gripes," a newly promoted Snafu gives all his fellow GIs two women each, while he enjoys the attentions of three women dressed in scanty harem attire. Indeed, sexy, buxom women are everywhere—at home, in the dance hall, in the cinema, and often in the bushes—and are usually being willingly groped by Snafu or some other soldier.

Except for Snafu's mother and his girlfriend in "The Home Front," who becomes a WAC, the sole asset these women contribute to the war is their sexuality. Their purpose is to please the soldiers, and although this innuendo could not have been displeasing to the legions of lonely young men watching these cartoons, the other side of the issue constantly lurks in the background, as demonstrated in "The Home Front." In this cartoon, Snafu imagines his girlfriend succumbing to the ministrations of a suave lothario. The implication is that all the beautiful babes back home are making love, but not necessarily to lonely soldiers. Thus, even the supposedly faithful girl back home is a potential whore.

Woman as whore is, in fact, the predominant image of women in the *Snafu* series. The *Snafu* cartoon that does not have a pinup prominently displayed is rare. Some of these pinups, although partially clothed, are all too ready to remove their clothing for the GI, as seen by the pinup whose dress billows up in rhythm to Snafu's snoring breath in "The Goldbrick." The symbolic stripper defrocking for the GI in this cartoon is more explicitly portrayed in "Coming Snafu" and "The Home Front." In the former, a stage stripper gyrates sexily before letting her clinging gown slip down to her hips. The "Restricted" signs that appear over her breasts and navel only serve to allow imagination to embellish the image that the clinging gown and sexy gyrations have already revealed almost completely. In the second cartoon, a stripper writhes explicitly before taking it all off as the camera angle drops for a shot downward from mid-thigh. Again, the suggestion is more powerful than the actual image, and in case the viewer didn't get the idea, the stripper is followed by a trio of high-stepping female dancers in fringed g-strings and strapless brassieres.

Doubtless, the soldier watching the strippers in this *Snafu* cartoon was too busy whistling and pounding his chair or dreaming of a buxom babe of his own waiting back home to worry about the social implications of demeaning sexist images. And just as likely, he also consciously missed the implication of events surrounding Snafu's attention to women. This implication is aptly demonstrated at the very outset in the first *Snafu* cartoon, "Coming Snafu." Snafu, walking by a sexy pinup, turns and whistles and promptly falls into a hole. The message was made a little more obvious in "Spies" when Snafu, bragging to his girlfriend, who is a seductive sexpot spy with microphones hidden in her brassiere, unwittingly discloses vital military secrets. The trend continues in "Private Snafu vs. Malaria Mike." Snafu gets jabbed by Mike because he exposes his bare ass while kissing a pinup. And in "Gripes," the sexual license of Snafu and his troops results in defeat by the Germans. In the event that some soldiers still had not understood the message, one entire cartoon was devoted to expounding on the hidden but definite dangers posed by women.

This cartoon is "Booby Traps," set in North Africa. The name is not, at first, the dead give-away that it probably ought to be, for the piece ostensibly deals with the need to be aware of the dangers of hidden explosive devices designed to kill careless soldiers. Snafu finds one such explosive device integrated into a shower, but his next encounter paves the way for the real booby traps of which he should be aware. In this scene, Snafu comes upon a camel with a bulging udder. A sign reads, "Free milk." Snafu grabs a teat before realizing the udder is really a mine strapped to the camel's belly. If this was the only reference linking booby to breast as well as explosive danger, it might be innocent enough, but Snafu next finds himself in a harem full of booby traps that are definitely of a human variety.

In the harem, Snafu rushes through the midst of some of the most pulchritudinous images ever seen in a cartoon before Ralph Bakshi's *Fritz the Cat* (1972) and *Heavy Traffic* (1973). A score of shapely chiffon and bikini-clad beauties lounge around, and the camera pans across the shadowed but extremely explicit and pneumatically lifelike figure of a totally nude woman who almost completely fills the screen. Just to make certain the viewer did not miss her the first time, the camera pans across her again as Snafu makes his way toward a piano. If his immediate interest is the piano, booby trapped with explosives, he quickly turns his attention to a nearby buxom babe. Snafu slips his hand around her waist to cup her butt, and he marvels at the firm gluteal roundness. But the audience sees that she is a dummy with twin bombs for buttocks. A second later, her flowered bra, toned in such a way as to resemble bare breasts, falls off, revealing another pair of bombs. Even a booby like Snafu now gets the message that booby traps are not only explosive devices but women, too.

The most self-revealing note on lust in the Snafu series occurs in "A Lecture on Camouflage." Although the Technical Fairy, who does everything right, gains his buxom sexual reward, it is a pair of mermaids, or, women without vaginas—

with camouflaged vaginas. What becomes evident is that underlying the pandering to carnal desire and the promises of sexual reward, there is a deeper level that indicates that lust, although a useful spur to prod the soldier into action and compliance, is a gratification at best impossible to achieve and at worst deadly and thus futile to pursue.

Women in the *Snafu* series are dangerous. Even if they are not outright seductive spies trading sex for death and destruction, they invariably cause fatal inattention, leading to the same devastating results. This message extends to the other pleasures in which Snafu engages. Alcohol leads to drunkenness which leads to divulging military secrets, as is shown in "Spies." Recreation does the same, demonstrated also in "Spies" when Snafu is a dancing fool blurting out things he should not to his dance partner. The desire for recreation also leads, as shown in "The Goldbrick," to laziness, laxness, and inevitably, death. And in "A Lecture on Camouflage," Snafu's yen for a smoke causes him to be so totally unaware of his surroundings that he does not realize that the tree he is leaning against contains a German.

The subtexts of the *Snafu* cartoons emphasize that soldiers are, or should be, a brotherhood of dedicated, directed, and determined men who have banded together to do work that is necessary but dirty and potentially deadly. The devices that the filmmakers use to make these points are specifically engineered to gain the attention of their viewers and to lull them into complacency through humor, sympathy, and pandering to common vices. Just as clearly, however, the cartoons also psychologically reverse the imagery that they use to depict these apparently positive themes and elements. Humor becomes intimidation, for laughing at Snafu—the common soldier—quickly translates into fear of being held up to public ridicule. Sympathy for the plight of the soldier transforms into fear of death, for sympathy brings weakness and lack of attention, and these are fatal. And apparently innocent and innocuous desires, like those for sex, alcohol, tobacco, and even friendship, likewise seduce attention, foster weakness, and bring about death and destruction—an idea that blatantly trades pleasure for paranoia.

Thus, the *Private Snafu* cartoons wield a double-edged sword that not only incised indoctrinational and informational material but attempted to excise any attachments the soldier might have that could impair his single-minded attention to fighting and winning the war. The informational success of the series may be judged by Mel Blanc's anecdote about the aerial gunners quoted above, but more, the army must have felt that the Snafu series also was serving its indoctrinational purposes, because a new Snafu cartoon appeared about once a month until the end of the war.

If, as often has been noted, extraordinary circumstances demand extraordinary means, the *Private Snafu* cartoons certainly provide a vivid example of extraordinary means. The kind of social engineering pioneered by the series has left a pervasive legacy in world culture by aptly demonstrating the effectiveness of social engineering that plays on those desires, drives, and fears that form the foundation of human thought and emotion. The same techniques pioneered in the *Snafu* cartoons form, in fact, the basis of modern media advertising. Unfortunately, even ostensibly beneficial manipulation and modification of thought and emotion require care and foresight to ensure that positive values are not trodden beneath self-destructive imagery. The *Private Snafu* cartoons should stand as a cautionary reminder of the arbitrary and often dark depths that social and behavioral conditioning can plumb beneath an apparently benign facade.

Part II
Literature

John Donne's Metaphorical Voyage

DURING THE RENAISSANCE, THE WISDOM and knowledge of classical Greek and Roman writers provided fertile ground for the new-found flowering of Renaissance learning and philosophy. At the same time, Renaissance expansion into the physical world provided invaluable cross-pollination that increased the fecundity of Renaissance intellectual expansion. Of particular importance for the English was the physical exploration of the globe, necessary to garner wealth and maintain national security in the face of the rising might of other European countries, particularly Spain. A prime exponent of English exploration was Richard Hakluyt, whose encyclopedic work, *The Principal Navigations, Voyages, Traffiques and Discoveries of the English Nation*, widely and favorably publicized the exploits of English explorers and travelers. Records of journeys such as those detailed in Hakluyt's work endowed English literature with new metaphors based on exploration and discovery. These metaphors are strongly and particularly expressed in the literary work of John Donne, and indelibly mark his writing with an evolution that provides an insight into the poet's work.

Hakluyt's *Voyages and Discoveries* was first published in 1590. While the great age of European exploration and travel was waning even before the second edition appeared in 1600, there was still tremendous interest in voyages for adventure and profit.

The sagas of those who ventured with Renaissance curiosity and boldness across uncharted seas into the unknown beyond were enough to stir any man's imagination, and few writings of the time are without some reference to the exploits they record.[1]

Moreover, adventures of the sort Hakluyt publicized are of particular interest to the hearty, curious, and adventurous young. John Donne, born in 1572, was an eighteen-year-old student when the first edition of *Voyages and Discoveries* appeared, and he could not have helped being inspired by these tales of adventure. As A. C. Partridge points out, "Donne's imagination was powerfully influenced by his most recent reading, not of the poems of his contemporaries, but of encyclopedic treatises."[2] Donne was sufficiently influenced that he undertook his own voyages. "Donne not only went abroad but travelled so extensively that several of his friends actually thought of him as a traveler."[3] Initially, he spent time on the European Continent, and "it is probable that his travels [there] extended over the three years ending in 1591."[4] He also joined two sea expeditions, the first to Cadiz in 1596 and the second to the Azores the following year.[5]

While much of Donne's work cannot be dated accurately, certainly *Juvenilia: Or Paradoxes and Problems* belongs to the period of his own great explorations.

The evidence suggests that the 'Paradoxes', the verse satires, most of the elegies, some verse epistles, some lyrics, a few prose letters and 'The Progress of the Soul' predate Donne's marriage in 1601. Most of this work seems to be the product of Donne's time at the Inns of Court and just after.[6]

Even as early as this, Donne was making use of the metaphor of exploration. The section of *Juvenilia* titled

"Problem: Why Does the Pox So Much Affect to Undermine the Nose?" refers to mice as "Indian vermin" that "defeat elephants by gnawing their proboscis."[7] A few lines later he says that the "Cold was able to show the high-way to noses in Muscovia."[8] The first of these two references alludes to one early aim of English exploration: the establishment of an easy and profitable overland route to the Orient. Journeys by men like Anthony Jenkins, who traveled through Russia into the Middle East during 1558 and 1559[9], were originally undertaken to discover such a route and were subsequently publicized by Hakluyt. The second quote is a more specific reference to the abortive pursuit of a Northeast Passage to the Orient. Hakluyt mentions several such voyages, beginning with the expedition lead by Sir Hugh Willoughby in 1553, and ending with Stephen Burrough's exploration as far as the mouth of the River Ob and inland to Moscow from 1556 through 1557.[10]

The youthful excitement of adventure is particularly notable in Donne's early poems, written during the years of the first edition of *Voyages and Discoveries* and his own travels. One excellent example is "Elegy XVIII: Love's Progress," attributed to the early 1590s.[11] The poem itself is constructed around a conceit that mimics exploration. As the title, "Love's Progress," indicates, the pursuit of love is like a journey of exploration. The poem treats the body of the poet's lover as if it is a new world to be explored. As with any exploration, this journey has a beginning, incidents of discovery and adventure, and an end. Donne begins the poem, in fact, by immediately referring to the end: "Whoever loves, if he do not propose / The right true end of love, he's one that goes / To sea for nothing but to make him sick."[12] What Donne says in these first lines is that love, like any voyage of exploration and discovery, should have a profitable outcome. Indeed, at the end of the poem he says that "Rich Nature hath in women wisely made / Two purses"[13], conflating the fiscal rewards of exploration with the physical rewards of love.

Donne continues his extensive use of the metaphor of exploration in the third line, which intimates that the turmoils of love can be likened to the tossing of a ship in storm, for both cause sickness.

> Donne's experience with ships...is enough to prepare us for one of the main currents of his imagery from this source—the tendency to recall the more unpleasant aspects of sea travel and to consider all such travel as symbolizing progress through any medium beset with countless and inexorable perils.[14]

The metaphor is extended when he refers to a woman's brow as the sea, which causes problems for voyagers no matter what its aspect. "The brow becalms us when 'tis smooth and plain, / And when 'tis wrinkled, shipwrecks us again."[15] He then likens her nose to the major meridian that divides the hemispheres of the earth, which are her cheeks.[16] Her lips are a creek of safe anchor[17], her breasts Sestos and Abydos flanking the Hellespont[18], and her abdomen "a boundless sea" dotted with "island moles."[19] All these geographical features are encountered on the journey to "her India."[20]

> Again and again among these images we find the "East," and "India" serving as symbolic of all that is precious and desirable.... In Elegie XVIII, "Love's Progress," it becomes the goal of the lovemaker's explorations.[21]

India, whose deltaic shape, fabulous treasures, and frank and exotic sexuality successfully merge the pleasures of love with the profits of a successful voyage, is a particular and potent metaphor.

As with any exploration, there are adventures and difficulties along the way. From the beginning of the actual search, Donne is pregnant with allusions to journeys of adventure and discovery. "The hair a forest of ambushes, /

Of springes, snares, fetters and manacles."[22] On a literal level, these lines allude to aboriginal attacks in the jungles of both Africa and the Americas. But Donne engages the conceit of exploration even more fully than as simple descriptive detail. He utilizes an explorative methodology that literally reflects the entire thrust of the English endeavor to explore and exploit the world.

The English people had entered late in discovering new trade routes to the East and new lands to the West. As a nation, England had to make the effort to discover new and apparently circumspect routes, like the Northeast and Northwest Passages. It was hoped that these routes would lead more directly to the treasures that were the goals of exploration and, at the same time, avoid the perils of the known trade routes. Donne's conceit of exploration in "Love's Progress" becomes thematic as he mirrors the English method in his metaphoric pursuit of the sexual reward of love. He begins the journey of love by describing the route most often followed, which is downward from the head of the woman to "her India." There are, though, he points out, many difficulties in following this standard route —storms, shipwrecks, becalmings, savage ambushes, dangerous straits, and vast oceans to cross—before arriving at the source of the treasure. He suggests that the lover, like the English explorer seeking alternative, although less-direct routes to the Orient, would do better to embark upon a different and less traveled route which leads more leisurely and with fewer difficulties to the treasured prize.

"Love's Progress" is a plethoric catalogue of exploration metaphors. Few other of his poems utilize the conceit as fully, but even so, metaphors of voyage abound in other works.

Scattered through Donne's imagery are other items connected directly or indirectly with the records of exploration: the storminess of the Bermudas, the Mediterranean as transition between two worlds, the energy of the Russian merchants (who came to London after the Willoughby and

Chancellor expeditions to "Muscovy"), and that epitome of all that is opposite—the Antipodes.[23]

In "Elegy XIX: To His Mistress Going to Bed," for example, Donne says his mistress's girdle is "a far fairer world encompassing,"[24] giving her hips a planetary image circumnavigated by her apparel. Farther down, his explorations of her body become explorations of new lands:

Oh my America, my new found land,
My kingdom, safeliest when with one man
    manned,
My mine of precious stones, my empery,
How blessed am I in thus discovering thee![25]

The poet equates his lover's body with the tangible reality and treasures of new land that he physically explores and, in the exploration, achieves personal possession.

"The Sun Rising" has two metaphors of voyaging. "Both the Indias of spice and mine"[26] refers to journeys to the East, which, by this time, might be reinforced by Hakluyt's rendition of Ralph Fitch's epic travels across India and Southeast Asia to the Pacific shores of the continent.[27] And the last line reads, "This bed thy centre is, these walls, thy sphere."[28] Here Donne likens love to possession by encompassing the sphere of the earth, an accomplishment achieved by Sir Francis Drake and other Englishmen within Donne's lifetime.[29]

Some of Donne's poems make relatively minor use of metaphors of exploration. The one reference in "The Canonization" asks, "What merchant's ships have my sighs drowned?"[30] Other poems make somewhat more extensive use of exploration metaphors. "A Valediction: Of Weeping" contains one stanza replete with imagery of travel.

On a round ball
A workman that hath copies by, can lay
An Europe, Afric, and an Asia,

And quickly make that, which was nothing, all,

. . . .

A globe, yea world by that impression grew.[31]

The importance of this stanza emerges upon closer examination. The earth is referred to as a "round ball...A globe, yea world." The intimation is that the earth is now looked upon as a single unit whose boundaries, if not complete details, are now known. Indeed, "A workman that hath copies, can...quickly make that, which was nothing, all." In fact, the world is so thoroughly explored that a workman—a common craftsman, not an artist—can easily make copies, such as maps and globes. But copies are not original discovery, and these lines mark a subtle change in Donne's attitude, or perception, of exploration.

"The Good Morrow" expresses this change more succinctly. "Let sea-discoverers to new worlds have gone, / Let maps to others, worlds on worlds have shown, / Let us possess one world, each hath one, and is one."[32] Clay Hunt suggests that in these lines "the imagery of exploration and discovery expands the intellectual and emotional suggestions of 'makes one little room, an every where' in a dramatically powerful and richly significant conceit."[33] While this may be true, the lines also provide an almost prophetic definition of the change that the metaphor of exploration begins to take for Donne. He says, in effect, that maps provide only a counterfeit form of exploration that is in no way comparable to authentic tactile possession of the world. Unfortunately, as pointed out above in reference to "A Valediction: Of Weeping," the boundaries of that world are now fully known and mapped, and the excitement of original exploration and discovery are at an end.

For Donne, until now, the metaphor of exploration has demonstrated a personal and sensual immediacy. The world, symbolized by woman, is not something to be simply looked at and thought about, but should be physically embraced and explored with a voluptuous sense of discovery and wonder. As Donne matures, however, the tactile imagery he has utilized to deliver the metaphor of exploration alters. The alteration finds full expression in two poems: "A Valediction: Forbidding Mourning" and "Hymn to God My God, In My Sickness."

"A Valediction: Forbidding Mourning" contains Donne's perhaps best-known conceit. The poem likens the affections between the poet and his lover to a compass—an instrument of cartography and other drafting work.

> If they be two, they are two so
>   As stiff twin compasses are two,
> Thy soul the fixed foot, makes no show
>   To move, but doth, if th'other do.[34]

The compass imagery occupies much of the poem and is complex, but at the same time, it is curiously distant and uninvolving. David Novarr says:

> The compass image comes as a surprise. Neither souls nor compasses strike us as subjects conducive to a concession about the humanity of love. If the appeal to the souls seems rarefied, that to geometry seems totally lacking in humanity. Moreover, if the argument about the nature of their love has to this point been made quietly, indirectly, associatively, the demonstration of the force of the compass analogy is made with attention to detail and logic.[35]

These observations point to Donne's progressive tendency away from the personal and visceral toward the more distant and purely intellectual. The preponderance of cartographical images in the work of his middle years furthers this interpretation.

The interesting thing about this group [of poems] is that the only sizable cluster of related images in it...are the figures drawn from the use of the compass and various technical phases of navigation.[36]

But as the old saying goes, a map is not the terrain. For Donne, the world is no longer a tactile sensation but at one remove from immediacy, where the cartographical image—maps and navigational instruments—replace direct sensation as both medium of interaction with the world and expression of that interaction.

"Hymn to God My God, in My Sickness" continues and embellishes the cartographical image:

> Whilst my physicians by their love are grown
>   Cosmographers, and I their map, who lie
> Flat on this bed, that by them may be shown
>   That this is my south-west discovery
>   Per fretum febris, by these strains to die,
>
> I joy, that in these straits, I see my west;
>   For, though their currents yield return to none,
> What shall my west hurt me? As west and east
>   In all flat maps (and I am one) are one,
>   So death doth touch the resurrection.
>
> Is the Pacific Sea my home? Or are
>   The eastern riches? Is Jerusalem?
> Anyan, and Magellan, and Gibraltar,
>   All straits, and none but straits, are ways to them,
>   Whether where Japhet dwelt, or Cham, or Shem.[37]

This extensively quoted passage certifies Donne's loss of the world of immediate sensual experience and its replacement by the cartographical image.

In considering Donne's images from navigation we saw how he was led—almost without consciousness, I venture to say—toward the technical niceties of the compass; so in these images from exploration we find another curious direction, another semi-technical field mined for the peculiarly accurate, mechanically precise parallels to experience that it can provide.[38]

In "The Good Morrow," Donne had said that those who experience the world through maps, or representations of reality, have an inferior experience to the immediate and tactile. Now it becomes apparent that, in his own later use of the metaphor, exploration has moved away from immediate experience into the cartographical realm.

> Donne introduces a refinement on the stock analogy between man and the world: as he lies in his sickbed, he is not the world itself but rather a map of it. To see the implication of this new twist in the analogy, one must recognize a special connotation which maps often had for the Renaissance imagination and particularly for Donne: he regularly thinks of a map as a scanty and inadequate picture of the world which it represents.[39]

But even if Donne thinks of maps as scanty representations, it is also true that he now peruses these cartographical representations of reality with greater regularity and pursues expression through them instead of directly embracing tactile experience of the world.

At last, in the final years of Donne's literary output, the focus becomes even farther distanced from the immediate sensory experience typified by his earliest work. Just as sensory experience has run aground on the cartographical metaphor, the cartographical metaphor dissolves into the optical image. If immediate experience allowed Donne to directly touch and explore the world, and cartographical metaphors reduce that exploration to representative maps of a world already explored, then the optical imagery of "A Sermon Preached at St. Paul's for Easter-Day, 1628" makes of the world a distant reflection that is not only unreachable and untouchable, but dim and distorted as well.

The specific optical instrument Donne refers to in this sermon is a mirror.

> The old writers in the optics said that when we see a thing in a glass, we see not the thing itself but a representation only; all the later men say we do see the thing itself but not by direct but by reflected beams. It is a useless labor for the present to reconcile them.[40]

He goes on to say:

> The greatest flat glass that can be made cannot represent anything greater than it is.[41]
> As the glass which we spoke of before was proposed to the sense.[42]
> A glass [is] this which he calls an aenigma, a dark representation.[43]
> The creature was our glass, and reason was our light.[44]

Interestingly, rather than the word "mirror," Donne uses the word "glass," which, by extension, includes other meanings besides mirror. First, it is the eye, the glass through which we all observe the world.

> The connotations of the metaphor of the lovers' eyes as "glasses" and "mirrors" enforces further the general metaphysical implications of these lines. This image is, of course, concretely descriptive of the reflecting surface of the eyeball, on which the phantasm of the beloved impinges. But both of these words...suggest also the merely mediate knowledge of ultimate reality which is all that most mortals can attain during earthly life.[45]

But "glass," particularly for explorers, also signifies the spyglass, or telescope. This instrument is employed on ships to perceive distant objects, and its use was being extended into explorations of the heavens—God's realm—by men like Galileo, who made many of his major observations during Donne's lifetime.

The eye is a primary human sensory organ, and the mirror and the telescope are major tools that aid it in perceiving reality. But sight is also one of the least involving of the senses, for it does not touch the world or act upon it. Sight merely records, and as such, is more distanced from tactile sensation than even the cartographical image, for cartography at least furnishes, through its instruments, a physical intermediary between the poet and the world, for through these instruments the poet can still touch the world, or its representation. The instruments of the optical image, however, lend no such tangible contact and, in fact, can distort the images they provide.

Donne's reliance on optical imagery in his later writings finishes the voyage of the metaphor of exploration which he began as a young writer inflamed with love and adventure. Perhaps optical imagery is more appropriate to the spirituality of the subject matter of his sermons, but it also indicates that his journey through the metaphor of exploration has not circumnavigated the globe but merely arrived at the Antipodes. While imagery of tactile exploration is immediate and clarifying, optical imagery is distant and distorting.

Yet, though the specifics of Donne's imagery might have polarized and his means altered, his goal has never really changed—he is still looking beyond the known in the best way he can. Tactile involvement with the world is the province of the young, and age naturally brings distance from the tactile. All along, however, he has steadfastly sought the treasures that lie at the end of the voyage, even as he turns that exploration inward.

Discrimination's Double-edged Sword
Exclusion and cultural demise in Douglas Turner Ward's
Day of Absence

THE THIRTEENTH AMENDMENT OF 1865 made slavery illegal in the United States. Even so, many members of the white population retained a perception that slavery was a necessary—and even desirable—institution. In post-Civil War America, legalized discrimination, with its policy of social, political, and economic repression, extended the form of slavery without its formalism. In his drama, *Day of Absence*, Douglas Turner Ward examines the ramifications of slavery and racial discrimination less as a record of personal repression than as a look at how racial discrimination has affected the structure of American culture. First, he observes that separatism has created ostensibly different functional and ethical roles for blacks and whites. He then deconstructs these mythologized differences. At last, he emerges with the idea that slavery and discrimination create a fatal weakness within the culture. This weakness is as ruinous to the perpetrators as it is to the more obvious victims, for by denying wholeness to blacks, white supremacists deny wholeness to themselves.

Cultural importance of individuals or groups derives from their functional contributions that sustain the physical organization and constitution of the culture and from their ethical contributions that encompass the psychological and emotional constructs and qualities that give to a culture its unique character.

Most obviously in *Day of Absence*, Ward looks at how blacks function within American culture. As John MacNicholas notes, "Ward depicts the enormity of the contribution of blacks to American life and in the same stroke the enormity of the exploitation that blacks have historically suffered."[1] This dichotomy arises because the attitude espoused by perpetrators of white supremacy is that blacks have no functional purpose in and make no contributions to American culture.

The first indication in the play that the dominant society does not accord functional importance to blacks is that it takes Clem and Luke all morning to realize that the black inhabitants are absent from the town. If blacks were considered truly functional, their absence would have been noticed immediately, as much as an absence of automobiles on the street would be. The appropriately named Mr. Clan gives voice to this attitude when he says that blacks "ain't supposed to do nothing 'til we tell 'em,"[2] implying that blacks cannot think constructively and, thus, are incapable of self-determination. For Clan, denying that blacks have the awareness of what to do and when to do it justifies denying that blacks have the aptitude of leadership—that they can be operators of the machinery that supports culture instead of being relegated to the position of the machinery itself. Even the Announcer echoes this idea when he refers to the vanished blacks as "nonessential workers" and "uncrucial personnel,"[3] further negating their functional roles.

Mrs. Aide carries prejudice from the functional to the ethical when she says that the main purpose of the Nigra Git-A-Job Program is "to improve their ethical behavior."[4] She implies that blacks are not human enough to be innately ethical, but must have their lives set within rigid parameters to compel ethical behavior. Further, she says that blacks are "notorious shirkers,"[5] as if to say that the supposed lack of ethics in blacks is as much intentional as it is a fact of nature. Intentionality implies innate corruption, a belief echoed by the Reverend Pious, who calls the disappearance of the blacks "a reversion of the Nigra to his deep-rooted primitivism" assisted by Satanic voodoo.[6] Blacks are, to the white supremacist, degraded examples of humanity all too ready to indulge in base instincts and corrupt practices. According to Aide and Pious, not only are blacks functionally unable to construct culture, they are unable, because of a lack of ethical commitment, to affect culture in a positive way at the levels that transcend the functional.

But Ward shows from the outset that blacks fill significant, if unrecognized, functional and ethical roles within the culture. "Negroes constitute a numerical minority, but Negro experience, from slavery to civil rights, has always been of crucial importance to America's existence," Ward writes in another context.[7] The most overt contributions are visible at the functional level. When all the blacks vanish, the results belie the idea that blacks have no function in American culture, for the economic structure of the entire town is thrown into dysfunctional turmoil. After all, as the Mayor remarks, "Half this town is colored."[8]

One immediately felt result is that retail sales are radically down. The Businessman tells the Mayor, "The volume of goods moving 'cross counters has slowed down to a trickle."[9] Worse, despite the implication that blacks fulfill only nonessential, non-crucial functions, production of goods also is at a standstill. "Seventy-five percent of all production is paralyzed," says the Industrialist.[10] On the home front, the absence of black domestics has created voids that completely disrupt home life. Infants remain unchanged, meals remain uncooked, floors remain unswept, and bathrooms remain uncleaned. By removing blacks, Ward shows that they do perform vital functions, that they are not nonessential and uncrucial to society at all levels at which they are permitted to act. And the fact that among the absent are the vice mayor, two city council members, the chairman of the Junior Chamber of Commerce, the chair-lady of the Daughters of the Confederate Rebellion, and other highly ranked cultural, political, and economic icons indicates that the functionalism of blacks, even if not recognized, extends far beyond domestic duties and manual labor, even if those who perform these higher duties must cross racial lines to perform them in "white face"—either knowingly or not.

But being functional goes much deeper than the fact that black Americans simply comprise a significant part of the government, the work force, and the consumer base. In speaking of the evolution of black drama, Genevieve E. Fabre says that "the dramatist induces [the audience] to develop new forms of action and thinking; he confronts them with new images that often invert the old stereotypes."[11] Blacks are not simply machines that labor and consume. Their functional roles open culture to their ethical effect upon that culture. Ward demonstrates this through the characters of John and Mary and their missing maid, Lula.

Early in the play, John and Mary are awakened by their infant, who is crying because Lula, their maid, is not there to care for it. Because Lula is absent, Mary must care for the child, but since Lula has always performed the tasks associated with motherhood, Mary finds herself unprepared to perform even the simplest duties of child care. Her unpreparedness extends to the kitchen, where Lula has done everything to such an extent that Mary cannot even prepare coffee or fry eggs. Mary is, in fact, so dependent on Lula's functional abilities that she tells John, "I couldn't accept your wedding proposal until I was sure you'd welcome me and her together as a package."[12] The functional importance of blacks within the culture is well portrayed in this microcosm, but John and Mary's dilemma goes on to demonstrate the truth of the assertion that functionality and ethics are inseparable.

The bond between mother and child is one of the most ethical of all human relationships. "Among the Ashanti, the union of mother and child establishes the very foundation upon which societal relations are erected," says Paul Carter Harrison,[13] and this is true for most cultures. Even more pointed is Mary's name, which links her to Christ's mother—that ultimate mother of ethical behavior. But in this household microcosm of society, something is askew. When

John, whose name recalls that of John the Baptist, another nurturing figure associated with Christ, tells Mary to get up and take care of the baby, she replies, "What baby...whose baby...?"[14] This mother is so disconnected from her motherhood that she doesn't recognize the cry of her own child. The situation is pronounced enough that her initial response is "Smother it!"[15]

The repugnance is mutual, for the baby "yells louder every time [Mary tries] to lay hands on her."[16] The child is the crux here, for, as a basic and unmolded human being, it espouses basic values. Love is food, comfort, and a change out of a dirty diaper. At its most basic level, ethics equals functionalism. Mary's ethical difficulty with the child is a direct outgrowth of her lack of functional ability with the child. She has not done the dirty work associated with child care, and her functional incapabilities have rendered her ethically vacant. On the other hand, Lula has consistently fulfilled the functional role, and the infant recognizes this manifestation of love as truly ethical behavior. Lula, despite her absence, is the dominant individual of this household, for she has single-handedly held it together on both levels: the functional and the ethical.

With these details, Ward delves to the foundations of separatist culture. There he discovers that they are cracked by the perceived differences in function and ethics between the races and that this flaw is only shoddily mended by a patchwork acceptance of the idea that blacks are inextricably interwoven in the cultural matrix. C. W. E. Bigsby claims that Ward's "humor is largely at the expense of a white community which is seen as insipid and stupid, unconsciously manipulated by a Negro world which it holds in contempt."[17]

This may be true, but Ward indicates something that should be far more disturbing to whites than being the butt of a joke. Paul Carter Harrison comes closer when he speaks of "the daily struggle for survival which rewards individual initiatives toward the easy life, that life so highly esteemed in the oppressor."[18] White supremacist society has achieved the "easy life" through oppression, but Ward indicates that in doing so, whites have damaged not only their ethical well-being, but their own cultural wholeness as well as that of blacks. Mary says it most succinctly when she confesses, "I'm lost wit'out Lula, I need her, John, I need her."[19] This is not simply a confession of physical need, but a plea for deeper wholeness. Lula is, after all, her other half.

Adam David Miller decries Ward for not speaking to black consciousness:

> We see a black audience laughing at whites in their helplessness at the loss of the Negroes for a day. . . . The image of the black woman who raises [white] children at the sacrifice of her own is one all too familiar to blacks. What Negroes need to know is not that they are needed by whites, but that they are needed by one another.[20]

But Miller misses the mark. Ward is not just portraying the humor of incompetence or expounding upon who needs whom or what side is better. Ward's point is that functional competence is what both advances culture and ensures its vitality. Those who relegate to others tasks they consider demeaning forget how to perform the most basic functions of life that ensure economic, cultural, and physical perpetuation. John shows a vague awareness of this when he says, "I might've [married Lula] if it wasn't 'gainst the segregation law!"[21] He intuits that Lula, despite her nominally low cultural station, is a more complete human being than is Mary.

Ward's message is that people who relegate the operation of their daily lives to others—any others—separate themselves from true living and sign away their personal independence and deeper connections to humanity and the reality within which we live. Such apportionment, when carried to a cultural level, violates natural law by making the assignor unfit to survive. The privileged class, like John and Mary, will eventually find that it is unable to perform, without artificial aid, even the most basic functions that continue life. In a sense, Ward is warning of a cultural schism similar to that of the Eloi and Moorlocks depicted in H. G. Wells' *The Time Machine*, where the cultural separations have become so extreme that the proletariat runs all the machinery and literally preys on the aristocracy.

Mary might desperately need Lula, but it's obvious that the reverse is not true. The institution of slavery and racial separatism, while ostensibly boosting the economic and social status of whites, is unnatural and severs them from their basic vitality. The Mayor says, "It is my solemn task and frightening duty to inform you that we have no other recourse but to seek outside help for deliverance,"[22] tacitly admitting that his oppressive culture is unfit to survive without those it oppresses.

Hidden in the bark of *Day of Absence*'s overt humor is the bite of a grim realization. If survival is for the fittest, then white supremacy, or any culture that thrives by separatist oppression, debases itself through self-enslavement to the fatal flaw of separation from its own basic morality and self-preservation.

Let Me Talk with This Philosopher

Edgar's role in Shakespeare's *King Lear*

EXCEPT FOR LEAR, EDGAR IS the most crucial character in Shakespeare's *King Lear*.[1] Edgar's significance stems neither from his ascension to the throne at the end of the play nor from his admittedly vital role in settling the political disturbances that form much of the plot. Instead, Edgar is essential for his advisory relationship to Lear and for the results that his advice have on the king.

When Lear meets Edgar in III.4, the king is in the midst of an identity crisis, confused about how to deal with the loss of his position and power. In an attempt to regain his identity, Lear fixes upon madness, and he does so in direct response to Edgar's behavior as "Poor Tom." Thus, Edgar directly catalyzes Lear's descent into madness by providing a model of behavior that Lear believes will both release him from suffering and give him a means to construct a new identity.

Lear's personal identity has always been bound in the fabric of his social context: his position as monarch and head of state, his authority and power, the presence of subjects for him to rule, and most important, possessing heirs to whom he could bestow his kingdom. His view of personal identity is, therefore, entirely dependent on external definition. For him, people are defined by, and only by, their social context. As a result, Lear can consider only external manifestations of personality when he inquires into the identity of other people. Thus, the lies of Gonerill and Regan when, as a condition of inheritance, they profess to love him (I.1), seem to him to be accurate reflections of their true feelings. The deep and very real feelings Cordelia has for Lear, however, are not as easily verbalized as the lies of her sisters. Her emotions are beneath the surface, where Lear cannot visibly discern them, and so, for him, they seem not to exist.

By the end of Act II, Lear finds himself bereft of all external definitions that have formed his identity: kingdom, power and authority, and subjects. Even that most basic external definer, family context, has vanished, for he has rejected or been rejected by all his children. Lear, a person totally dependent on external definition to delineate his identity, has lost every single one of his definers and, so, has become a person without an identity. Further, since Lear's identity has always come from external sources and not internal resources, he finds himself without the inner means to construct a new identity for himself. Instead, he must seek personal identity, just as he always has, through an external definition. He must be told who to be.

But despite being in the throes of an identity crisis, at the beginning of Act III, Lear is not insane, merely lost, angry, and emotionally distressed. He vents his feelings in a fury that damns his oppressors and his present condition when, in apostrophe, he rages at the storm:

> Rumble thy bellyful! Spit, fire! Spout, rain!
> Nor rain, wind, thunder, fire are my daughters.
> I tax not you, you elements, with unkindness;
> I never gave you kingdom, called you children.
> You owe me no subscription. . . .
> . . . .
> But yet I call you servile ministers,
> That will with two pernicious daughters join
> Your high-engendered battles 'gainst a head
> So old and white as this. (III.2.14–24)

These are words of righteous anger rather than madness, for though Lear personifies the elements, he does so out of familiarity with their action upon himself, not because he actually believes the elements have consciousness or volition to conspire with his daughters against him.

In fact, given the choice to go mad or remain sane, Lear chooses the latter. He responds to Kent's suggestion that they seek shelter with a speech that starts: "My wits begin to turn" (III.2.67). This line shows that Lear understands that his mind has not been focused on the exigencies of reality that the storm have forced on him and his companions. The following six lines expand this understanding into a reply indicative of sane responsibility overcoming Lear's indignation and adverse circumstance rather than of imminent irrationality threatening his mind:

> Come on, my boy. How dost my boy? Art cold?
> I am cold myself. Where is this straw, my fellow?
> The art of our necessities is strange
> And can make vile things precious. Come, your hovel.
> Poor fool and knave, I have one part in my heart
> That's sorry yet for thee. (III.2.67–73)

Here, Lear is clearly not mad, for he retains all the qualities of sanity: sense of self, awareness of the necessities of life, the ability to heed the counsel of his advisors, and kingly responsibility toward other people. The frequent repetition of self referents—I, my, myself—further emphasizes the qualities of self possession, or sanity. And at the same time, these referents reinforce the idea that Lear's sense of self is determined by external definition, for here he is "himself" most when acting as "ruler" of others.

But even if not mad, Lear is in a precarious mental state. Because he cannot create an identity for himself, he desperately needs an external force—an advisor—to give him identity. Thus, not only is he open to any influence that may bring him relief from his loss of identity, he actively seeks such an influence. Outside Edgar's hovel, Lear cries:

> Poor naked wretches, wheresoe'er you are,
> That bide the pelting of this pitiless storm,
> How shall your houseless heads and unfed sides,
> Your looped and windowed raggedness, defend you
> From seasons such as these? Take physic, pomp;
> Expose thyself to feel what wretches feel,
> That thou mayst shake the superflux to them
> And show the heavens more just. (III.4.28–36)

Here Lear's externally dictated personality has been wiped away by the external turbulence of his life—symbolized by the storm— and he calls on the most wretched of humans to give him personal knowledge of how to survive in his present state and to teach him how to create from within himself his own identity. He calls on these people because, though homeless, poverty-stricken, and near-naked, they nonetheless manage to survive.

Enter Edgar, or rather, enter Lear into the sphere of Edgar's influence. Immediately after Lear ends his call for guidance, Edgar replies, "Fathom and half, fathom and half! Poor Tom!" (III.4.37) Edgar introduces himself as the "poor naked wretch" Lear has just called for, and he does so in terms a mariner uses when sounding the depths. Perhaps Lear must drown in order to live.

Significantly, Lear and Edgar meet in III.4, the central scene of the central act—the major balance point of the tragedy. Lear's sanity pivots on the axis of this scene; before meeting Edgar, Lear is sane, and afterward, he is mad. Although Lear does enter this scene in a vulnerable state, the genesis of his madness develops from the particular circumstances and occurrences depicted here. First, is the importance of the setting. Lear meets Edgar at the door of the hovel—the boundary between the external world which Lear has inhabited both physically and as head of state, and the interior world of Edgar's persona, mad Tom. Lear, wishing to gain identity for himself, must learn to create his own identity, and to do that he must enter into an interior world that has, until now, been foreign to him—a world in which interior identity isn't always as ordered as is externally defined identity, a world where stereotypes yield to archetypes, a world in which mad Tom is at home.

The setting also is a vital indication of the forces at work, for the hovel belongs to Edgar, the rightful future Earl of Gloucester. Thus the meeting is a grimy likeness of a visit by a royal monarch to the castle of a lord of near-equal status for the purpose of aid and advice during a time of state crisis. The submerged context of king seeking a mode of operation from an advisor is pointedly paralleled earlier in the play when another monarch, Regan, speaks to Edgar's father, the present Earl of Gloucester, during her visit to Gloucester's castle:

> Thus out of season, threading dark-eyed night—
> Occasions, noble Gloucester, of some price,
> Wherein we must have use of your advice.
> . . . .
> Lay comforts to your bosom, and bestow
> Your needful counsel to our business,
> Which craves the instant use. (II.1.118–127)

This speech counterpoints, in its ordered neatness, Lear's wild words outside Edgar's hovel, but its intent echoes and emphasizes Edgar Gloucester's capacity as advisor, teacher, and role model when Lear pays him a visit "out of season, threading dark-eyed night, for counsel which craves instant use." Considering Lear's unconscious need to have his identity externally defined, his awareness of his lack of identity demonstrated by his verbalized cry for instruction, and his present vulnerability to external influences, Edgar's role as Lear's advisor takes on paramount importance. The fact that the advisory persona is not Edgar, a rational nobleman, but Tom, a wretched madman, provides the key to Lear's own madness.

The Fool immediately senses the danger, for the instant he sees Tom he cries, "A spirit, a spirit!" (III.4.41) Edgar is not actually mad, but as Tom, he does carry the shade of madness like a sort of infection. Even Edgar intuits the danger and says, "Away! The foul fiend follows me. Through the sharp hawthorn blow the cold winds" (III.4.44–45). He is warning Lear that a brittle mental state, even if it is well-armed against tangible foes, affords no protection from the winds of unreason. He tells Lear to "Go to thy bed and warm thee" (III.4.46). Lear should retreat to a place where his response to confused identity will not be madness but rest and recuperation.

Lear does not retreat, however, but immediately seeks to understand Tom, a person who survives without an externally defined identity, for his is a feat that Lear himself must now accomplish. When Tom asks, "Who gives anything to Poor Tom?" (III.4.49), the condition of withheld identity so directly mirrors Lear's own fate that Lear immediately begins to equate himself with Tom. Further, the sentence leads a prose passage where Tom openly voices Lear's personal conviction that "the foul fiend hath led [him] through" adversity, thrown him at the mercy of corrupted domesticity by having "laid knives under his pillow and halters in his pew, [and] set ratsbane by his porridge," and forced him into a raging wilderness devoid of human context (III.4.49–59).

As a result of this passage, Lear begins such a complete identification with Tom that he insists Tom's "daughters brought [Tom] to this pass" (III.4.60), or in other words, that he and Tom are equal, even though Kent points out that Tom "hath no daughters" (III.4.66). Lear ignores Kent and persists in his delusions and equating himself with Tom, indicating that the king now prefers the advice of Tom over the counsel of his former advisor, Kent. Lear now views Tom as a role model to be emulated for his ability to exist in the new context in which Lear finds himself.

In direct response to Lear's acceptance of him as advisor, Tom delivers the recommendation to "Take heed o'the foul fiend, obey thy parents, keep thy word's justice, swear not, commit not with man's sworn spouse, set not thy sweet heart on proud array" (III.4.77–79). The truth and sanity of this exhortation to remedy the social ills of disobedience to parents, dishonesty, adultery, greed, and pride strikes so close to the conditions of both Lear and the state that it cements Lear to Tom. He asks Tom, "What hast thou been?" (III.4.81) Ostensibly Lear here asks for personal background information from Tom, but underlying the question is a hidden request for identity, as if Lear is subliminally asking Tom to teach him how to create identity from within.

At this request for further identity from him, Tom enters into a second prose passage describing the fictitious life of a member of the serving class: a proud, vain gigolo who was "false of heart, light of ear, bloody of hand; hog in sloth, fox in stealth, wolf in greediness, dog in madness, lion in prey" (III.4.82–94). While the particulars of this fabricated life do not mirror Lear's own life experiences, the general condition of descent from a higher to a lower station of life reflects Lear's circumstances. More important, Lear identifies with the results, for both men are outcasts.

Lear replies to Tom's account with his own prose passage, as important for its prose form as for its content. Prose speech, lacking the structured music of the blank verse spoken by the majority of the characters, is indicative of formlessness and disorder. Prior to Tom, the only other character who has spoken extensively in prose has been the Fool. Due to its unmusical formlessness, prose is the manner of speech proffered by fools and the insane. Before listening to Tom, Lear has had only two minor prose passages (I.4.40–44, 66–71). However, after Tom speaks prose, Lear instantly replies extensively in the same form. Afterwards, until recovering his sanity in IV.7, nearly half of Lear's speeches of more than two lines are prose. Lear has decided to learn from Tom, and in keeping with his reliance on externals to define identity, naturally mimics this external aspect of his model when he replies in kind to Tom's prose.

In content, Lear's prose speech proclaims that he believes that man in his natural state owes nothing and is owed nothing:

> Thou owest the worm no silk, the beast no hide, the sheep no wool, the cat no perfume. Ha! Here's three on's are sophisticated. Thou art the thing itself! Unaccommodated man is no more but such a poor, bare, forked animal as thou art. (III.4.98–105)

The line, "Thou art the thing itself," shows that Lear has an inkling that personal identity can come from within, and to him, the madness manifested by Tom seems to be a means to self-create identity. At this moment, he decides to completely imitate Tom. As an outward sign of his emulation, Lear tears off his clothes. "Off, off, you lending! Come, unbutton here" (III.4.98–105). Naked now, like Tom, Lear formally invites Tom to be his mentor: "First let me talk with this philosopher" (III.4.146). Then he asks Tom to join him: "Noble philosopher, your company" (III.4.166). And finally, he voices his desire to have Tom's continuing example: "With him! I will keep still with my philosopher" (III.4.169–170). Thus Lear's rapidly growing identification with Tom progresses from the somewhat removed "this philosopher," to the more familiar "you," and finally ends as the completely identified "my philosopher." Lear is now totally reliant on Tom's advice and example.

Unfortunately for the king, Lear's intuition that Tom is able to self-create identity is supported by a dark undercurrent. Tom indeed has the ability to create himself, but on a much deeper level than Lear suspects. The persona of Tom is, indeed, truly self-created—completely and convincingly manufactured from whole cloth by Edgar. This means that Lear accepts as teacher and role model an individual who is totally false and unreal. Ironically, in his search for an internally created identity, Lear has not only once again accepted another external definition of identity, but worse, has fabricated an identity that is based on a persona invented in another person's imagination. As if this isn't disastrous enough, Lear's newly adopted persona is that of a madman. In his search for identity, Lear now finds himself once removed from any identity and from sanity itself.

Lear's conversion to madness has now taken place, though only afterward do the other members of the company notice a change in his mental state. By the end of the third act, Kent says of Lear, "His wits have given way to his impatience" (III.6.4–5), but this is not so. Lear's wits have given way in a misguided attempt to emulate Tom. Even Edgar, who had not recognized the king's vulnerable mental state, much less considered that Lear might mistake Tom's behavior as a valid response to loss of identity, begins to consciously realize that he has unwittingly caused Lear's degeneration. He says, "How light and portable my pain seems now, / When that which makes me bend makes the King bow— / He childed as I fathered" (III.6.96–98). In this last line, Edgar himself accepts that he is the father, the genesis, of Lear's madness.

The darkly humorous aspect of Lear's acceptance of Tom's madness is the fact that, after the king's descent into insanity, Edgar "recovers" and assumes a role of externally defined responsibility. This indicates that he accepts that a completely self-created identity is insane precisely because it is disconnected from the social fabric. Lear's misunderstanding, madness, and demise are predictable since he has consistently considered only the exterior of people when trying to understand identity. In the final analysis, the real tragedy might be that Lear met a madman rather than a saint.

An Equestrian Tragedy
The image of the horse and the fall of Troy in Chaucer's
Troilus and Criseyde

MANY IMAGES EMERGE FROM THE story of the Trojan War.
Achilles, the nearly invulnerable hero is legendary, as are the
beauty of Helen, the lusts of Paris, and Odysseus's long and
eventful voyage home at the close of the war. One image,
however, rises above all others in memory and imagination—that of the huge and hollow equestrian statue known
as the Trojan Horse. The beauty of Helen and the lusts of
Paris precipitated the Trojan War, and the exploits of
Achilles provided many of its memorable moments, but the
Trojan Horse was the specific and immediate means by
which it ended. Troy, secure behind its walls and facing a
demoralized enemy, fell only because of the horse. Geoffrey
Chaucer does not explicitly allude to the Trojan Horse in his
epic poem about the Trojan War, *Troilus and Criseyde*[1], most
obviously because the action of the story ends well before
the statue figures in the war. Chaucer does, however, make
interesting use of equestrian imagery in connection with his
main characters, their relationships, and the fates of Troilus
and Troy.

The parallels between love and war often have been noted. *Troilus and Criseyde* juxtaposes the armorial conflict of the
Trojan War with the amourial conflict of the love affair between Troilus and Criseyde, and Chaucer extends the equiva-

lencies into definition of character and delineation of plot. Indeed, Chaucer defines the characters of Troilus and Criseyde in direct relationship to the partisan forces of the historical war, and the particulars and results of the love affair offer analogies to the historical outcome of the conflict.

That the character of Troilus personifies the city of Troy is most directly indicated by their nearly identical names. The parity of Troilus and Troy is lent further weight by the fact that the identity of a nation's ruler, particularly for Chaucer's Medieval audience, is equated with national identity. Troilus, as prince of Troy, acquires a comparable identification as the state. Chaucer further connects the man and the city in the first two lines of the work when he refers to "The double sorwe of Troilus to tellen, That was kyng Priamus sone of Troye." (One, 1–2) In addition to their coincident naming in these first two lines of the work, Troilus and Troy are conjoined by the double sorrow—Troilus's private sorrow at being defeated in love and Troy's public sorrow at being defeated in war.

Thus, Troilus personifies Troy, and Chaucer carries the analogy further by presenting, within the context of the love story, the Greek enemy. Criseyde, being Troilus's counterpart in the love affair, is that enemy. Even Troilus eventually comes to think of her as such. After she has left the city, Troilus realizes that she will never return and that she has transferred her love to Diomede. He says, "O herte myn, Criseyde, O swete fo!" (Five, 228) He agrees that Criseyde represents the Greeks, but his understanding comes too late, for this characterization of Criseyde as the Greeks is not new in Book Five. From the outset, Chaucer has presented it as a major motif. Just as the Greeks oppose the Trojans in the war, Criseyde consistently has played the antithesis of Troilus. That she is the feminine side of the love affair and he is the masculine is the most basic level, but the metaphor grows from that foundation.

Unlike Troilus, an inexperienced lover who has until now completely scorned and rejected love, Criseyde has been married. Not only does this demonstrate her experience and acceptance of love, but having been married also implies that Criseyde has prior binding loyalties. What sets the distinction between her past marriage and her present affair with Troilus is that though she married for love, the affair with Troilus is contrived through the machinations of Pandarus rather than because Criseyde is drawn to the prince through innate affection. And there is another, more significant aspect of the lovers' manifold roles that invites further examination: the unusual paring of masculinity with innocence on the one hand and femininity with experience on the other.

Troilus, the soldier, is shown to be strong externally, for among the Trojans, he is a warrior second only to Hector. At the same time, he is internally weak, for he vacillates and finds it nearly impossible to initiate advances toward Criseyde. She, on the other hand, is weak externally, for she is a woman with no political rights living in a city her father has betrayed. At the same time, Criseyde possesses internal strength shown by her willful self-determination. These contradictory attributes in the two lovers mirror the forces they represent. Troilus's strong exterior and weak interior portray the powerful walls of the city protecting the militarily weak population of Troy. Criseyde's weak exterior but strong interior depicts exactly the state of the Greeks who, though devoid of externally protecting walls, maintain a determined will to conquer the Trojans.

Another specific connection between Criseyde and the Greeks is her identification with Helen. The two women are first linked when Pandarus asks Troilus the identity of the object of his affections. He says, "Ne, by my trouthe, I kepe nat restreyne Thee from thi love, theigh that it were Eleyne That is thi brother wif." (One, 676–678) By mentioning them in this manner, Chaucer creates an immediate correlation between Helen and Criseyde, a correlation that is reinforced by the fact that Criseyde and Helen are the only two Greek women in *Troilus and Criseyde*.

The two women are reciprocal in other respects as well. Both are in love relationships with princes of Troy, but both have only reluctantly entered into these relationships. Helen is kidnapped by Paris, and Criseyde is coerced into her affair with Troilus. Furthermore, by being maneuvered into these relationships, both women lose positions of personal influence and power. As wife of Menelaus, Helen had been a queen, but as wife of Paris she is only a princess to a prince who is not even the direct heir to the throne. Similarly, the widowed Criseyde possesses freedom and self-determination that she is reluctant to give up by becoming involved with Troilus.

The bonds between the two women and the Greeks extend even deeper. Although Helen appears only briefly in Troilus and Criseyde, her actions demonstrate a symbolic significance within the context of the historical tale. At the end of Book Two, Helen pledges to protect Criseyde from those who might conspire to harm her: "Joves lat hym nevere thryve, That doth yow harm...If that I may, and alle folk be trewe!" (Two, 1607–1610) Because Helen only appears this one time, it is important to examine this vow in relation to Criseyde as a symbol of Greece.

The legend of the Trojan War relates that Helen was forcefully taken by Paris. Though she may have submitted to his charms while captive, at heart she remained loyal to Menelaus and the Greeks. Within Troy was a statue of Minerva, reputedly fallen from the heavens, that protected Troy as long as it remained within the walls. Odysseus and another warrior entered Troy in disguise and stole the statue. While on the mission, they were spotted by Helen, who recognized Odysseus. Her loyalty to the Greeks was such that, although she recognized Odysseus, she did not raise an alarm but let the Greeks escape with the protective talisman of Troy. Thus, in offering to protect Criseyde from her enemies, Helen is symbolically fulfilling her role as secret protector of disguised Greeks as they work mischief within the walls of Troy. The scenario is equally applicable to the Trojan Horse, the ultimate in Greek disguise, which was devised by none other than crafty Odysseus. And what truly cements this subtle conspiracy is that the warrior who accompanied Odysseus was Diomede, the Greek prince for whom Criseyde forsakes Troilus.

Criseyde, therefore, in the context of the love story, represents the Greeks to Troilus's Troy. Thus, since the Trojan Horse was the downfall of Troy, horses in *Troilus and Criseyde* need to be examined in the context of the lovers and of Troilus's downfall. Chaucer does, indeed, continue his analogy by presenting in the fate of Troilus a mirror image of the fate of Troy—fallen because of an equestrian image.

A symbiosis exists between a knight and horse that signifies military power and success, for a knight depends on his horse to lend him strength, mobility, and superior position in battle. Just as the knight who controls a horse in battle possesses the power of victory, the tribe or nation that lays claim to the equestrian image symbolically possesses the power of dominion. Throughout the rising action of Troilus and Criseyde, Troilus is the premier knight of the story, and as the primary representative of the dominant power, he has a special relationship with the equestrian image.

In fact, during the first four books, Troilus is the only person seen in a direct and personal relationship to a horse, and the only other people seen riding are the warriors under his direct command: "Troilus...Com ryding with his tenthe som y fere." (Two, 1248–1249) Troilus is referred to as a knight who "sat on his hors aright." (Two, 1261–1263) Furthermore, the steed that Troilus rides is the only one in the entire work that is given a name—Bayard—and it is a powerful steed. (One, 218). Troilus's personal control of the horse suggests that he controls the symbolic potency of this powerful image. This, in the representation of Troilus as Troy, is consonant with Troy's superior position in the war, for the city, secure behind its walls, is in possession of the victory that is alluded to by the military power of the horse. It is, in essence, a warrior sitting in a strategically and tactically superior position.

The symbolic linking of knight and horse is a general motif, but Chaucer wastes no time in conflating Troilus and the horse in specific terms. He does so, though, in ways that gradually erode Troilus's control of the image. No sooner has Troilus been introduced in person than he makes a prideful boast in defiance of love: "I have herd told...of...Ye loveres....O veray fooles, nyce and blynde be ye!" (One, 197–202) Troilus is ostensibly speaking for himself, but since he represents Troy, his statements are equally indicative of the situation of the city. The blind lusts of Paris have precipitated the war, and the foolish pride of Priamus convinces the city that it should and can defend the illicit acts of Paris in the face of the armed might of Greece. Immediately after Troilus makes his boasts, Cupid's arrow smites him in the eye. Love is to be Troilus's personal downfall for the hubris of pride, just as love precipitated the downfall of Troy for a similar sin.

Horse imagery immediately surfaces following this fore-shadowing of the "double sorrow," merging love and pride and Troilus in a special way in the very next stanza when Troilus mounts his horse and says, "'Yet am I but an hors, and horses lawe I moot endure, and with my feres drawe.'" (One, 223–224) The law, or influence, of the power of the horse will rule Troilus, just as it rules the fate of Troy. Fealty to the equestrian image may seem appropriate to the young Troilus, warrior and knight, but the following stanza demonstrates the lack of foresight inherent in the vow when the narrator points out that "So ferde it by this fierse and proud knyght...Wax sodeynly moost subjit unto love." (One, 225–231) Troilus may be the leader of the horses, but right away his control over the image begins to wane, for at the same time, he is now ruled by love. If Troilus controls the horses but is himself controlled by love, then love actually controls the equestrian image, not he. Since Criseyde is the object of Troilus's love, Troilus thus transfers the essence of the power of the image to her. Now she, symbolically, is in control of the equestrian image. So, although the horse initially lends its power to Troilus and Troy, there is intimation that the power is as subject to the wheel of fortune as is love.

Even Pandarus confirms that Troilus's claim to the equestrian image has begun to deteriorate when he awakens Troilus with, "'Artow like an asse?'" (One, 731) Wily Pandarus senses that Troilus's equestrian power has degenerated into a laughable imitation. From the moment of being stung by Cupid's arrow, Troilus's claim to the image and power of the horse progressively disintegrates. At the end of Book One, he mounts his powerful bay steed to do battle with the Greeks (One, 173–175), but when he returns, "Wownded was his hors, and gan to blede." (Two, 626) Troilus's control over the equestrian image has not only begun to deteriorate, but the Greeks have contributed to its weakening by physically wounding his horse, indicating that the Greeks are beginning to lay claim to the power of the image.

Criseyde, the symbolic Greek foe, further usurps Troilus's proprietorship of the power of the image when she says, "Shal noon housbonde seyn to me 'chek mat!'" (Two, 754), then refers to Troilus, only seven lines later as "this knyght." (Two, 761) The proximity of a reference to the game of chess and the word "knight" creates a distinct visualization of the chess piece called the knight, which is shaped like a horse. Unfortunately for Troilus, he is not a player in this game, but merely a piece to be manipulated by Pandarus and Criseyde, both of whom are more experienced and subtle players.

After Troilus's bay steed is wounded by the Greeks and his claim to the equestrian image is checkmated by Criseyde, both of which indicate the Trojan's near-total loss of control over the power of the equestrian image, the action turns at the beginning of Book Five to favor the Greeks. At this time, Criseyde leaves the city to join the Greeks, taking with her both Troilus's love and the equestrian image. This move destroys Troilus and at the same time heralds the destruction of Troy.

Criseyde's appropriation of the horse image for the Greeks is blatantly demonstrated by the fact that she, accompanied by Diomede, rides a horse out of the city gates. Until now, no one else has been seen in direct and personal relationship to the equestrian image except for Troilus. Now, Criseyde and Diomede, representatives of the Greeks, are in control of it, and they irrevocably remove it from Troy in much the same way that Diomede and another crafty Greek removed another important talisman of power from the city. As if to emphasize the completeness of the transfer of power, Troilus, while waiting for Criseyde to ride out of the city, is "So wo-bigon, al wolde he naught hym pleyne, Than on his hors unnethe he sat for peyne." (Five, 34–35). In some way, Troilus is uncomfortably aware that all the power is departing from the city, leaving it vulnerable.

Soon after this, Troilus, devoid of both love and power, "sodeynly doun from his hors he stert" (Five, 200) and is never again seen mounted on a horse. He, and Troy, have lost control of the power of the horse, and that power is conferred completely upon the Greeks.

And after this he to the yates wente
Ther as Criseyde out rood a ful good paas...
Ans to hymself ful ofte he seyde, "Allas!
Fro hennes rood my blisse and my solas!" (Five, 603–607)

Hereafter, instead of riding, Troilus can only stand on the walls of the city watching Criseyde, the representative of the Greeks, blatantly exhibiting her control of the equestrian image as she rides about on the open ground beyond the walls.

More subtle elements accompany the transfer of the power of the horse from the Trojans to the Greeks. As Criseyde exits Troy, she is accompanied by Diomede, who, ironically, is described as the second greatest warrior for the Greeks, which makes him the Greek parallel to Troilus. But Diomede does not simply accompany Criseyde. He leads her horse out of the city by the bridle. (Five, 92) This action overtly indicates both his growing relationship with Criseyde and complete Greek mastery of the equestrian image. With the conflation of "bridle" and "bridal," not only will Diomede become the new object of Criseyde's love, thus contributing the personal blow that will result in the death of Troilus, but his presence is significant in relation to the public sorrow of the defeat of the city.

Very important is that fact that Diomede and Criseyde are in joint possession of the image of the horse as they appropriate it from the city. The parallel to the theft of the statue of Minerva is unmistakable. In that instance, Diomede and a disguised Greek jointly removed another symbol of power from Troy. While the statue represented spiritual protection for the city, the symbolic horse that Diomede and this disguised Greek, Criseyde, remove from Troy represents tangible Trojan military power. Thus, Diomede has had a personal hand in both destroying the will of Troy to defend itself and compromising its defensive capabilities, thus ensuring the defeat of the city.

Diomede and the Greeks now control the love and the equestrian image that formerly had been the provinces of his opposite number, Troilus. From this point onward, it is Diomede rather than Troilus who is consistently referred to as "the knight," and the Greek wields the power of the equestrian symbol for his people. He tells Criseyde:

> For trewliche he swor hire, as a knyght,
> That ther nas thyng with which he myghte hire plese,
> That he nolde don his peyne and al his myght
> To don it.... (Five, 113–116)

The meaning is unmistakable. The Greeks have control of the horse, and it will do anything to serve them.

The tide of battle turns immediately toward Greek victory. Troilus, his aggression purloined along with his heart, becomes a slipshod warrior, indicating that the interior weakness of the city has begun to adversely affect Trojan defenses, which the impregnable walls should ensure. Indeed, it will be sloppy military strategy that will allow the Trojan Horse within the walls of Troy.

Punctuating Greek control of the power of the equestrian image, Diomede wins Troilus's bay steed in battle. He gives it to Criseyde and she gives it back to him (Five, 1038–1039), reinforcing the transference of the power of the equestrian image from Troilus/Troy, though the intermediary Criseyde, to Diomede/Greece. Finally, Troilus is slain by Achilles—a Greek who is also the most powerful warrior of the war. With his death, the fate of Troy is sealed. Superior Greek forces will infiltrate and overwhelm the city.

Chaucer brings the Trojan War to neat closure with an ironical juxtaposition: The Trojan War begins because a Trojan prince betrays an alliance with the Greeks by seducing a Greek woman and kidnapping her, and it ends because a Greek woman betrays an alliance with Troy by seducing a Trojan Prince and escaping. Specifically, Troilus falls because a disguised Greek penetrated his defenses and destroyed him from within by taking from him his strength and power, symbolized by the weakening effect of his unrequited love and the theft of the equestrian image.

Mirroring the tragedy of the Trojan prince is the destruction of his city, which also falls to disguised Greeks who now employ the equestrian power the Trojans have lost. Ultimately, it is a specific equestrian image—this time of heroic proportions in the Trojan Horse—that wins the war when it is turned against Troy, reentering the city by the very gates through which Criseyde removed it.

T. S. Eliot Consults the Oracle
The Sibyl and "The Waste Land"

IN HIS REVIEW, "ULYSSES, ORDER, and Myth," T. S. Eliot argues that "instead of narrative method, [writers] may [and should] now use the mythical method."[1] His groundbreaking poem, "The Waste Land" bears out this dictum, and in it, mythical people, places, and incidents abound. However, nothing resonates so fully in this arena as does the presence of the numerous prophets within the poem. Some, like Tiresias, are mythic in origin, and some, such as Buddha and Christ, come from religious traditions. Others, like Shakespeare's Prospero, hearken to literary sources, and Madame Sosostris is of a definite modern cast. But the first prophet to appear, the Sibyl of Cumae, her aged and withered form suspended in a jar, is the most significant, for she provides a focus to define the roles of Eliot and "The Waste Land" within the mythic continuum.

The Sibyl of Cumae is an oracle of Apollo. She appears in the epigraph, quoted from *The Satyricon by Petronius*:

> For I myself saw with my own eyes the Cumaean Sibyl hanging in a bottle, and when the boys said to her, "Sibyl, what do you want?" she would reply, "I want to die."[2]

Her appearance before the poem actually begins both demonstrates and fulfills her role, which is at once symbolic and prophetic. In a great many mythic journeys, the traveler consults an oracle before beginning his or her pilgrimage through the wasteland of an unknown and alien wilderness. By calling on the oracle before the poem begins, Eliot, the poetic traveler entering unknown poetic territory, immediately invokes a resonance with the mythic by conforming to this well-established mythic pattern. Traditionally, the adventurer asks a question of the oracle, who presages particulars of the journey, its outcome, or both. In the epigraph, the Sibyl is asked a question by more than one boy, a significant point when the following epigraph to Ezra Pound is considered, for "The Waste Land" was nearly as much Pound's work as Eliot's, so this particular poetic journey is, indeed, being undertaken by more than one poet.

Prophets perform a duty within mythic journey that is more important than simply revealing highlights and outcomes. Often mythic journeys and the cultural and political changes they bring about are directly motivated by prophecies. The stories of Oedipus, Jason, Theseus, and Heracles are prime examples of journeys begun not simply by chance or by the intention of the traveler, but specifically because an Apollonian oracle directly inspired their undertakings. The idea that prophets actually impel mythic journeys has a strong relationship to the appearance of the Sibyl at the opening of the poem.

The epigraph, like the Sibil's jar, is a self-contained unit, and both contain the Sibyl. In a sense, the epigraph is the jar. Prophets and prophecy are the entire world of the epigraph, just as they are the entirety of the jar. The conflation between the epigraph, jar, and prophecy suggests a relationship between the content and form of the epigraph that is focused by the question the boys ask. Notably, the question does not concern the boys, but relates to the Sibyl and asks how she feels about herself, indicating that the prophet is the real subject matter under debate. The Sibyl's answer further turns the world of prophecy inward, for her reply also deals with herself and is not really a prophecy, but more of a cry for surcease.

Both question and answer indicate that the real subject matter of prophecy is prophecy itself. Thus, prophetic vision becomes, in a sense, both the entire world of the prophet and the force that motivates that world. Since the contents of the oracular reading are equivalent to its form, and since that form is equivalent to the prefatory words of the poem, the Sibyl's presence in the epigraph effectively foretells the importance of prophets and prophecy as primary motivators of the poetic journey.

Further, prophets not only launch but continue to propel the very incidents and adventures whose ends they foretell. In many Greek myths begun with auguries by the Sibyl of Cumae or one of her pythonic sisters at Delphi, Gryneium, or Clarus, the prophetic function is either continued by the oracle or, just as often, is taken up by other prophets such as Tiresias, or even the gods themselves. The continuation or assumption of the prophetic role from the Sibyl by others once the journey has begun is an obvious element in "The Waste Land," as Madame Sosostris and Tiresias enter to foretell and redefine particulars of this poetic journey. More subtly, it is also an indication of the role of Pound, who takes the work begun by Eliot, and through a process of re-vision, refines and redefines it to its finished state.

Since the presence of the Sibyl conflates subject matter and form, and prophetic words both motivate and propel myth, the epigraph envisions the prophetic role within myth not simply as descriptive but as a unifying motif. There emerges from the epigraph a clear progression of unity that begins with the cohesive quality prophets bring to individual myths. Much of this has already been discussed with regard to individual myths, since most Greek myths and legends of distinction contain seers who appear and reappear to motivate and propel the journey or incidents. But the functions of motivation and continuation extend beyond the boundaries of particular myths.

The Sibyl of Cumae, being an oracle of Apollo, becomes, in essence, all Apollonian oracles since all speak with Apollo's voice. The voice of Apollo is what is significant, not the vocal cords of an individual oracle. Because of this, it is important to consider the overwhelming effect this one voice has had on Greek mythology. Nearly every significant Greek myth detailing the rise of Greek civilization and culture owes either its existence or its continuation to Apollo and his oracles. Century after century, the voice of Apollo, coming from the lips of his oracles, represented here by the Sibyl of Cumae, ordered and manipulated not only the inception but the growth and flowering of Greek culture. From myth to myth through a millennium, no other single force has played a more significant role in creating Greek culture, and more importantly, sustained that culture sufficiently enough to allow it to become the foundation of modern civilization in general, and Western literature in particular.

Thus, the idea of mythic unity established by prophecy extends simple cohesion within individual myth into a sense of cultural continuation. Prophecy is not simply the root, but the tradition that flowers from that root, making the Sibyl of Cumae an important image with which to begin the poem. Of all the prophets mentioned in the poem, the Sibyl not only represents the single most pervasive cultural voice in human history, she is, personally, by far the oldest and most individually continuous of Apollo's vocalists. But the idea that prophecy empowers and is empowered by a tradition that extends to the beginnings of time delineates more than the primordial nature of prophecy. Prophecy, being as old as creation, is a gift from the gods. The fact that the Sibyl is a primordial being whose life and influence extends across several millennia and whose power is, in fact, to speak with the actual voice of a god, suggests that the ancient and lasting quality of prophecy makes that art a continuing and pervasive influence directly connecting humanity to universal principles.

Traditionally, all the functions enacted by prophets can be ascribed to the poet. The word "poet," from the Greek, means "maker," implying that poets produce material which contains new thoughts and new modes of expression. They are, in other words, motivators of cultural progress. In addition, as Robert Graves and others have made equally clear, poetry is an ancient and time-honored occupation that continually carries the substance and tradition of culture. And poetry, like prophecy, is strongly associated with transmission of absolute and eternal knowledge and understanding. Finally, the words of all classical prophets are transmitted through the medium of poetry, the creators of which have helped fix myth and legend into a tacit historical continuum that forms the basis of Western tradition, culture, and civilization.

Clearly, Eliot sees poets in the same light as prophets. Both are creators, motivators, and maintainers of cultural knowledge and tradition, and both unify the integrity of a particular myth and cement myth to myth. And last, both provide vital links between worldly human actions and universal truths and constants. Just as clearly, Eliot sees himself as a member of the poeto-prophetic clan. Prophecy concerns times of change, and mythical prophets always warn of danger in times of transition. In the same way, "The Waste Land" is a prophetic polemic of Modernism, and Eliot is the modern prophet warning the twentieth century, poised between the worlds of Tradition and Progress, of the potential dangers that lie before it.

By invoking the Sibyl of Cumae, Eliot immediately establishes a direct link between his poem and a continuous tradition so ancient that it is primordial. This connection is ideal for Eliot, who purports, through production of writings in the mythic tradition, to be the modern embodiment, carrier, and transmitter of tradition, for it allows him to claim the Apollonian voice as his direct and most ancient antecedent. And, by placing himself within that same chain of tradition, Eliot justifies the idea that he embodies a link in the chain of being which connects humanity to the higher realm of universal principles and truths. This connection, due to its mythic nature as well as to its universality, further legitimizes Eliot's claim to the importance of his pronouncements and their right to immortality.

In the last analysis, it would seem that Eliot received, or created for himself, an auspicious divination by invoking and consulting the Sibyl.

Charting Terra Incognita

Maps, Guidebooks, and Guides in Joseph Conrad's *Heart of Darkness*

BY THE TIME JOSEPH CONRAD wrote *Heart of Darkness*[1], the great age of European global exploration and colonization begun during the Renaissance had drawn to a close. The globe had been circumnavigated, the seas charted, and the shapes of the continents mapped. The last major exploratory discoveries—those by Burton, Speke, and Livingstone during the middle of the nineteenth century—mapped the heart of Africa and charted its two major water courses, the Nile and the Congo River. Like all seekers into the unknown, these later explorers depended on existing maps and guidebooks to take them as close as possible to unknown territories and then relied on the personal, first-hand experiences of others who had delved into terra incognita to guide them safely into and through its mysteries and dangers. Conrad's Marlow follows a similar pattern as he wends his way up the Congo in search of the renegade Mr. Kurtz.

Marlow, in common with many Europeans, "had a passion for maps...[and] all the glories of exploration" (10-11). As a boy, he would look at maps, at the blank white spaces of terra incognita, and wish to go there. "There was one yet," he says, "the biggest, the most blank, so to speak—that I had a hankering after." (11) Marlow wishes to be not simply an explorer, but a discoverer of great mysteries. During

Marlow's boyhood, these could be found in Africa, but by his adulthood, this particular terra incognita "was not a blank space any more. It had got filled...with rivers and lakes and names" (11). The map in the office of the company he works for reaffirms this repletion, showing a patch-work of colors filling what was formerly white terra incognita (14-15). Marlow thus finds himself in the unfortunate position of desiring to be an explorer in a world whose major physical boundaries and features already have been discovered and documented.

Even so for Marlow, the lure of the Congo River is irresistible. "It fascinated [him] as a snake would a bird" (11). The fascination, begun with his boyhood view of the blank whiteness on the map, is further exacerbated by two encounters. The first is with the two women who knit at the door to the company office. Marlow sees in the look of one that she does not expect to see him again. This indicates to him that his journey might be perilous, even life threatening. As an experienced seaman, he is familiar with the possibility of physical danger, but the second encounter, that with the company doctor, redefines the nature of the danger.

The doctor reaffirms the physical danger by saying he has not examined anyone who has returned from Africa, as if to say that no one does return, but he also measures Marlow's skull, saying, "The changes take place inside" (17). He then asks Marlow if there is madness in his family and expresses an interest in observing psychological changes of individuals as they occur. The encounter with the doctor indicates that there remains a vast unknown territory that has yet to be mapped—the terra incognita of the psyche, which is exactly where Marlow is about to journey. Perhaps the two women at the door were right. Even if Marlow returns physically intact from his sojourn to the Congo, would he still be the same man?

The intimation of undiscovered territory is all the inducement Marlow, the thwarted explorer, needs to spur him on. Like any good explorer, he seeks maps, guidebooks, and signposts that will lead him to the terra incognita of the mind. He finds his first aid in Towson's text, *An Inquiry into Some Points of Seamanship* (62). The book is not a guidebook in the usual sense of speaking about places; instead, it describes techniques of traveling. The text is meticulously written, though its subject matter, "the breaking strains of ships' chains and tackle" (63), appears, at first glance, to be mundane. What really intrigues Marlow is the marginalia, written, he believes, in cipher. This cipher, this unknown language, gives Marlow the clue that the journey into the territory of the psyche requires a knowledge deeper and more arcane than the simple facts and figures that govern the mundane world of ships' chains and tackle. It also implies that such a journey must have its own language. Thus the book invites scrutiny on a symbolic level, hinting that the terminus of Marlow's journey is knowledge of the breaking strain of the chains and tackle of the human psyche.

As Marlow's journey continues, he tries to maintain a form of quantifiable progress and guidance by attempting to use trees as if they were mile posts. But this effort fails, for he cannot focus on the trees long enough to give meaning to their demarcations (64). Already, as foreshadowed by Towson's book, Marlow's ability to rely on the dependability of maps and recorded facts is breaking down, and it culminates when he stops the boat the night before reaching the Inner Station. "Eight miles meant nearly three hours steaming for us" (65), he says, as if still believing that the quantifiers of known territory apply equally to terra incognita. But as terra incognita of the mind represents an altered state of consciousness or of being instead of simply altered location, there are no exact equations or correspondences that lead from known territory into the unknown. Instead, a quantum leap is required to take Marlow from reliance on external patterns of behavior to an understanding of psychological motivation and complexity.

The nature of that quantum leap is hinted at when the manager urges Marlow to stop for the night before proceeding at dawn to the Inner Station (64). It is significant that this act of caution is motivated by the voice of personal experience—or, a guide. The manager has been to the Inner Station and knows there are dangers. Thus the manager's warning suggests the importance of real experience over second-hand knowledge gained from maps and guidebooks. Maps can delimit unexplored territory and guide one to it, but within the blank whiteness of terra incognita only the word of personal experience—of those who have been there—is sufficient guide. And then Marlow personally enters psychological terra incognita.

His entrance is symbolized by a physically tangible counterpoint to the white space on the map—a fog that enshrouds the river in blank whiteness that both obliterates the physical features of the terrain and leaves Marlow in a state of psychological limbo. Marlow says, "Were we to let go our hold of the bottom, we would be absolutely in the air—in space. We wouldn't be able to tell where we were going to—whether up or down stream, or across" (70-71).

Lost in the blank whiteness, Marlow experiences a condition in which maps cease to have validity—a condition in which only the internal sense of psychological direction has meaning. Contemplating the implications of being lost in psychic terra incognita gives him understanding of the dangers inherent in the situation. While the pilgrims, rooted in the physical world, fear physical attack by the natives, Marlow says that "the danger...was from our proximity to a great human passion let loose" (72). Without a solidly physical foundation in which to anchor the psyche, reason and morality are set adrift. He realizes that it is no longer sufficient to look at the world as a merely physical place with physical dangers, but that the human psyche and its pitfalls must be understood as well.

The fog lifts, and Marlow immediately faces his first personal decision when the river splits into two channels. He chooses the path of logical expediency, steering the boat into the channel that passes closest to the station. The channel quickly grows narrower, arrows rain down, and, most significantly, Marlow's pilot is killed. Still trying to cling to the logic of the physical world, Marlow has only succeeded in endangering the boat and losing his pilot, his last symbol of guidance by external means.

Luckily for Marlow, he quickly meets a guide—the Russian. The Russian's motley makes him an embodiment of the archetypal Fool—the man who, through his seemingly mad criticism of the temporal realm, helps guide kings. And it also recalls Edgar, in Shakespeare's *King Lear*, whose tattered and patched clothing is quickly noted by Lear and equated with madness, yet who becomes Lear's own guide into the realm of the psyche. But even more to the point, the Russian's motley recollects the multicolored map hanging in the company office.

Further indicating the Russian's function as guide is the fact that Towson's book belongs to him, and the marginalia were written by him in his native language. Instead of testifying to Marlow's foolishness in considering the marginalia a mysterious cipher, the revelation of the truth of its language indicates that Marlow, having entered the terra incognita of the psyche, now discovers that there is, indeed, a real and decipherable language that can begin to describe the new territory. Marlow may not personally understand this language, but it is intelligible to those who have been to the terra incognita of the mind. With study, such a language can become comprehensible—one simply has to have the key.

But the Russian, like all Marlow's previous maps and guides, can only point the way further into terra incognita. The Russian has not personally traveled deeply into it but only skirted its edges. To get the final word, Marlow must hear Kurtz, who has delved there more deeply and dwelt there longer than any other. This is exactly the reason Marlow must talk to Kurtz—Kurtz has "been there" and has a first-hand knowledge of the way through the terra incognita of a psyche loosened from the restraints of the world.

Marlow places much emphasis on Kurtz as a voice, as speech, for what Kurtz has done is not as significant as the information he has to impart about where he has been. Ultimately, however, the reader hears none of what Kurtz says firsthand. It is as if Marlow suggests that such knowledge is so tied to personal experience that without that experience to inform the facts, the facts become just so many disconnected words that can mean anything. Kurtz's final, "The horror!", taken out of context, is open to a variety of interpretations, any of which are probably false without the meaning supplied by context. The point is that the geography of the mind cannot be mapped because it is too personal, but even so, understanding may be possible for the individual within the limits of that individual's context.

Realizing that physical exploration of the world had gone about as far as it could, Conrad indicates that now human exploration must go inward. If he denotes that such a search is necessary through his depiction of the casual brutalities inflicted by so-called civilized Europeans, he also connotes that the search is inevitable by showing that humans have the drive to journey to the ends of every tributary of knowledge, even if all that is to be found at the end of some of them is horror.

But Conrad also has an important message about the external world as we know it. In essence, the world is composed entirely of terra cognita stained by dark hearts. *Heart of Darkness* exposes European colonialism at its worst as an attempt to impose a system of order for the purpose of plunder. But what is significant is that this system of order does not hold in the new territories carved from terra incognita, for these territories embody, not disorder, but antiorder, at least in terms of the European concept of order.

What Conrad is saying is that the very act of exploration, whether in the real world or in the realm of the psyche, changes the parameters of life so drastically that the old concepts of order must, perforce, give way to new paradigms. In a sense, he's espousing a sort of humanistic version of

Heisenberg's principle that any observation of any system alters that system. In other words, if the world is opened up to encompass a global awareness for all peoples, then all peoples must take part in shaping that world and its meanings.

It is interesting to note in this regard the context in which Conrad tells his story. He puts it into the mouth of Marlow, who, in turn, tells it to an audience composed of archetypal representatives of the British empire—the Director of the Companies, the Lawyer, and the Accountant. While their motives were, admittedly, exploitative rather than benevolent, these men, and other Europeans like them, did open up much of the world and create, for the first time, an awareness among all men of the extent of the global community.

But, having done so, their influence immediately begins to wane, symbolized by the fact that Marlow's narrative begins at dusk and ends in full darkness, for now the sun has set on the British Empire at last, and the new world of tomorrow belongs to all peoples of the global community.

Good Science, Bad Science, and Nons(ci)ence
Jonathan Swift's Satiric Backfire

NO ONE IS BETTER SUITED to expose the foibles and follies
of a culture than a person who is born into, trained by, and
completely immersed in that culture. Jonathan Swift, intellectual and Anglican cleric, is an ideal example, and in *Gulliver's
Travels*, he exposes eighteenth-century European and, particularly, British culture to critical scrutiny. His critiques are well
aimed in books I, II, and IV. "A Voyage to Lilliput" examined pettiness in politics and religion; "A Voyage to Brobdingnag" looked into licentiousness and sexual mores, greed
and acquisitiveness, and arrogance disguised as magnanimity;
and "A Voyage to the Houyhnhnms" inspects basic human
nature by comparing and contrasting its best and worst parts.

Because elements of human nature and behavior like the
ones surveyed in these three voyages have no objective reality, they lend themselves easily to Swift's satiric methodology.
There is no way to prove one custom or mode of behavior
better than another, for appropriateness of custom and behavior depends as much on personal, social, and cultural per-
spectives as it does on objective truth. However, when Swift
turns his pen to the third book of the tetralogy, "A Voyage
to Laputa," he faces a very different foe than custom or behavior. His adversary is science, and while science provides
specific targets for his satire, this very specificity causes him

to over-shoot his own arguments. As a result, his satire of Laputa fails in its effect and, in fact, backfires on Swift.

In "A Voyage to Laputa," Swift makes the mistake of attacking tangible reality with the same methods he uses against social custom and behavior. The primary problem with this approach is that reality exists independent of opinion or beliefs about it. Arguments about the uncertain nature of reality—mind or spirit create reality, or reality has no permanent or objective existence apart from its apprehension, for example—are, perhaps, possible at the abstract theoretical levels of science, philosophy, and theology, but not at the basic, practical, and demonstrative levels of daily life in the here and now. Despite any possible wishes to the contrary, water in the presence of gravity always seeks the lowest level (ancient knowledge), gravity attracts with equal velocity objects of different densities, sizes, and weights (Galileo, 1564–1642), an object will displace its own volume of water (Archimedes, 287–212 B.C.), and the universe obeys certain mechanical laws (Newton, 1642–1727).

All these truths were known to scientists by the time Swift wrote *Gulliver's Travels* in 1726, and scientific discoveries were totally transforming the way Europeans viewed the reality of the world around them. It was, after all, the beginning of the Industrial Revolution, and the general attitude of Europeans toward science and new discoveries was, for the most part, positive. Joseph Addison, Swift's friend, contributor to the first prototype magazine, *The Tatler*, and coproducer of the second, *The Spectator*, characterized the age thus:

> There are none who more gratifie and enlarge the Imagination, than the Authors of the new Philosophy, whether we consider their Theories of the Earth or Heavens, the Discoveries they have made by Glasses, or any other of their Contemplations on Nature. We are not a little pleased to find every green Leaf swarm with Millions of Animals, that at their largest Growth are not visible to the naked Eye. There is something very engag-

ing to the Fancy, as well as to our Reason, in the Treatises of Metals, Minerals, Plants, and Meteors. But when we survey the whole Earth at once, and the several Planets that lie within its Neighbourhood, we are filled with a pleasing Astonishment, to see so many Worlds hanging one above another, and sliding around their Axles in such an amazing Pomp and Solemnity.[1]

People were excited by new scientific understandings of the world. But the very quality of scientific understanding also profoundly shook more than thirteen centuries of Christian orthodoxy and dogmatism. The world, no longer a sort of homunculus of God, was now considered a machine that obeys certain rules. Further, the new rules of science were not only as complex and esoteric as sophisticated ecclesiastical arguments for the existence of God, they were becoming more immediate and tangible and thus more convincing. Scientists could prove their theories, while ecclesiastics, even after a millennium, could not definitively prove the existence of God.

The realization of this popular philosophical turn must have been particularly odious to a man like Jonathan Swift, a high-ranking clergyman in the Anglican Church, who understood that the new mechanistic view of the universe jeopardized the authority and power of orthodox religion he served. He symbolizes this threat in Book I of Gulliver's Travels when the Lilliputians theorize that Gulliver's watch is the god he worships because he constantly consults it to regulate the actions of his life.[2] If the workings of the universe are reducible to the schematic of a clock, then there is the danger that the holy spirit will receive no more consideration than the internal rumblings of a mechanism.

Of even graver consequence to religious orthodoxy was the debate concerning the inaccuracy of the Julian calendar raised by scientific observations of the regular motions of the heavenly bodies—a sort of universal clock mechanism. This inaccuracy had caused, by 1582, a ten-day error in the observance of the equinoxes. That year, by decree, Pope Gregory XIII adjusted the calendar, creating the Gregorian calendar. Use of the new calendar spread through Europe until 1752, when it was finally adopted by England.

The choice between the two calendars was a point of religious and philosophic contention throughout Swift's lifetime. Even a quarter of a century after the publication of *Gulliver's Travels*, and one year before the official adoption of the Gregorian calendar in England, *The Gentleman's Magazine* printed a series of articles on the topic.[3] The articles argued that a significant implication of the debate, with respect to orthodox religion, was that the new calendar would facilitate accuracy in regulation of ecclesiastic festivals. Of even greater urgency was the need for an unequivocal observance of Christ's birth, the exact date of which had been thrown into question due to the inaccuracy of the Julian calendar. In fact, one item on the content page of that issue reads: "Time of Christ's Birth Uncertain."[4]

Swift would have preferred a simpler notion of the calendar. Gulliver says of the coldly rationalistic but sage Houyhnhnm:

> They calculate the Year by the Revolution of the Sun and the Moon, but use no Subdivision into Weeks. They are well enough acquainted with the Motions of those two Luminaries, and understand the Nature of Eclipses; and this is the utmost Progress of their Astronomy.[5]

Astronomical observations were well and good when it came to practical regulation of the seasons, but astronomical meddling was not well and good when it advanced doubts as to the date of Christ's birth. The idea of the uncertainty of Christ's birth date is a critical notion, for it meant something far worse than the fact that the orthodox establishment had been celebrating this supremely important holy day at the wrong time. The foundation of power and authority of orthodox Christianity lies on two pillars of belief: that the Church is infallible and that the hierarchy of the established Church possesses a direct connection to the deity and serves as the ordained intermediary between man and God. The uncertainty of Christ's birth date not only called into question the infallibility of the Church but was, by extension, conspicuous evidence that the orthodox Church did not actually have the direct connection to God that it claimed to have. If it did, why was it now so wrong that the date of Christ's birth was in doubt? That, horrors, might even extend to doubting the existence of Christ. Confronted with the implacable and undeniable discoveries of science, the ecclesiastics had proven as ignorant as the laymen they supposedly guided.

In fact, ecclesiastics were, perhaps, even more ignorant. By and large, the clergy deprecated science, but science was, at least at the time, the ultimate in non-elitist self-confirmation. Laymen not only could witness scientific wonders but could personally participate in important new discoveries. The microscope, invented in 1654 by the Dutch naturalist Antonie van Leeuwenhoek, revealed to one and all a world as formerly unseen as that of Heaven, and the denizens of it could have been no less mysterious and intriguing than the angels of the empyrean reaches. Here was tangible evidence of a multitude that could, indeed, dance on the head of a pin. Magazines printed articles like the several by an unknown contributor pseudonymously referred to as "Convexo," who studied microscopic animals and observed their transformations through four stages of development: egg, larva, pupa, and adult.[6] Convexo also relates finding microscopic mites on a common housefly, and speculates that they are either tick-like parasites or the fly's brood, which she has taken under her wing.[7]

But at least the tiny creatures actually could be seen, unlike angels, which even telescopes had failed to behold, though the telescopes did reveal that the wandering stars called planets were actually spheres—apparently whole other worlds—floating in space. Other celestial phenomena that just a few years earlier had been considered portents from God also were being looked at in a new light. Comets, usually thought of as omens of public disaster, became intellectual curiosities. A letter to *The Gentleman's Magazine* describes what must have been an unusually bright emanation of the aurora borealis, giving particulars of location and time as well as a vivid physical description.[8] Common people were studying the unseen, the unsuspected, and the unknown, and in their hearts was neither fear nor awe but excitement. Nature was relinquishing its secrets to those who studied, and if nature could be studied, eventually it could be understood.

Swift, however, despite his intellect and education, failed to understand theoretical science.

> Although I cannot say that I was ill treated on this Island [of science], yet I must confess I thought my self too much neglected, not without some Degree of Contempt. For neither Prince nor People appeared to be curious in any Part of Knowledge, except Mathematicks and Musick, wherein I was far their inferior, and upon that Account very little regarded.[9]

Perhaps it is true, as Allan Bloom remarks, that Swift felt that:

> Science in freeing men, destroys the natural conditions which make them human. Here, for the first time in history, is the possibility of tyranny grounded not on ignorance, but on science. Science is no longer theoretical, but serves the wishes and hence the passions of men.[10]

But since Swift, as will be seen, proved to be such a poor prognosticator of the implications of science, a more accurate appraisal of his antiscience stance is that it was based as much on anger and resentment at personal losses as on a real philosophic concern for posterity, for science had effectively undermined both Swift's professional authority as a clergyman and his position of intellectual superiority.

The democratic implications engendered by science must have struck negative personal chords within him, as well. Swift, who had strived so hard to rise to eminence within the elite establishment, saw in the non-elitism of science a dangerous sanction of egalitarianism. Gulliver says:

> This made me reflect, how vain an Attempt it is for a Man to endeavor doing himself Honour among those who are out of all Degree of Equality or Comparison with him...where a little contemptible Varlet, without the least Title to Birth, Person, Wit, or common Sense, shall presume to look with Importance, and put himself upon a Foot with the greatest Person of the Kingdom. [11]

Curiously, this statement can be viewed in a reverse light —that of Swift's own personal failures on exactly these points. Swift was only of modest birth, and while he aspired to the post of Archbishop of Canterbury, he never actually attained that exalted position. And though he did rise to literary eminence, he was, by his own admission in "Verses on the Death of Dr. Swift," a writer inferior to his contemporaries Pope and Gay. Even worse, Queen Anne had been repulsed by his "Tale of the Tub," squelching his pretensions to greatness and social prominence. He was, in effect, rejected by the same high-born he aspired to join because of his lack of title and wit, because of his crudity, and because he was of the proletariat.

Egalitarian threat to Swift's status excited more than his vanity and self-interest. It inflamed his racist and xenophobic tendencies. His dread of racial differences were obvious when Gulliver says of the Yahoos:

> The Face of it indeed was flat and broad, the Nose depressed, the Lips large, and the Mouth wide: But these Differences are common to all savage Nations, where the Lineaments of the Countenance are distorted by the Natives suffering their Infants to lie groveling on the

Earth, or by carrying them on their Backs, nuzzling with their Faces against the Mother's Shoulders.[12]

His dismay at equality with "savage Nations" is easily noted when Gulliver concludes, "I expressed my Uneasiness at his giving me so often the Appelation of Yahoo, an odious Animal, for which I had so utter an Hatred and Contempt."[13] Swift obviously viewed himself as superior to the majority of Europeans, and especially to anyone from other continents.

The Houyhnhnm Master, who represents wisdom, albeit a frigid sort, is in concordance with Swift's elitism:

> He made me observe, that among the Houyhnhnms, the White, the Sorrel, and the Iron-grey were not so exactly shaped as the Bay, the Dapple-grey, and the Black; nor born with equal Talents of Mind, or a Capacity to improve them; and therefore continued always in the Condition of Servants, without ever aspiring to match out of their own Race, which in that Country would be reckoned monstrous and unnatural.[14]

For Swift, intelligence, superiority, and breeding are not simply linked but synonymous. The Houyhnhnm Master's attitude of superiority and the facile compliance of the lower-bred Houyhnhnm to Houyhnhnm classicism must have been a great comfort to the elitist Swift.

Most telling of all with respect to egalitarianism is that the Yahoos are immigrants:

> Many Ages ago, two of these Brutes appeared together upon a Mountain, whether produced by the Heat of the Sun upon corrupted Mud and Slime, or from the Ooze and Froth of the Sea, was never known.... These Yahoos engendered, and their Brood in a short time grew so numerous as to over-run and infest the whole Nation.[15]

Aside from being a sort of devilish parody of the creation of Adam and Eve from the clay, this description is equally a precursor to the prevalent racist myth that the darker-skinned races are "mud people"—people created from the soil and bereft of a soul and thus not really human. That Swift only expected wickedness from social intercourse with the inferior subhumans of other countries and different racial types is shown when Gulliver tells the Houyhnhnm Master:

> In order to feed the Luxury and Intemperance of the Males [of England], and the Vanity of the Females, we sent away the greatest Part of our necessary Things to other Countries, from whence in Return we brought the Materials of Diseases, Folly, and Vice, to spend among ourselves.[16]

In essence, Swift implies that England would have none of these malignancies—diseases, folly, and vice—had they not been imported from inferior and probably degenerate foreign cultures.

Adding personal urgency to Swift's evidence against the religious and social changes wrought by science were psychological implications of events from his early life. Louis Landa postulates:

> If Part III of Gulliver's Travels, where Swift attacks the corruptions of learning, is the object of consideration, the commentator is certain to make an excursion back to Swift's student days at Trinity College, Dublin, to explain that here began his life-long hatred of science and philosophy.[17]

But, truly, the ill-will began much earlier.

Swift made an ominous start in life when he was snatched from his cradle by a loving but misguided nurse, who carried him to Whitehaven, where he remained separated from his mother for three years. From the age of six, Swift (now restored to Dublin) attended the grammar school in Kilkenny, while his mother went to live with her sister in Leicester.[18]

Early, devastating personal changes had to have given Swift a profound fear of change, which had, from his earliest moments, only resulted in trauma and separation. Now, science was threatening to separate Swift from everything that gave meaning to his life.

The bitter enmity of such a man had to emerge, and it did so with invective and choler in his attack on science in "A Voyage to Laputa." Swift hated science and the radical changes it promised, and from the outset, he makes his position clear by naming the floating island "Laputa." Gulliver says that the etymology of the word Laputa is obscure. It could mean "High Governor," from the old Laputian language, signifying its position of physical, intellectual, and technological superiority over the lands it rules. Alternately, by Gulliver's own conjecture, it could have the more poetic meaning, "The Dancing of Sunbeams on the Sea Wing," or, in essence, a chimerical phantom masquerading as reality.[19] Both of these definitions may be applicable, but certainly Swift also means "the whore," from the Spanish definition of the term. Whatever the meaning is, one fact remains paramount: The "flying island is built on the principles of the new physics founded by Gilbert and Newton,"[20] and Swift, through acrimonious, intense satire, utilizes every element of his personal prejudices to attack his hated enemy.

He immediately associates scientists with evil by giving the Laputians crooked bodies, recalling the Platonic concept that spiritual corruption manifests as physical deformity. He gives them eyes that are slanted, indicating that science leads to an invasion of foreign thought, which in this case may be Oriental in origin. Their eyes also look in different directions, superficially symbolizing a world view split irreconcilably between external vision and introspection, but resembling more the erratic oculation of madmen. He even equates science with pagan and primitive belief systems when he shows some of the astronomers on Laputa discussing the potential destruction of the Earth by comets. "This Conversation they are apt to run into with the same Temper that Boys discover in delighting to hear terrible Stories of Spirits and Hobgoblins, which they greedily listen to, and dare not go to Bed for fear." [21] For Swift, science is clearly an irreligious, alien, insane, and superstitious activity.

Swift also evinces a definite lack of faith in the intentions of scientists, or, as he calls them in the chapters on the Lagado, "projectors." "Swift distrusted science and did not care for scientists," James Gunn points out, "particularly those who tried to find practical uses for their discoveries." [22] The projectors insistently pursue scientific schemes that are inherently impractical, causing an almost total collapse of Laputa's socioeconomic system. Worse, they destroy existing and useful, if simpler, public works to build impractical, useless ones, and then do not even complete their work. [23] Gulliver's "host, the genial and wise Lord Munodi, tells him that work of the Academy has had the effect of destroying the country's traditional prosperity." [24] Heaping sin upon stupidity, the scientists use the power of government and law to compel practical people to pay obeisance to their impracticality. [25]

> These People suppose, that because the smallest Circle hath as many Degrees as the largest, therefore the Regulation and Management of the World require no more Abilities than the handling and turning of a Globe. [26]

If scientists cannot be practical even within their own disciplines, then they cannot possibly be able to adequately regulate the larger issues of political and economic stability and social welfare. More particularly, Swift attacks a wide range of specific scientific subjects during Gulliver's visit to the Lagado. At this institute, a parody of the Royal Academy of Sciences, Gulliver witnesses examples of contemporary scientific inquiry that Swift read about or actually saw in the Royal Academy.

Marjorie Nicholson and Nora M. Mohler located in the Philosophical Transactions of the Royal Society specific sources for many of the experiments in the Academy of Lagado: the sundial upon the weathercock (1719), the use of a pair of bellows to cure the colic (1717), the making of silk stockings and gloves from spider webs (1710), the conversion of calcine ice into gunpowder (1693), the use of hogs to dig up and simultaneously manure the field (1702), and other things.[27]

Swift attempts to use these experiments and others to portray contemporary scientific experiments and the experimenters as misguided, ignorant, foolish, and even idiotic. An old homily declares that one may more easily tear down than build. Despite the venerableness of this wisdom, Graham Green shows in his story, "The Destructors," that thorough, and therefore "correct," destruction is truly as difficult as construction.[28] Of course, Swift could not have heeded the words of a man born a century and a half after his death, but had he the opportunity, he could, perhaps, have avoided collapsing his Laputian edifice around his own ears. One must have knowledge and foresight to prevent being crushed by faulty demolition techniques.

In fact, Swift was able to argue this point quite well when he saw this tendency in others, and he would have been one of the first to denigrate the mediocre poet or critic of poetry for lack of breadth or depth of knowledge in the classics of literature, as, indeed, he does in "The Beasts Confession" and "On Poetry." By the same token, an adequate critique of science must have a firm grounding in scientific principles. Superficial acquaintance with science married to antiscientific cant is not an adequate basis for valid criticism of science.

Swift often exhibits a lack of understanding about the workings of science, though he does try to feign knowledge of it. Gulliver is a ship's surgeon, a sort of practical medical scientist, and he also claims that he "had always been a Mechanical Genius."[29] Gulliver is, as well, an expert in the sciences of navigation, geography, and cartography. Indeed, his navigational skills elevate him to the position of captain of his last ship. But despite the pretensions of his character, Swift did not really understand the basic tenets of science. In Glubbdubdrib, the ghost of Aristotle says:

> New Systems of Nature were but new fashions, which would vary in every Age; and even those who pretended to demonstrate them from Mathematical Principles, would flourish but a short Period of Time, and be out of Vogue when that was determined.[30]

Swift did not understand that, although some scientific theories are indeed superseded by more comprehensive theories, it is not true, as he implies, that new theories completely supplant the old. In fact, ironically, modern science can be traced, in part, to Aristotle, directly countering the assertions Swift places in the mouth of that philosopher.

Beyond his basic misunderstanding of science, Swift often falsifies scientific facts, or fails to maintain convincing verisimilitude with respect to the logical functioning of reality. While it may be true that Swift was either feigning ignorance or simply exploiting exaggeration to further his story line and make his philosophic and satiric points, lapses in verisimilitude, even if intentional, can only weaken the effect and the force of the argument. Satire depends on the reader believing the thing or idea lampooned to be actual or at least potentially so. As A. D. Nuttall puts it:

> All the great ironists, since Socrates said that he knew he knew nothing, have at some level always meant the thing they said in jest. Even tragic irony (a different but related thing) actually works most potently through an un-

looked-for coincidence with truth rather than by any pleasure we may take in the manifest error.[31]

Swift, however, departs from this axiom by ignoring potential scientific reality within the contexts he criticizes. Without a firm basis in reality, his words become merely prejudiced rhetoric based on falsified principles of science rather than valid examples that reveal the shallow falseness of human behavior.

Science is falsified, for example, in the first chapter of "A Voyage to Brobdingnag," when Gulliver delivers a lengthy description of the operation of his ship, the *Adventure*, during the storm that blew the vessel to Brobdingnag.[32] Though the sequence is an obvious parody of the great number of sailing adventure and shipwreck stories of the period, the fact must be remembered that Gulliver claims to be an expert navigator and sailor. His expertise in an arcane yet precise and practical lore lends him scientific pretensions, and veracity is therefore given to his description of sailing the ship. But viewed critically, the description is also a fatuous catalog of pseudo-scientific jargon. Swift tries to fool the reader, but his effort, through the transparency of its fabrication, does not convince of genuine parody, only of inauthenticity.

A serious lapse in scientific logic occurs also in Brobdingnag, when Gulliver notes that proportions there are twelve times larger than in England and that "Nature in that Country [observes] the same Proportion through all her operations."[33] Gulliver comments that because of these proportions he could not sail on Brobdingnagian rivers because the water itself was proportionally larger and therefore more violent.[34] This condition, however, raises several important issues. Logically, water, being of uniform composition everywhere on Earth, should behave no differently in Brobdingnag than in Lilliput, where Gulliver makes no mention of the water being twelve times "smaller." And if the Brobdingnagian water is twelve times larger than water elsewhere on the planet, there must be, as Gulliver does mention, proportionally larger precipitation.

But if there is "big" rain, then this rain must come from special (very large?) clouds that hover only over Brobdingnag, since similarly large rain fails to fall elsewhere on the planet. Then there is the problem of what happens to the large water of the rivers when it reaches the ocean, where the water, perforce, must be of normal composition. Further, if the water is actually larger in Brobdingnag than England, then Gulliver would soon die of thirst because it would be too large for him to swallow and certainly too large for his body to assimilate. And if the water is twelve times larger, are the molecules air, also? That would make it impossible for Gulliver to breathe.

However, nowhere does Swift err as fully as he does in his descriptions of Gulliver's visits to Laputa and the Lagado. Robert Scholes puts it simply by saying, "Swift detested the science of his time, which drove him to dogmatic posturing in Book III of Gulliver."[35] Dogmatic posturing leads Swift into lapses of extrapolation as serious as his lack of consistency and insight with regard to the reasonableness of "big" Brobdingnagian water—extrapolation that is not grounded in scientific fact or logical extension. In the Lagado, says Bloom, "Gulliver's critique, although funny, impresses us less than it does elsewhere. He seems to have seriously underestimated the possible success of the projects."[36] In Laputa and at the Lagado, Swift mentions with sarcastic skepticism ideas that today have validity and proven applications or that are presently in serious developmental stages.

Already mentioned is the discussion by Laputian astronomers of the potential destruction of Earth by comets. Swift mocks this belief as being like a horror story with which boys frighten themselves, but we now know the more terrible truth. Comets and meteors have often in Earth's history bombarded the planet, causing widespread destruction and mass extinctions of life on a global scale. And this is not Swift's only astronomical blunder.

The island of Laputa floating above the Earth's surface may have seemed fanciful in Swift's day, but people now are accustomed to humans—usually scientists—in spacecraft orbiting the Earth. There is even a working orbital space station, so the idea of scientists inhabiting an island floating above the Earth is less fanciful than it is real. Swift, indeed, populates Laputa with scientists, specifically astronomers. The demographics of Laputa are appropriate, for Laputa's vantage gives the inhabitants a very clear view of the heavens, enabling them to see celestial phenomena unobservable from the ground. The astounding astronomical discoveries made possible by the orbiting Hubble Space Telescope point out the legitimacy of an idea Swift attempts to ridicule.

By Swift's time, astronomers had examined most of the planets and had seen multiple moons orbiting Jupiter, and their observations added evidence to postulations of a mechanistic universe. But Swift questions the veracity of scientific proof for a mechanistic universe by making statements he modeled on contemporary speculation but which he probably considered preposterous. The Laputians have

> discovered two lesser Stars, or Satellites, which revolve around Mars; whereof the innermost is distant from the Center of the primary Planet exactly three of his Diameters, and the outermost five, the former revolves in the Space of ten Hours, and the latter in Twenty-one and a Half.[37]

Swift is poking fun at astronomic prognostication, for the existence of the two moons had been

> predicted as long ago as 1610 by Kepler, on the basis of Galileo's discovery of the four bright satellites of Jupiter and a bit of fanciful numerology. With Venus having no moons, the earth one, and Jupiter four, it seemed only celestially correct that intermediate Mars should have

two and that the missing planet between Mars and Jupiter should have three.[38]

To cinch the parody, Swift gives the two Martian moon orbits that probably seemed dangerously low, for Luna is eighteen times as far from Earth as Swift places Mars's furthest moon from its parent planet. He also describes the two moons as having absurdly fast periods, so that these worldlets would race frantically around their parent planet, in sharp contrast to the stately procession of Luna around Earth.

Swift must have felt himself safe in postulating these two Martian moons and their characteristics, for Mars is considerably closer to Earth than is Jupiter, and yet in his day, no moons had been seen orbiting it. Unfortunately for the effect of the parody, there actually are two moons orbiting Mars, first observed in 1877 by the American astronomer Asaph Hall. Amazingly, the periods Swift gave to the two orbits were very nearly correct: that of the inner moon being seven and a half hours and that of the outer moon thirty-one hours.[39] He was even closer to fact concerning the orbits, one of which is approximately three Martian diameters above the surface, though he placed the wrong moon in it. The other orbit is far lower than he depicted. So, while he tries to lampoon astronomers by having them erroneously predict lunatic celestial phenomena, he only succeeds in actually predicting very nearly real facts about phenomenon that behave in even more erratic manners than he thought possible.

When Swift shows concern for the mass destruction of war, his prognostications seem even more fruitful and accurate, though it is doubtful that he ever considered his ideas actually possible. In his conversation with the King of Brobdingnag, Gulliver describes the misuses of science by Europeans, who employ scientific discoveries for war and destruction.[40] By the third voyage, Swift had not altered his bleak outlook. He places in the hands of the Laputian scientists three means of conquering their enemies that even the vicious Europeans had yet to develop. One method the Laputians use to quell uprisings is covering the rebellious people with perpetual shade by interposing the floating island between the rebels and the sun.

This action has the twofold effect of destroying the rebels' crops and infecting the people with disease. In modern terminology, these tactics are called chemical and biological warfare. The Laputians' second method of control is to throw rocks down upon the rebels, or, in essence, to perform aerial bombardment. Swift even anticipates air-raid shelters by having the rebels retreat to cellars to escape the falling rocks. Finally, there is the Laputians' ultimate weapon of lowering the island onto the offending city, crushing it—an action tantamount to total nuclear destruction of an entire city. When the island attacked Lindalino, the inhabitants there built four towers atop each of which they placed a lodestone and "a vast Quantity of the most combustible Fewel, hoping to burst therewith the adamantine Bottom of the Island."[41] This is a neat anticipation of anti-ballistic missiles, complete with homing devices and explosive payloads.

The problem with Swift's predictions is not his intention of demonstrating abuse of power conferred by science. Instead, since Swift had no sense that human flight might become possible, the difficulty lies in his failure to realize that his literary inventions foreshadowed reality as much as they served his personal agenda. Swift made the same mistake numerous time in the Lagado. "A great many things that Swift mocked at as chimerical," points out Bonamy Dobree, "have come to pass."[42] Though it is true that not all of the experiments of the projectors are amenable to interpretation of future worth, many have figurative if not actual applications.

The first projector Gulliver meets is trying to extract sunshine from cucumbers. Scientists in fact do "extract sunshine from cucumbers, though we put it into gel globules and call it Vitamin C."[43] A second possible interpretation of this projector's work is the successful storage of intense energy within relatively small containers so that the energy can later be released in useful ways. Modern equivalents this anticipates are fossil fuels carried in tanks, electric batteries, or more pointedly, atomic reactors that derive energy as powerful as that of the sun from quantities of matter even smaller than cucumbers. And, at any rate, there are the amusing scientific facts that a potato is, essentially, a low-voltage battery and that a pickle charged with electricity will glow. And a pickle is a cucumber!

The second projector is trying to reduce human excrement to its original food. People have for a millennium used animal and human wastes as fertilizers, but scientific extraction of the useful chemical components of natural fertilizers began in the nineteenth century. This science continues to be an important aspect of agriculture, increasing food production in quantity, quality, and variety, thereby aiding humankind.

Although the eighteenth century had gunpowder, most of the explosives now know were discovered in the nineteenth century. The third projector is trying to cook ice to produce gunpowder and has written a treatise "concerning the Malleability of Fire."[44] While ice never produces gunpowder, other, superior, explosives are developed through the cooking and distillation of equally unlikely base materials. Ironically, Swift ridicules the idea that explosives can be manufactured from ice, which is a solidified liquid. Some of the modern high explosives, like nitroglycerin, are liquids, and others, like cordite and TNT, are melted at some point in the manufacturing process. In fact, almost all modern explosives are made, in part, from liquids such as acids and petroleum distillates.

Though Swift also derides this projector's belief that fire can be malleable, or shaped for a purpose, fire often is shaped and otherwise altered in welding applications, manufacturing processes, heating of homes and buildings, and in jet and rocket engines. And explosive charges can be shaped to produce specific results. Perhaps the most extreme example of malleable fire is the controlled atomic reaction of nuclear power plants.

Architectural projects concern the fourth projector. He is an architect who builds from the roof downward in the manner of the bee and spider. While Swift may have thought this a ridiculous concept, it is also a very accurate description of the work of Buckminster Fuller. This mathematician, philosopher, and architect invented the geodesic dome, a structure consisting entirely of roof and which resembles both a spherical honeycomb and a webwork.

The fifth projector is a blind man who experiments with sensing colors through the medium of his skin. Disregarding the several reported cases of blind people purportedly able to accurately distinguish colors through touch, there is the movement among physical therapists to substitute heightened aspects of functioning senses for inoperative ones, enabling handicapped people to compensate to some degree for their handicaps.

Another projector's experiment uses hogs for plowing. The hogs plow and fertilize at the same time. Although animals were being used for such tasks in Swift's own day, Swift does not foresee that the mechanism of Gulliver's watch might one day be developed into sophisticated machines that perform the duties of plowing, planting, fertilizing, irrigating, and harvesting. Modern farmers are even experimenting with agricultural robots, or, mechanically and independently operating plowing and fertilizing hogs.

The textile experiments of the next projector, who employs spiders to not only spin but weave, predicts the ready availability of a plethora of modern fabrics produced by automated spinning and weaving machines. The projector feeds his spiders colored tinctures so their weaving automatically is dyed, and, with respect to fabrics composed of artificial fibers like nylon and rayon, the machines not only spin and weave but produce the fibers in colors as well. And these days, scientists are breeding natural fibers that lend themselves to autopigmentation. Innovations in the cotton industry have produced cotton strains that are naturally orange, brown, and green, and other colors are in development. In addition, some animals have been bred with exotically colored fur or wool.

Another projector combines a primitive weather-telling device and a primitive time-piece with astronomical observations of the seasons. This man's stated objective is "adjusting the annual and diurnal Motions of the Earth and Sun, so as to answer and coincide with all accidental Turnings of the Wind."[45] Though this is absurd on face value, his device does prefigure modern meteorological techniques and instruments.

Last, and most significant, is the projector who has a "Project for improving speculative Knowledge by practical and mechanical Operations.... The World would soon be sensible of its Usefulness; and he flattered himself, that a more noble exalted Thought never sprang in any other Man's Head."[46] This invention is a sort of mechanical calculator composed of blocks of wood turned by cranks. Upon these blocks "were written all the Words of their Language."[47] In this projector's experiment the cranks are turned at random, producing, or so he hopes, new combinations of learning.

While this particular experiment sounds like the proverbial monkey sitting for an eternity at a typewriter and producing all the world's writings through random chance, it also presages the electronic computer, data banks, and the Internet. In fact, early computing devices were very much like this projector's project. Charles Babbage's Difference Engine and Analytical Engine, both conceived in the 1830s, come to mind, as do the various Enigma-type cryptography devices of World War II. Babbage, along with others, also contributed to the development of punchcards, first used to give instructions to automated weaving machines. This was simply an extension of rolls of heavy paper with punched holes used to activate various sorts of equipment, including player pianos. What would Swift have thought of a piano that played itself via a mechanism he'd ridiculed?

The innovations of the modern computer during the course of less than thirty years totally transformed the depth and breadth of humankind's knowledge, enabling people to make better-informed decisions in nearly every area of endeavor. Further, computers have effected almost instantaneous world-wide communications, giving humankind, for the first time in history, an immediate awareness of global community.

The argument can be made that many of the discoveries and inventions Swift lampoons that have borne fruit in subsequent times have produced as much ill as good, such as the aerial warfare carried out by the Laputians. Certainly in such a debate Swift would be foremost among those against science. Swift blamed science and scientists for the ills of his day, but a more accurate appraisal could be taken from his critiques in Books I, II, and IV, which show that politicians and the business community, not scientists, pervert, misuse, and prostitute scientific discoveries in the name of power, greed, and political and economic expediency. The King of Brobdingnag may be disgusted by the techniques of European warfare, but he uses the most up-to-date science of weapon-making he has at his disposal to maintain a militia for the purpose of quelling insurrections.[48] And the Houyhnhnm Master informs Gulliver of the Houyhnhnm plan to systematically, or scientifically, exterminate the Yahoos.[49] Both the King and the Master are virulently antiscience, yet both are politicians and use the science of their cultures to maintain the status quo of their own regimes.

Misuse of science for aggression, domination, and genocide is not proof that science is inherently bad, only that people can be. Had Swift greater extrapolative powers or less prejudice against science, he may have had greater insight into potential uses for scientific discoveries that would prove beneficial to humankind. The dichotomy is succinctly apt in the case of modern explosives. On the one hand, they have been extensively dedicated to martial use and mutual destruction, but on the other hand, they have aided immeasurably in the domestic front in development of mining, agriculture, road building, and construction. Nitroglycerin even has found application in medicine.

Scientists are sometimes wrong and sometimes egregiously foolish, as are members of any human group, but neither fact negates their efforts to understand the workings of nature or their considerable successes in advancing knowledge and information systems, generating energy, increasing agricultural production, facilitating transportation, and improving medicine and the general quality of life.

Although Swift was witness to many of the vast advances achieved from the end of the seventeenth century to the end of the eighteenth century, such as the discoveries of the microscope and the circulation of the blood, his problem was that he lived in an age where science had yet to produce the profound changes it would following his death. His life-long hatred of science can be viewed as the opinion of a man who had never seen science really work. Swift, for example, rants against physicians and medicine:

> To remedy [disease], there was a Sort of People bred up among us, in the Profession or Pretense of curing the Sick.... Their Fundamental is, that all Diseases arise from Repletion; from whence they conclude, that a great Evacuation of the Body is necessary.... Their next Business is [to introduce substances] most abominable, nauseous and detestable, that they can possibly contrive, which the Stomach immediately rejects with Loathing.... [And] besides real Diseases, we are subject to many that are only imaginary, for which the Physicians have invented imaginary Cures.... One great Excellency in this Tribe is their Skill at Prognostics, wherein they seldom fail; their Predictions in real Diseases, when they rise to any Degree of Malignity, generally portending Death, which is always in their Power, when Recovery is not: And therefore, upon any unexpected Signs of Amendment, after they have pronounced their Sentence, rather than be accused as false

Prophets, they know how to approve their Sagacity to the World by a seasonable Dose.[50]

These are virulently condemnatory words, but it is unlikely that Swift would have so thoroughly castigated doctors had they been able to provide cures, or at least relief, for his own many physical disorders.

Perhaps Swift should have heeded his own advice in "The Beasts Confession," and refrained from encroaching on territory foreign to him. His aggregate disposition against science was, in the final analysis, simply subjective opinion formed more by personal proclivity than by real evidence against science. And Swift also proved himself equally erroneous in an ontological sense. There exist far too many specific scientific experiments and ideas that Swift mocked but which have since produced real, positive effects for humankind to give credibility to his blanket condemnation of scientific inquiry. He tried to attack science using its own precepts on its own territory, but he was bereft of rule book and map. Further, though he accused the scientists of shoddy thinking, he was equally guilty of that defect. His criticisms of science fail not because he was not right, but because he was not correct.

Journey to Freedom
The Adventures of Huckleberry Finn and the American Civil War

SOON AFTER THE PUBLICATION OF *The Adventures of Tom Sawyer*, Mark Twain began a sequel to the popular book, starring Tom's friend, Huckleberry Finn. Commentators on Twain's *The Adventures of Huckleberry Finn*[1] often point out that while Twain constructed the opening sequences early on, he eventually lost interest in the novel and put it aside. Apparently, it just wasn't gelling for the author. Only when he again returned to the manuscript after a gap of many years did the characters and story fall into thematic place, allowing Twain to complete it and create an enduring and important piece of American literature.

What happened in the intervening time to bring *Huck Finn* into focus for Twain? The answer is tied to the meaning of Huck's journey down the Mississippi River with escaped slave Jim. Both of them seek freedom, but their southward journey only takes them deeper into the land of servitude. So why would they travel in that direction to achieve freedom? Twain has purpose, here. While there is not a thorough one-to-one correspondence between events, the book can be viewed as a document of the momentous trauma through which Twain, like all Americans, has just lived: the War between the States.

The Civil War was a central issue of American writers during Reconstruction, and it was no different for Twain. A symbolic chronicle of the causes of, events leading up to, and physical collision between the North and South, Huckleberry Finn also examines the war as a conflict between states of being, between truthful adherence to the tenets that govern the United States and a hypocrisy that abuses and games the system for profit and power.

The opening chapters of the book lay out the major players in this strife. Besides Huck, there are Jim, Pap, Tom Sawyer, Judge Thatcher, and the Widow Douglas and Miss Watson. Each represents an aspect of American society that is revealed through their characteristics and actions and through Huck's interactions with them. Huck, however, as the narrator and focal point of the narration, is not an aspect. Rather, he is the American everyman dealing with those aspects—the protagonist young America in first person. These early chapters also lay out the idea of conflict between opposite frames of reference and opposite states of mind. On the one hand, there are the Widow Douglas and her spinster sister, Miss Watson, representatives of cultural stability enhanced by slow but definite social progress. They are the ones educating Huck by teaching him to read and otherwise "sivilizing" him with religion—the two great pillars of civilization. Significantly, both women are unmarried. Or rather, they are married to humankind as a whole rather than to individual men. Like nuns, theirs is a higher calling than personal attachment and fulfillment: the task of bringing order to society from within. For Huck, however, that society seems as restrictive as it is enlightening.

Ironically, the story with which Miss Watson tries to impress Huck of the need to earn an education and to live with and impart order is that of "Moses and the Bullrushers." Huck on his raft is Moses in his basket, washed up among the bullrushers—the bushwhackers, bull artists, and those who would rush headlong like maddened bulls, all of whom destroy social and cultural order. From here on out, Huck encounters such people with great frequency. Equally ironic is that, although Huck hates having to learn to read and write, that skill becomes vital during his journey, and finally, it allows him to "author" this book.

At odds with the Widow Douglas and Miss Watson is Huck's father, Pap, who is cultural stagnation personified. Exhibiting the full range of negative human attributes, he is the lowest of the low in his town: a vicious, dirty, lying, drunken, lazy, thieving, poverty-stricken, and almost bestial scoundrel. Yet, because he is White, he still is qualified to possesses a slave. That slave is Huck. Pap takes all Huck's money for his own. Then he absconds with Huck to a rude cabin in the wilderness across the border in another state. There, he imprisons Huck, keeping him locked up at night and forcing him to labor during the day without compensation under the threat of corporal punishment. This is metaphorically tantamount to taking African people—or anyone—from their homes, transporting them to a foreign land, housing them in slave shacks, and making them perform slave labor or face corporal punishment or death.

And the corporal punishment and threats of death are the same for Huck as for a Black slave. Pap beats him with sticks and whips and threatens him with a gun. The abuses Pap visits upon Huck form an almost verbatim inventory of the treatment of Black slaves by their White masters as recounted in abolitionist literature, particularly Frederick Douglass's *Narrative of the Life of an American Slave*. As Pap succinctly puts it, he was "boss of his son." (p. 42)

Sometimes the brutality comes when Pap doesn't think Huck has worked hard enough, but just as often, it happens when Huck asserts his rights as a free individual. Most of all, Pap does not want Huck to get an education—something he himself lacks—and he resents the little that Huck has picked up from the Widow Douglas and Miss Watson—mostly because it has made Huck "uppity." Huck might be resistant to education, but despite complaining vociferously about it, he already understands the value in it—something Pap cannot conceive or perceive.

Even Pap's name—synonymous with mushed-up food for infants, political patronage, and lacking solid value or substance—further expresses Pap's representation as the Southern White man with his prevailing moral corruption in differentiating Blacks from Whites, enslaving them, and treating them as inferiors. Indeed, sick whiteness becomes a trope with regard to Pap. His narrow mindset and shallow, selfish, and ignorant reasoning mark his critique of the government as pure pablum. And while pap is White, it is not the pure white of goodness but an off-white that, like pablum, quickly sours and becomes sickly. Huck describes Pap thus: "There warn't no color in his face where his face showed; it was white; not like another man's white, but a white to make a body sick, a white to make the body's flesh crawl—a tree-toad white, a fish-belly white." (p. 39)

And let's not forget Huck's name. The huckleberry is a common and widespread fruit native to North America. Even aside from the idea that Huck is the American everyman and thus representative of Americans, who are becoming common and widespread on the continent, the colors of the huckleberry are notable. It comes in three—red, black, and blue—which makes Huck's name very possibly a play on red, white, and blue in the context of a book whose subject is slavery and whose method is reversal. In this context, White Huckleberry takes on the characteristics of the black huckleberry—the Black slave—since Huck is Pap's slave. This continues later on when Jim, in essence, becomes a father figure for Huck. Finn, of course, refers to the piscine nature of Huck's journey down the Mississippi River as he swims with the currents of his time.

As the episode with Judge Thatcher shows, Pap is eloquent in his use of deceit and religion to subvert authority to his will so that he can continue his depredations on Huck —the American everyman who has become as much a slave to the slaveholding system as are the Black people who are held in bondage. (p. 42–44) From his title and position, Thatcher is obviously the law of the land, the rules that govern us as well as the administration of those rules. In that capacity, he should be critical of and watchful for acts that defy those laws and rules. However, he is so entrenched in the prevailing and corrupt slaveholding culture that when Pap is brought before his court, he cannot help but abet Pap's prevarications, depredations, and criminality despite his clear knowledge of Pap's notoriously bad reputation. To do otherwise would be to deny—in a legal sense—that slavery was a valid concept—something the entrenched Southern culture would never tolerate and Judge Thatcher, as that culture's arbiter, would never do.

Pap's representation as the Southerner entrenched in a backward-looking, slaveholding, agrarian economy is solidified by his rant against the federal government.

> Call this a govment! why, just look at it and see what it's like. Here's the law a-standing ready to take a man's son away from him—a man's own son, which he has had all the trouble and all the anxiety and all the expense of raising. Yes, just as that man has got that son raised at last, and ready to go to work and begin to do sutin' for him and give him a rest, the law up and goes for him….Sometimes I've a mighty notion to just leave the country for good and all….Says I, for two cents I'd leave the blamed country and never come anear it agin. (p. 49)

Pap's mindset emerges more fully as his rant takes in the North, free blacks, and education, all of which are rolled into the image of a black man Pap once encountered. This black man lived in the North, was free, was a college professor, and even had the right to vote. Contained in this single image is Southern fear that Blacks might be equal to Whites—or even superior—endangering the core of White supremacy in economics, politics, and social prestige. More pointed is that Pap, as the prototypical Southern slave owner, takes the first formal step toward civil war. He says, "When they told me there was a state in this country where they'd let that nigger vote…I says I'll never vote again." (p. 49–50) By eschewing participation in national politics, the Southern slave owner gives notice of secession from the Union.

Huck, however, is of a new generation, and his personal experiences of being exploited by the same system that enslaves Black people have given him a new awareness of human injustice. So, when he meets up with Jim, who has decided to escape bondage, they quickly realize they both have the same goal: freedom from indentured servitude—freedom to live one's life as one chooses, just as laid out in the founding documents of the United States: the Declaration of Independence and the Constitution. To do that, they must, in the modern parlance, take the roles of mismatched buddies seeking to escape villains in a chase movie. Of course, like the heroes in chase movies, they cannot help but run straight into their enemies right before the end. That's the nature of drama, and often life itself.

After Huck and Jim join forces, they begin their sojourn together. It starts on dry land, but very soon, they must take to the water of the Mississippi River—the major artery of America's heartland, the one mighty and irrevocable linkage between the North and South—to preserve themselves from capture. Their first craft is a flimsy skiff, but they soon create enough of a society together that they graduate to a solid raft with a wigwam shelter. As noted, their journey is ostensibly to seek freedom—Jim from slavery and Huck from the fetters of his society and civilization, represented on its extremes by Pap's cultural stagnation and the Widow Douglas and Miss Watson's cultural restrictions. But as noted before, if freedom is their literal purpose, the journey they take is illogical because the Mississippi River flows south. Every moment they remain on its currents ferries Jim deeper into slave country and Huck closer to New Orleans, the quintessential bastion of the very culture whose appurtenances and restrictions make Huck uncomfortable and where that culture is at its most overt and corrupt.

But Huck and Jim—the nation—can't go to the freedom of the North without first moving against and confronting the slavery of the South. So, before the journey, proper, begins, Twain has to prepare the way thematically, which he does in the episode where Huck, dressed as a girl, converses with the woman in the house. These themes, which are played out time and again through the course of the novel, are outgrowths of the tensions surrounding the notions of identity and direction. The former questions who we are as a nation, and the second denotes conflict because, in choosing the direction the nation should take, it is impossible for its people to go in two directions at once. One cannot espouse personal freedom while enslaving others. And both identity and direction imply choice—making deliberate and thoughtful decisions about these critical matters.

One of the first bits of information Huck learns from the woman is that the people back home think he is dead—that Jim killed him and fled. On the eve of deep national conflict, the American everyman has lost his identity and even his former life, and it is because a slave has killed him—because slavery has killed the American Union. Even his name is now in question. Huck gives the woman one name, then another, then a third and fourth, none of which are his own. The American everyman, just like his country, is undergoing an identity crisis and has yet to figure out who he is. Further, Huck's dressing as a girl lends him a dual sexuality. He is is not just everyman but everywoman, too. And this dual context also mirrors the idea of opposites contained within a single body.

Huck tells the woman he's going to Goshen. In addition to being the name of a town in Missouri, Goshen is the Biblical name for an area of the Nile Delta in ancient Egypt. Further, in popular parlance, Goshen euphemistically refers to a sort of promised land, linking the name Goshen with the North and freedom. But if Huck intends to go to Goshen, the woman tells him, he's going the wrong way. She lives in St. Petersburg, and Goshen is ten miles north. Huck has overshot his mark. He's not headed toward Goshen but toward New Orleans, which is just about as far south as one can travel on the Mississippi River before it empties into the Gulf of Mexico. But despite her warning that Huck seems to be going in the wrong direction, he and Jim resume their journey south as soon as he returns to the raft.

This episode might seem contradictory, but with it, Twain blatantly acknowledges that Huck and Jim's journey south along the river is illogical. Freedom, like Goshen, is not where Huck and Jim are heading, at least not literally. Just the opposite. However, Twain sends them South for reasons of his own, and their journey has an internal logic that is not at odds with their purposes. On the raft, Huck and Jim form a microcosm of ideal American society, where Whites and Blacks are unified through living, working, and playing together. However, their journey also is symbolic of the journey of this American ideal, carried by the natural currents of historical imperative through America's heartland, toward the inevitable physical confrontation over slavery, which is the antithesis of the concept of freedom espoused by Americans. This is why Twain sends his racial fugitives south, into the arms of their staunchest enemies. The mismatched buddies in the movies always must confront the chief villains in the climax.

But before Americans could confront slavery, they first had to become aware on a deeper level of the inherent wrongness of that institution and demonstrably acknowledge that it and racism are ethically and morally corrupt. Huck, as an American everyman, starts out with a view of Blacks and slavery that was conventional for his time. His first mention of Jim is his casual introduction of Jim as "Miss Watson's big nigger" (p. 22), but Huck isn't being vicious or intentionally derogatory here. He's simply reflecting the language and tenor of his times, unaware that the literal meaning of his words implies that Jim is somehow not fully human and has no identity beyond that of his color, owner, and large stature, which gives him a superior ability to perform manual labor. In fact, Huck could be describing any farm animal—"Miss Watson's big horse."

And the casualness of Huck's words illustrates how deeply ingrained and normalized such attitudes were. For American everyman Huck, Blacks are less important than are Whites, and so Huck automatically and without reflection considers them inferior. His attitude isn't surprising. It is the prevailing attitude of an American culture that thrived on slavery, which in turn required the dehumanization of Black slaves.

So, the novel's first step is to rehumanize Black people for the White American everyman. For Huck, this occurs after he denies that he and Jim were separated in the fog, when he sees in Jim's reaction employment of all his own positive qualities. First, Jim is intelligent. Once he sees the physical evidence of the trash littering the raft, he immediately deduces the truth behind Huck's lie. Second, Jim demonstrates deep emotion in his sorrow at Huck's apparent loss and in his concern for Huck's well-being. "'My heart wuz mos' broke bekase you wuz los', en I didn' k'yer no' mo' what became er me en de raf.'" (p. 121) Third, Jim reveals his human dignity through his hurt at being deceived. "'Trash is what people is dat puts dirt on de head er dey fren's en makes 'em ashamed.'" (p. 121) And fourth, Jim's affront at Huck's cruelty indicates ethical and moral depth of character.

Jim and his behavior are such a direct contrast with Huck's major male role model, Pap, that he does not have to think long about Jim's reaction and its implicit and explicit proof of Jim's humanity before he "humble[s himself] to a nigger." (p. 121) With this action, Huck and, symbolically, the average White American openly admits that his past behavior towards Blacks has been demeaning, dehumanizing, and just plain wrong.

From Huck's new awareness of Jim's inherent humanity emerges a realization that slavery is a profoundly corrupt evil, followed by the inevitable conclusion that Black people must be released from bondage. Thus, it is not long before

Huck begins to actively work for emancipation. The very next people Huck and Jim encounter are two men looking for runaway slaves. Huck saves Jim by telling them that Jim, hidden in the wigwam on the raft, is his father. He further ensures their hasty departure by saying there is sickness on the raft. By calling Jim his father, Huck has, in one stroke, rejected his own racist, backward father/heritage and professed intimate kinship and a new future between Blacks and Whites. Further, he indicates that slavery is a virulent sickness that infects society. And on top of that, in protecting Jim by subterfuge and hiding him away, he uses the same tactics many White Americans were employing to abolish slavery and help runaway slaves escape North via the Underground Railroad.

But even before Huck comes to his awareness, there has been a strong signal that the dominance of the South's former way of thinking is at an end and that the inevitable imperatives of cultural progress are destroying the Southern way of life. Right at the beginning of their river journey, Huck and Jim find a house floating on the swollen water. Just as the river represents the forces of cultural imperatives bearing the nation toward war, the house symbolizes personal lives and families, as well as social traditions, uprooted and carried away by the flood. Significantly, though Huck does not yet know it, this house contains Pap's dead body. Huck's roots in the old way of life, the old thought patterns and behaviors, are severed by the rising flood of conflict in the heartland, and by extension, so are those roots severed for all Americans.

Soon after the encounter with the house, Huck comes ashore in the midst of the feud between the Grangerfords and Shepherdsons. While the surface level of the feud follows the ages-old outlines of clan or tribal warfare, the two families become stand-ins for the warriors of a new intertribal combat that was of significance during Reconstruction. In 1867, established farmers and landholders began an agrarian society called the Grange, whose immediate purpose was to protect established agrarian interests against incursions of other, newly arrived land users. These might be freed Blacks or immigrants—or even Yankees!—but the single major foe of the Grangers was the sheepherder, and bloody battles over pasturage were not uncommon. In the end, the sheepherders emerged victorious, with legal and moral rights to equal pasturage upheld.

So the range war, like the Civil War, was a fight for liberation and equality—and diversity. The significance, though, is not simply in the thematic similarity of the two conflicts, for there is a deeper level to this feud that has a direct bearing on America's progress toward Civil War. Twain depicts the Grangerfords as Southern patricians. The head of the family is called the "Colonel," an honorary title customary in the South. The Colonel wears white suits and a Panama hat, and he possesses considerable property and many slaves. All these elements typify him as the aristocratic Southern plantation owner.

While the representation of the Grangerfords as Southern slave holders is fairly obvious, what the Shepherdsons denote, besides being sheepherders, is less so. That they are the enemies of the Southern slaveholding Grangerfords provides the first hint that the Shepherdsons must represent the abolitionist movement. While this might not seem obvious at first glance, a closer look strengthens the supposition that the Shepherdsons are, in fact, not only leading their flocks to freedom but are abolitionists in the guise of the most famous abolitionist of all—John Brown.

Brown fathered twenty children and, so, was patriarch of a clan. And like the Shepherdsons, Brown was known for his violent attacks against his opponents. In 1855, he and five of his sons killed five pro-slavery men in Potawatomie, Kansas—the same number as that of the Grangerfords killed by the Shepherdsons in their final fight. Also, that fight takes place at a ferry crossing, further linking the Shepherdsons to Brown, who was hanged in 1859 following his aborted raid on the federal munitions dump at Harper's

Ferry. But the fact that clinches the relationship between the Shepherdsons and Brown is that immediately prior to his years as a violent abolitionist, Brown owned a sheep-raising and wool brokerage business.

The Potawatomie killings resulted from the Kansas–Nebraska Act of 1854, which gave territories the right to enter the Union as slave or free states. This was a major issue before the war because the act repealed the Missouri Compromise, which had made slavery illegal in newly admitted states. The South, a proponent of states' rights principally because supporting that doctrine supposedly legitimized slaveholding, viewed the Missouri Compromise as a weakening of its political power. Instead, the South rallied around the Kansas–Nebraska Act, which asserted popular sovereignty, strengthening the South's political position.

The Kansas–Nebraska Act was sponsored by Stephen A. Douglas, and though the South lauded the act, Douglas's later antislavery, pro-Union stance destroyed his popularity there. A beaten man, he died, almost symbolically, on June 3, 1861, the same day as the first skirmish of the Civil War— the Battle of Philippi. And he, too, has his place in Huck's tale in the form of Stephen Dowling Bots, Emmeline Grangerford's poetic subject. Beyond the similarity in names is that Botts falls down a well and drowns—a fitting metaphor for Douglas, who could be said to have perished in a hole he'd dug for himself.

The states' rights connection is reinforced by the presence in the Grangerford library of speeches by states' rights advocate Henry Clay. Clay did, however, try to ameliorate the political difficulties caused by slavery and the states' rights issue, and he predicted that bloody civil war would result from secession. Thus, the Grangerford–Shepherdson conflict is linked to both of the major causes of the Civil War: the abolitionist movement and the states' rights issue.

Soon after leaving the Grangerfords, Huck falls under the control of two confidence men. The extensive tenure of these two hucksters aboard the raft also has significance in relation to the Civil War. The younger of the conmen says he is "the rightful Duke of Bridgewater," (p. 163) and the older claims he is the "pore disappeared Dauphin, Looy the Seventeen," (p. 164) the rightful heir to the throne of France. These two individuals portray European involvement in the Civil War, with the Duke personifying England and the King acting the part of France. Their names—Bridgewater and the Dolphin, as he is often termed—indicate their transatlantic nature, and their titles confer a counterfeit legitimacy.

During the war, England and France provided aid to the Confederacy. Thus, the Duke and King ostensibly offer attachment to all the cultural, economic, and political benefits of Europe that aristocratic Southerners craved: culture in the form of theatrical drama; economics and kinship, represented by their offer to support the Wilks sisters in England; and politics, which comes both from their offer of implied protection for the Wilks and the political nature of the dramas they perform.

While aboard the raft, the two hucksters spend most of their time huddled in the wigwam, plotting means to fleece gullible townsfolk. England and France helped the Confederacy not out of ideological affinity but in a united effort to weaken America politically and economically and to profiteer from the South's conflict with the North. This is why all the culture and supposed aid presented by the Duke and King is really just false pretense. The Duke's bogus offer to support the Wilks sisters, both economically and politically—to make them English—is simply a sham to rob and weaken them in the name of false kinship. And instead of genuine high culture, the Duke and King foist off farcical dramatic adaptations that are culturally vapid and artistically hollow. Instead of bestowing value to the viewers, the counterfeit dramas are politically void and serve only to divest the Southerners not only of their money, but of their caution regarding such formidable international powerhouses as England and France. Amusingly, the dramas the King and

Duke perform give a clue to the true nature of the performers, for all of them—*Richard III*, *Hamlet*, and even *Romeo and Juliet*—dramatize not only political intrigue and betrayal, but portray societies in the throes of antagonisms, feuds, or open civil war.

Huck then discovers that the King has sold Jim, who is being held by the Phelps family. He goes to see what he can do, only to be mistaken for the Phelps' nephew, Tom Sawyer, who is due to arrive for a visit. The real Tom soon shows up, and after Huck tells Tom that he plans to help Jim escape, he is dumbfounded that Tom agrees to help. "I couldn't believe it. Tom Sawyer a nigger-stealer!" (p. 285) Huck's wonder is sparked by the fact that Tom, despite his frequent shenanigans, is an upstanding citizen. As Huck puts it, Tom "was respectable and well brung up…had a character to lose…was bright…, knowing;… and yet here he was, without any more pride, or rightness, or feeling, than to stoop to this business, and make himself a shame…." (p. 295)

The problem for Huck is that Tom is an avowed disciple of proper social form and political doctrine. Using romance and adventure literature as his behavioral bibles, Tom always strictly adheres to accepted cultural tenets. But not only does Tom help, he does so with such enthusiasm that he takes control of the enterprise, concocting elaborate plans based on literature—on fictions. Although these plans ostensibly create an aura of propriety around Jim's liberation, their actual purpose in the context of the novel is to thwart and subvert authority by weaponizing the literary canon established by that authority in the first place. After all, if America's founding documents—the rules by which our nation is supposedly governed and which we all tacitly agree to follow—proclaim that all men in America are equal, why is the Black man enslaved? Tom, however, is not really subverting authority, nor has he ever had any intention to do so. For Tom, liberating Jim is just a technical game, because he knows that there is a new authority: Miss Watson has already officially liberated Jim.

There is more going on here than two boys rescuing a Black man from a shed. The Phelps are at the southernmost tip of Huck and Jim's voyage, close to New Orleans. Huck and Jim have journeyed here, passing through incidents and issues leading to the Civil War, and they now face the inevitable physical confrontation over Jim's bondage, and, by extension, the bondage of all Black people in America. In this context, the Phelps represent the social norms, economic prerogatives, governmental authority, and military forces of the South. Not only do they keep the Black man—Jim—in bondage, they raise a rabble army of Southern farmers to prevent his liberation—the Army of the Confederacy. Amusingly, Tom's obligatory letter of warning to the Phelps cautions that the force that intends to free Jim "will sneak down from northards, along the fence." (p. 338) This is exactly what has already happened. Huck, the new abolitionist, has come from northwards, and when he first arrives at the Phelps' farm, he actually sneaks around the fence before climbing it and approaching the house from the rear. The allusion here is to the army of the North, quietly amassing along the Mason–Dixon Line prior to the war.

If Huck is the new everyman abolitionist, Tom also has an alternate role in this drama. Because the Phelps believe that Huck is Tom, Tom assumes the false and very common but somewhat stately sounding name of William Thompson—Tom's son. This indicates that he is no longer the individual, Tom Sawyer. Instead, like Huck, he has taken a larger role that fits his general character as a staunch upholder of social structure: that of the federal government.

On behalf of Huck, the common American, Tom is the one who takes charge of the mechanics of the war to free Jim. Tom is the general who possesses the arcane knowledge of strategy and tactics—learned with authority from books —and he engineers all the battles then leads his troops into the fray. And most importantly, he carries with him the official sanction enabling him to free the slaves with confidence. This is the *Emancipation Proclamation*, symbolized by Miss

Watson, a representative of established social order and cultural progress, setting Jim free.

Thus, Tom's elaborately wrought plans become the tactics and strategies of the Civil War, all the battles of which occurred on Southern soil. General Tom and Private Huck engage in battles all over the symbolic South of the Phelps' farm, leading armies of rodents, snakes, and bugs in a harassment of the Southern homeland. As the Union troops, they commandeer supplies from defeated Southerners in the form of clothes, food, tools, and the other items that Huck and Tom pilfer from the Phelps. The things they sneak into Jim's cabin, such as the witch pie and the rats, are equivalent to the supplies, war materiel, and reinforcements delivered across Southern lines to replenish the Union army. And finally, Jim's cryptic scrawls equate with coded military and spy communiqués.

At last the war ends, although in the process Tom, the Union, has been wounded. Only after he is restored to the Phelps, that is, after the North and South come together again as a single nation, is he made whole and well and able to wear the bullet that wounded him as a proud symbol that his efforts and pain have brought tangible rewards.

More important for the real protagonist of the story—a nation recovering from war—Jim, the Black American, is set free. He is allowed to travel where he wants, to take a wife of his own choosing, and to create a home life of substance and permanence to call his own. In sending Jim on his way, Tom, representative of the Union, presents him with $40, just as the federal government promised to give to each former slave forty acres and a mule.

Significantly, only after Jim has been freed does he tell Huck that Pap is dead. The Civil War, a war of liberation, must be won by the forces of equality before America can truly realize that the structure of the old slave culture has permanently shifted off its foundation and washed away. This fact is as liberating for Huck as it is for Jim, because Pap treated Huck, his own posterity, as property. The culture that enslaved Blacks also fettered White Americans with bonds of an inhumanity that would enslave the world. The success of the Civil War has lent a greater potential for freedom to all Americans.

So ends Huck and Jim's journey—America's journey—to freedom. American consciousness has gained awareness of the inherent humanity of Black people and reacted against the inhumanity of slavery. Secession, the abolitionist movement, the states' rights issue, European involvement, and other elements have formed benchmarks along the way to war. Emancipation proclaimed, battles fought, and the Civil War won have resulted in freedom for the slaves and a re-formed Union between the North and South. The bonds of slavery and inequality have to be broken for the bonds of brotherhood to flourish.

In the end, Huck, the eager new post-war American everyman, adamantly proclaims his intention "to light out for the Territory." (p. 366) He intends, like his namesake plant, to spread across the continent. Importantly, the end of slavery and the reaffirmed national unity allowed America to dispense with the political controversy surrounding the Missouri Compromise and the Kansas–Nebraska Act. This controversy, engendered by slavery and the states' rights issue, had seriously hampered America's potential to expand westward. Now, with these political impediments eliminated by the Civil War, America, personified by young Huck, can expand unhindered into the Western territories, where it can strive, in its rough-and-tumble way, toward maturity.

There are several contenders for the designation of the Great American Novel. Many great writers have vied and continue to vie to produce it. In vain. It already has been written. For my money, it isn't possible to do better than *The Adventures of Huckleberry Finn*, which so artfully and entertainingly charts one of the country's most severe growing pains, resulting in contention, a messy divorce, and violence of brother against brother. And the result was an equally contentious reconciliation that introduced a whole new way of life to the United States. This is a book about America like no other.

Through the message of the novel, it would seem that Mark Twain was expressing hope for a healed Union and eventual true equality for all Americans. If nothing else, the war should have proved the futility of the South remaining as it always had been in the face of scientific and technological progress and a burgeoning nation eager to expand its boundaries. The South was defeated precisely because of a lack of technological advancement. The future was upon the country, and the future waits for no one. And as one moves into the future, one must, by necessity, change.

A century and a half have passed since Twain published *The Adventures of Huckleberry Finn*, and during that time, the United States has been set free to expand to its utmost. Yet the other issues that came to a head in the Civil War—identity and direction—remain undecided. And the conclusion of the Civil War, which should have allowed the notion and practice of freedom to come to full fruition, did not. Equality has not fully materialized, despite a century and a half of continued, if often subterranean, strife. Even the fact that many of those decades were fraught with major international conflicts over identity, direction, and freedom seems to have brought little awareness within our own society of the need to truly live by the tenets of equality and freedom we espouse. Simply stated, understanding of identity and direction brings equality and freedom. Advancements have been made, but they are only battles in a larger, ongoing—and seemingly never-ending—Civil War.

Part III
Other Matters

The Ultimate Chicken

ONE EARLY MORNING, IN THE hour before dawn, I climbed through a shrouded, rocky gorge that lead up the east side of a fog-filled valley. At the top, I found a short flight of stone steps at the rear of an old stone and brick building and sat there to wait for daylight. Before me spread the valley, several miles wide and quite deep, though when I first sat, I could not see it. And not just because of the darkness. Dense fog filled it to the brim like an immense, tranquil sea of white whose edges drifted up onto the lawn less than a hundred feet from my steps. Nothing tangible could be seen on my side save the two steeples of a church jutting angular shadows above the fog's surface a hundred yards down the hillside to my left. Misty, indistinct treetops darkened the rim of the shrouded ridge on the far side of the valley. The sea was white and calm, the air above it quiet and still. The world was ethereal, and I was a sitter on its rocky verge.

From above the building at my back, the sun rose, illuminating first the opposite hilltop, then gradually the surface of the sea of mist filling the valley. As the sun's rays, first golden then brightening to white, bathed the mist and melted it away, shapes began to take form out of the blankness on the far slope, first in vague shadow, then in sharpening detail. A tan patch soon acquired edges and turned into a lone house. A dark, foreshortened rectangle spotted with color became a parking lot with automobiles.

A dense area laced with white and color resolved into a shady residential neighborhood.

This process of enlightenment and revelation continued for a couple of hours, and as the fog thinned, shrank, and flowed down the deepening valley to my left, I could see the town beneath the white surface—that a whole world of life and activity and variety existed where I would have seen nothing but blankness had I but casually glanced and passed on.

Two thoughts came as I sat there. The first was that I had witnessed a hatching process. When I first sat, I saw nothing but the surface of a large, white egg. Soon a crack began to appear in the surface, and that crack gradually widened, and the life within showed itself in ever-greater detail. As I watched, the crack finally split wide enough to release that life, and out it came to bustle about on its daily round. The white egg, now vanished, was only a memory, but bound up in that memory was that the sun had been the life-giving source of energy that had sparked the life within then split the egg, revealing the form and structure organized within. The sun was no less than a sort of cosmic chicken—one among many in the henhouse of our galaxy.

At this point, the second thought arrived. The white surface I had seen also was like a piece of blank paper on which the energy of the sun—of creation—wrote its stories. The shapes it finally etched out of the white void were neither words or pictures but glyphs of a language that could be understood. That lone house there was not merely a house or an image of a house but, specifically, the definition of house and, by implication, the necessity for shelter, appreciation of aesthetics, construction techniques, deforestation, the nail industry, and so forth. You could look at that house and follow the physical trails and meanings of it throughout reality.

Because the implications of any given object or situation can ultimately reach into infinity, we require definitions to help order our complex reality. Definitions are limiting factors, helping narrow the range of possibilities to manageable chunks. And words, which are the abstract elements—the building blocks—of definitions, also serve as limiting factors. That lone house across the valley, by the simple fact of its existence as house, limited the space it occupied from the pure abstraction of everythingness that existed prior to it being defined as a house, to a specific set of responses that correspond to house. It, and the space it occupied, was house, not automobile, parking lot, grove of trees, or anything else. And even in its individual imperfection, it was the perfect definition of house.

White is the complete spectrum—the unification and presence of all the visible colors. It can be fractured—defined—by inserting a single word—prism—into its structure, which is then broken into the limited categories of the visual spectrum that can be defined as specific colors, which can then be mixed in an almost infinite variety up to but not including white. So implicitly contained in that white sea was an almost infinite range of possibilities simply waiting for the creative energy of the sun—the nuclear reaction going on inside—to write on the sea's white field with a pen of photons and other emitted particles to define the limits of the space they touched. No less does the energy of the sun's rays draw the forms of life on our planet's blank landscape of dirt and rock. No less do the forces of creativity fill the blank spaces of the human mind.

Creation writes in certain, specific languages, each complete with definitions. It limits space/time, not only with definitions but with the physical forms those definitions take. The process holds true, for example, for these words on this paper. This paper is the white field of all possibilities. I could write anything here, and the words I do write are the shapes—the factors—that limit the infinite possibilities originally inherent in the blank sheet. They are the limitations that not only express thoughts but that say, "No, not poetry or fiction or article but essay."

The power of limitation through definition seems, perforce, to link the realm of ideas inextricably with the realm of the physical. There is no better example than the words on this paper. In the physical world, we have the simple fact that these words limit the amount of white space on the page by covering it up with ink. More important is that the exact form of these physical limitations—the spaces in and between the ink—delimit the meaning a writer intends as much as the letters do, themselves.

Thus, we can glean certain information from a secondary limiting power of the ink on this page: its mere structure, which is simply abstract form codified and amplified. For example, consider these samples of writing from the standpoint of structure alone:

Prose, obviously.

Rhymed couplets.


```
--------------
------------------
--------------
------------------

--------------------------
------------------------
--------------------------
------------------------

------------
------------
```

English sonnet.

In each case, the restrictions that the structure alone has placed on the field of all possibilities have served to limit our perceptions of that space. It is now recognizable as something specific that is not, and cannot be, anything else.

While both the intellectual and the physical serve as limiting factors by defining reality, the power of limitation on both of them is actually somewhat weak. Thinkers continue to strive for intellectual understanding—read, definition—but many basic philosophic points and concepts remain arguable. Besides, ideas continue to evolve, sometimes revealing greater clarity, other times just muddying the water. After all, variegation can be considered a move farther away from understanding if for no other reason than that the "right thing" is one thing, and all the rest are wrong. We all agree, for instance, that a chair is to be sat on, but what does the Platonic ideal of chairness actually embody? Is it a Morris chair, a throne, or early American? Or a stone step? What is the ideal government people should live by—democracy, totalitarianism, anarchy? What economic system? Where does economics end and politics begin?

Philosophers, politicians, critics, and pundits argue endlessly about the meanings of ideas because ideas are not easily limited by delineations and depictions of them. The problem is that, in the end, we cannot know a single fact to be universally, ultimately, and irrevocably true—we've learned that apparently even the speed of light has not remained universally constant through time, nor is it precisely the same in all regions of space. Could we know one singular, absolute fact, then the actual nature of the universe might eventually be deduced. Or revealed. After all, mystics the world over use single-pointed awareness to achieve satori.

But the reality within which we live encourages just the opposite. It demands outward perception because that is how we apprehend and know reality. If you don't know how to make a living, you will starve. But outward perception is, by definition, limited in range and scope—the eye can never see totality because it cannot see farther than light has traveled, nor can it ever itself. Further, as Albert Einstein pointed out, all things are relative, which, perforce, must extend to the idea that all ideas must remain in a permanent state of flux because no one thing in the universe—in reality—is absolute and permanent—or real.

Nor is the concept of structured physical reality easily defined to the satisfaction of all. On a purely tangible level, for example, what is the most perfect female form? Peter Paul Rubens might answer very differently than Hugh Hefner. (Again the physical is bound with the idea.) Buckminster Fuller's house would be distinct from Frank Lloyd Wright's and both from that of a Chinese mandarin, yet each would be satisfied that his house is the best. Even the very basis of matter is indefinable since we have learned that matter is not actually something tangible but merely energy vibrating at various rates in subatomic packets that are either waves or particles, depending on how you observe them. But while we have reduced our understanding of matter to subatomic particles and some of their constituents, we have yet to deduce the basis or source of energy—the vibration—itself.

Some might say it consists of the remains of the explosion of the Singularity at the Big Bang as it expands into space. Others might point out that explanation doesn't account for the source of the energy inherent in latent form within the Singularity to begin with. Nor does it explain the archaic universes that existed before ours and whose remnant shadows scientists have begun to detect. All we can truly say is that it seems that there was simply a state of pure Yin waiting to transform into pure Yang, and we exist in a time and place somewhere along in that process of transformation. Thus, not only is all life in flux, all life is in transformation, too.

The ultimate idea and the ultimate physical construct wrapped up together in a single state might be called, with a bit of tongue in cheek, the ultimate chicken—at once egg and creature, idea and construct. It would take something like that to discover a pure and accurate conception of universal truth and reality. But because such a "creature" is both unconceived and inconceivable—sort of a cosmic Schrödinger's cat—it would seem to be impossible to apprehend either intellectually or physically. There was one additional avenue, however, down which I might pursue this chimerical being, and that is emotion. What about the limiting power of definition on emotion?

In many ways, emotions, which at first glance seem impossible to define in an absolute sense and thus limit, are actually more amenable to human perception than is the realm of the idea and more substantial than the realm of the physical. The fact that the definitions of emotions are subjective rather than objective does not negate them but actually reinforces their power, for in the proportion that something is internally recognized and universally known it gains significance. We can discuss an intellectual viewpoint—such as "What is the best government?"—extensively and never come to a conclusion, all while living under different forms of rule, each of which has its proponents. And if I say to you, "I live in a house," you might ask for a description to determine what sort of house. But if I tell you "I love you," you know exactly what I mean. A few people are interested in philosophy and many more in scientific discoveries or the latest news, but almost everybody wants to hear about sex scandals.

Although there are varying degrees and shades of love, and the details of expression of love may vary from culture to culture, people from widely different backgrounds, societies, and cultures can, and do, share love and a firm understanding of what the concept means. And everyone recognizes that the basic emotion of love is at polar opposites to the basic emotion of hate. Most people can feel hate at the mere mention of the word—not necessarily hatred for anything or anyone in particular, just general hate. If I say I'm happy or unhappy, perhaps you cannot know or understand the cause of my state, but you can identify with the emotion I'm feeling. While the intellectual ideal of home and the physical delineations and definitions of a house may differ from individual to individual, the loneliness of the single inhabitant of that house can be felt and empathized with by most of us.

The limiting power of the ways in which we delineate and recognize emotional content—such as facial expression, body language, verbal tone, and so forth—are more powerful and affecting than are those for either the intellectual or the physical simply because they are more universally understood and accepted. Two enemy soldiers meeting on the battlefield need no dictionary of translation to read each other's hatred and fear—or relief at war's end. Further, emotional states can—and often do—dictate behavior. Most obvious are cases of neuroses or psychoses, but to some extent, the emotions of even "normal" people subvert the intellect and the body to their will, in essence controlling one's life in ways that can't be governed intellectually or physically.

The ultimate proof of emotions' universal power is that their effects and affects are true and authentic, even for those who live on the lower half of the IQ scale as well as for the most hardened realist who demands that a thing be quantifiable to be actual. Even pragmatists feel love, that most unpragmatic of emotions. Everyone responds to emotion, save, perhaps, psychopaths. This is true despite the fact that emotion is somewhat akin to a singularity, which is impossible to know except by peripheral phenomenon—like the eye/I, which is not visible to itself.

How odd that the concepts most definable—the physical and the idea—are the least susceptible to limitation, and that the concept most susceptible to limitation—emotion—is the least definable. And how interesting that, while the intellectual and the physical are occupied with scores of widely divergent or tangential possibilities, we distinguish only a few significant, basic, common human emotions, and those only in relation to and in distinction from their opposites: hate/love, happy/sad, anger/joy, and so forth. As the Pretenders' song says, "There's a fine line between love and hate."

At last the hatching process was complete, and the valley was fully revealed. The air was clear, as if there had never been a fog. I had sat on the steps overlooking the valley and watched as form and idea revealed themselves, but it was not the physical beauty of the scene nor the ideas contained in the revelation that had become important. Instead, it was the emotion that welled up from that ineffable place we have within us: a feeling of being at one with the mysteries of an external, idealized field of all possibility and with the mysteries within myself. For a short time, sitting there on the stone steps overlooking the valley, I felt as if I were, at once, both chicken and egg.

Illegal Alien and Drug Smuggling Checkpoint Just West of Del Rio

As I come out of the western desert, the first warning is a speed zone sign where no town ever thought to be. A few hills and curves later, stop signs and orange cones come into view. Beside the road is a small metal building shaded by a metal canopy, and parked next to it are a couple of Border Patrol SUVs. As I slow and approach, a sun-browned man in green uniform and pilot sunglasses emerges from the shade and waits at the stop sign.

There are questions. "Are you a United States citizen? Where are you coming from? What was the purpose of your visit? Where are you going?"

This is the third Border Patrol checkpoint I've passed today, and it's only noon. I'm reminded of movies about World War II and the Cold War, where the landscape of Europe seems littered with border crossings, suspicion, and guns attempting to control interlopers. When I first passed this way thirty years ago, there wasn't a single checkpoint, but these days, the government suspects us all.

The Border Patrol officer listens to my answers and looks me over. Satisfied, he says, "Move on." I do, with an inner smile and a flutter in my stomach. Once again I have fooled them into thinking I belong and that my journey has purpose and a beginning and end.

Not long afterwards, Amistad Reservoir comes into view. After miles of desert, its sheer volume and turquoise waters are a shock. It's as if a bit of sky has broken off and fallen into an alien residence of ravine and dry wash. All this water transgresses the border, washes Mexican and U.S. shores alike. Certainly that can't be legal. I wonder if the Border Patrol knows.

Throwing Down the Gauntlet

WHAT DO BASEBALL PLAYERS, JAI ali players, archers, the Music Machine, a bounty hunter named Tate, Rottwang, Dr. Strangelove, Mr. Han, Carl Hickman, and Michael Jackson all have in common?

While you ponder, I'll give you a few fun trivia tidbits. The Music Machine, led by lead singer Sean Bonniwell, was a band from the mid-1960s American garage band/psychedelic explosion. Their 1966 song, "Talk Talk," reached number twenty on the singles charts, and the group appeared on Dick Clark's American Bandstand. When Clark asked them what they called the kind of music they played, Bonniwell responded that it was "punk rock." I couldn't swear that they invented the term, but the music certainly was proto-punk and the term prescient.

Tate was a quirky, short-lived western that aired thirteen episodes in 1960–61. It starred David McLean, who made appearances in many other TV series, including *Bonanza*, *The Virginian*, *Perry Mason*, *Death Valley Days*, *The Streets of San Francisco*, *The Fugitive*, and *I Dream of Jeannie*. He also was in several low budget movies as well as a couple of better efforts, notably *The Andromeda Strain* and *Nevada Smith*. *Tate* was McLean's first role, and the show was the first TV western series shot on video tape. This was back in the black-and-white days of TV, and video cameras—which then used tubes instead of chips to gather light from visual images and convert it to electronic form—were still pretty primitive, giving a smeared look to the images on the screen. You can see the same sort of defect in the original *Dr. Who* episodes starring William Hartnell.

Rottwang is, of course, the mad scientist in Fritz Lang's 1927 masterpiece, *Metropolis*. Rottwang's machinations set off the near destruction—but ultimate revisioning—of the stultifying, impersonal, and demoralizing machine culture of the city of Metropolis. He is portrayed brilliantly by Rudolf Klein-Rogge, who played equally memorable villains in several of Lang's other films despite the fact that Lang had stolen his wife, Thea von Harbou. Von Harbou also wrote all the films that the director and actor later collaborated on. She later became the premiere filmmaker for the Third Reich, even as Lang was fleeing Germany for the United States.

Dr. Strangelove is the character for whom Stanley Kubrick's 1964 antiwar film *Dr. Strangelove or: How I Learned to Stop Worrying and Love the Bomb* is named, though he is not the central character. Actually, the central character is really the actor Peter Sellers, who plays three roles: Group Captain Lionel Mandrake, President Merkin Muffley, and Dr. Strangelove. As played by Sellers, Strangelove is a cross between Rottwang and the famous German rocket scientist Werner von Braun.

Mr. Han, played by kung fu movie veteran Shih Kien, is the lead villain defeated by Bruce Lee in *Enter the Dragon*. He's the one who talks about kung fu men forging their bodies in the fire of their wills. It's a good speech that probably has some truth to it even if it is a little histrionic. *Enter the Dragon* was Lee's best-realized film, and it made him into an international superstar even though he died just days before its premiere. He may, in fact, be the only international superstar to achieve that status post-mortem. As a result, the value of his earlier roles bounced dramatically—including *Return of the Dragon*, confusingly released before *Enter the Dragon* and bearing no thematic relationship to that film. *Enter the Dragon* was later parodied to hilarious effect in the

"Fistful of Yen" segment of *Kentucky Fried Movie*, with Bong Soo Han providing a telling caricature of Mr. Han.

The character of Carl Hickman was played by the talented William Fichtner, in the first two seasons of the television series *Crossing Lines*.

Although Weird Al Yankovich has done his best, no parody is necessary for Michael Jackson, who became his own best caricature. His most revealing artistic moment may have been when he morphed into a creature other than himself in the video for "Thriller." But despite Jackson's personal foibles, he did make the album *Thriller*, which stands as a fine piece of work. I guess Quincy Jones had something to do with that, too.

It is with Jackson's nickname that we glean a way to bring together our disparate cast of characters—and I don't mean "The King of Pop," as he was sometimes called. His other nickname refers to a wardrobe item that earned him the moniker "The Gloved One."

Yes, it is the glove—indeed, a single glove rather than a pair—that our cast has in common. There are a number of real people and movie characters—most often villains— who wear two gloves or have two weird or artificial hands: the electrical genius inventor Nicola Tesla often wore gloves due to a germ phobia, and Peter Lorre's character in *Mad Love* and Dr. No in the James Bond movie of the same name also readily come to mind. But the single glove is what sets our cast apart.

Baseball and jai ali players, archers, and some other athletes wear single gloves for obvious reasons. And I probably ought to mention Art Jimmerson here. Jimmerson is a retired boxer who fought Royce Gracie in the very first UFC competition, held in November 1993. The competitors did not wear gloves in the first UFC, but Jimmerson wore a boxing glove on his left hand during the match so he wouldn't injure his jabbing hand. He lost to Gracie by submission in two minutes, which promptly ended his mixed martial arts career, but he did earn the nickname "One-Glove" Jimmerson.

The reason many of the others wore a single glove, however, is at ironic odds with the idea of protection since some of them—at least the movie characters—wore not gloves, really, but fake hands to replace lost ones. And most of the gloves—or fake hands—were black in color, except for Carl Hickman, whose dark brown glove covers an injured, incapacitate, and painful hand, and Michael Jackson, whose glove was white instead of black. I'd like to be able to say that that is somewhat of an additional irony since Jackson is the only man of color among his fellow single-glovers, but that wouldn't strictly be true since Mr. Han was Asian. But I guess you could quibble by correctly stating that Mr. Han didn't wear a glove, exactly, but a collection of snap-on appendages that gave him considerable variety in usages. Some of the others also could use their fake hands, which presumably were made of some hard material, as permanent karate-chopping hands.

But it is interesting to note that most of our cast also has one more thing in common: They met a very public demise: villains Rottwang, Strangelove, and Han done in by heroes or circumstance; the Music Machine by changing musical taste; Tate and Hickman by poor ratings; and Michael Jackson by his own hand, so to speak.

I wonder if it has something to do with wearing a single garment designed by our basic anatomy to be worn in pairs. Is wearing a single glove somehow violating some esoteric law of nature that dooms the one who flaunts it with abject failure and death following swiftly on the heels of success? J. E. Cirlot has this to say about gloves in his book, *A Dictionary of Symbols*:

> Gloves, since they are worn on the hands, derive their symbolism from them. Of special interest is the right-hand glove, on account of the ceremonial custom of removing it when one approaches a person of higher

rank, or an altar, or the Lord. This custom has twin symbolic roots: in so far as it implies a glove of mail, it signifies disarming oneself before one's superior; at the same time, since the right hand pertains to the voice and to the rational side of Man, it is a custom which suggests candor and the frank disclosure of one's mind.[1]

Maybe wearing a single glove, particularly one that is black, is detrimental to one's well-being. As if to prove the point, Dr. Strangelove's gloved hand often takes on a life of its own and even attacks him. I don't know about this, but I do know that wearing a single glove has attracted more attention than, say, wearing a single sock, though perhaps not as much as wearing a single pant leg might. And then there's always the man with the one shoe. That one goes back to prehistory, and oddly enough, generally indicates a person of heroic stature. So, if you're going to wear one glove, maybe you also ought to consider wearing only one shoe. Just to be safe.

Busted!

DURING MY YOUNGER YEARS, WHEN I didn't have a car, I did a lot of hitchhiking. That was a lot safer then—back in the late 1960s and early '70s—than it now. Does anybody actually hitchhike anymore? My thumb got me around the city, to nearby cities, and a couple of times, across the country. One of the city-to-city trips was from my home in Houston to Austin, this time with a friend named Clay. We went to visit our friend, Ditto, who'd move there the year before. I don't know if Clay came up with the idea, or if I did, but suffice it to say that we got out on the road and stuck out our thumbs.

The trips to and from Austin must have been uneventful since I don't remember anything about them. After we arrived in Austin, we found Ditto's place, which was a house fairly near the university. Ditto had a roommate named Paul, and they'd lived in the house for only a week. Inside, it was a typical poor freak student pad, furnished with mattresses on the floor, crates for end tables, shelves made of cement blocks and boards, and cheap dressers and desks.

Shortly after Clay and I arrived, Paul came home with an ounce of pot, and the four of us spent the remainder of the afternoon and evening talking and smoking and having a good time. At last it was time for bed. Paul went to his room, Clay dossed-out in the living room on the mattress that served as a sofa, and I slept on an extra mattress in Ditto's room, which had a door to the back yard. I guess we went to bed about 11:30 or midnight.

About one o'clock, I was shocked from a deep sleep by a huge crash followed by the hurried trample of heavy feet. Lights were flashing confusedly in the darkness, nightmarishly silhouetting a handful of menacing forms moving quickly through the room from the busted-open back door. It was like some wild nightmare, but I was pretty sure I was awake, so I reached for my glasses. Just as I got a grip on them, a gun butt slammed into my arm, pinning it to the crate that served as a nightstand. Handcuffs were snapped around my wrists, and in seconds, I was dragged from bed by the chain, roughly hauled into the living room, and tossed onto the mattress next to Clay, who was sitting up in sleepy astonishment. With a plunk, Ditto, also in handcuffs, was deposited beside us, and a few seconds later, Paul was there, too.

By now, someone had turned on the overhead lights, replacing the confused flares of the flashlights lighting the scene, and the four of us—all in our underwear—found ourselves confronted by five large and menacing men in cheap suits, one man in slacks and a sport shirt, and a single uniformed cop. All were brandishing pistols or shotguns and flashing badges.

"Okay," said the bullying, overweight, florid-faced man who seemed to be in charge. "Where's the stuff?"

"What...?" we stammered.

"We know you're dealing," the boss said. "Tell us where it is."

"We're not dealing," Ditto said.

"Have it your way," the boss said, and he turned to his five colleagues. "Find it."

All the plainclothes cops disappeared into the other rooms, leaving the uniformed cop to guard us, and seconds later came the sounds of the place being torn apart. The uniformed cop stood halfway in the hall, staring toward Ditto's bedroom, watching the search in progress more than he was keeping an eye on us. But then, what could we do? Where could we go? We were in our underwear, lined up on the mattress with our backs to the wall, and two of us were handcuffed.

That's when we began to act like the Three Stooges, only there were four of us. As I recall, Ditto was on one end of our line and Paul was on the other. Ditto started it:

"Where's the pot?" he whispered in my ear. I surreptitiously passed the query on to Clay, who passed it on to Paul. Paul whispered the reply to Clay, who whispered in my ear.

"We're sitting on it."

I told Ditto, and we all grew quiet, somber, and very self-conscious sitting there on the mattress with the ounce of pot secreted somewhere beneath it.

A few minutes later, the plainclothes cop who was wearing slacks and a sports shirt came in, and the uniformed cop left to join the search. The plainclothes cop began asking us questions about who we were and so forth. I don't know if it was the good cop/bad cop routine with this guy playing the good cop to the six bad ones, but his behavior toward us was actually decent. After a few minutes of questioning and learning that Ditto and Paul had lived in the house only a week, that Clay and I were friends visiting from out of town, and that all of us were students, he seemed a bit chagrined. We could understand that—apparently these guys were looking for some big-time drug dealers, and they just weren't going to find large quantities of drugs here. We could only hope they wouldn't find the small quantity we were sitting on.

About the time the friendly plainclothes cop finished questioning us, the uniformed cop returned. He'd been allowed to help in the search, and now he was eager to use his own initiative.

"Did anyone look under there?" he asked, pointing to the mattress we were sitting on.

"Yes," said two of us as the other two said, "No."

The Four Stooges.

"Get up," ordered the uniformed cop. "Sit over there." He directed us to the far side of the room, where we sat on the bare wood floor by the wall, with the friendly plainclothesman standing in the doorway right next to us.

I was pretty nervous. The uniform—the lowly uniform—was going to lift the mattress, find the ounce of pot, and be the one to make the bust. I knew my friends felt much the same because none of us were breathing, and we were all staring, mesmerized, at the mattress.

The uniformed cop grabbed the mattress by one of its handles and hoisted the front edge about three feet off the floor. His initiative about to pay off, he bent and peered beneath.

All I could do was gaze with riveted, numb resignation. There, tucked back near the wall and now in full view of those of us on the far side of the room, was the plastic baggie full of pot. It was glittering in the light. No, it was flashing like a neon light. It was shouting, "Look at me! Here I am!" It was about to do a jig to draw more attention to itself when the uniform dropped the mattress, squashing it. He straightened and, without a word, left the room to search elsewhere.

"You boys get back on that mattress, and stay there," the friendly plainclothesman said quickly, giving us a peculiar look.

Amazed and shocked though we were, we moved very quickly back to the mattress.

Apparently, only the sagging curve of the mattress had kept the uniformed cop from seeing the baggie of pot where it was snugged up against the wall. But I know the plainclothesman must have seen it, could not have failed to see it. Even his attitude said he'd seen it. But for some reason, he let it ride

I think the reason was that the cops thought they were busting major dealers, not just casual users, and the friendly plainclothesman knew that even if we were arrested for possession of the ounce, the raid itself was a bust and an embarrassment.

By now, the sounds of the search were diminishing in the background, and the florid-faced boss cop reentered the room with a couple of other plainclothesmen and the uniform. The boss was carrying a shoe box.

"Did anyone look under there?" the boss asked, indicating the mattress.

"I did," the uniform said. The friendly plainclothesman quickly affirmed that, and we kept our asses planted firmly and confidently. We all knew the right answer, now.

"We know you've got five kilos stashed somewhere," said the boss, standing over us with his most menacing stance. "And we're going to find it."

"We don't," Ditto tried to tell him, but the boss wasn't listening. I suppose he'd heard false protestations of innocence too often to recognize the real thing.

"Look at this," the boss said, triumphantly holding out the shoe box, determined to save face.

It was empty.

He must have seen our puzzled expressions, because he amplified: "Dust."

Dust?

He wiped a finger inside the shoe box and held it up so we could see the dust on his finger.

"I know this is marijuana dust. You were using this box to clean your stuff. We're going to take it back to the lab for analysis."

The absurdity was enough to make us laugh, but we were too sobered by the events of the past thirty or forty minutes to even consider a chuckle.

"All right," the boss said to his goons. "Let's go." They retrieved their handcuffs from our wrists and left, with the boss giving one parting shot: "We'll get you sooner or later."

Well, no, they won't catch the big dealers unless they have the right people in the right house. Ditto later learned that the previous tenants probably were drug dealers, but it didn't say much for the Austin P.D. that their surveillance of the house was at least two weeks out of date when they decided to pull their raid. Which netted one empty shoe box coated with a patina of closet dust.

Once they'd gone, we inspected the damage, which was considerable. The back door was half kicked off its hinges, and the searchers had trashed the entire house. Everything was pulled out of closets and drawers and off of shelves and was lying jumbled on the floors.

We sat up a little while longer, amazed at the wonder of it all, trying to figure out why it had happened and astonished that we'd escaped unscathed, then we went back to bed. But the excitement wasn't over quite yet.

At six am, a heavy knocking on the front door roused us. It was a uniformed cop, though not the same one who'd been there earlier. He wanted to know if a certain underage runaway girl was on the premises.

Not in the last two weeks, at least, officer.

But we let him tramp through the house, anyway. It was easier to let him look than it would have been to argue with him.

When he finally left, his expression clearly showed that he was disgusted by the way those dirty hippies lived, with their stuff lying all over the floor and the back door gaping half-open on broken hinges. But he didn't find the girl.

Maybe Ditto or Paul had her stashed under a mattress.

A couple of days latter, Clay and I hitchhiked back to Houston, and after that, I never saw him again—in person, that is.

The Road Back

IT'S FUNNY HOW YOU CAN see things so many times that you don't see them anymore. Take the stretch of I-10 between Houston and San Antonio. I first traveled it in the late 1960s after I moved to Houston to go to college. My best friend and roommate, Ditto, was from San Antonio, and every so often, we'd go there to visit his family or friends. I didn't know the road well, then, and certainly there wasn't much to see. From the highway, most of the towns along the way exhibited little more than a sign, an exit ramp, and maybe a gas station or two.

Because of the relative austerity of the highway, I tended to exaggerate certain features beyond their actual importance. Take the old motor court, for example. It was a row of half a dozen rectangular, two-room structures made of cement blocks, probably built between the world wars. Lined up along the service road, it was old and abandoned when I first saw it, and its emptiness and dilapidation made it mysterious. I couldn't imagine anything taking place there but shady dealings in the past or hauntings in the present. Indeed, it had a reputation as an only recently defunct bordello.

A person's first few years away from home are incredibly formative. Ditto and I shared adventures and experiences that have remained alive in my memory and helped shape my understandings of the world. But even in the midst of growth comes waning, and Ditto and I drifted apart. I moved in with different roommates, and he left for Austin. We saw each other infrequently during the next couple of years, then lost touch entirely.

I still drove that stretch of road, though. During much of the 1980s, I had monthly business in the Alamo City, and I drove that part of I-10 a couple of hundred times. I watched the small towns grow and begin to peer through the forest and farmlands until they showed faces to the highway. And I watched the old, abandoned motor court take on a new life as a depot for decorative Hill Country stone bound for Houston. But its renaissance was short-lived, and as the 1980s ended, the little line of lonely rooms again was deserted.

By then, though, I no longer really saw it. I'd driven this highway so often that the sights became routine, and I came to mark my passage only by the small but growing towns along the way: Columbus, Luling, and Seguin. Maybe that was because development gave them a larger stance on the countryside, eclipsing the smaller, more intimate features. Or maybe it was because of the way travel was changing. Air conditioning and stereo sound systems have conspired not simply to make the occupants of vehicles faceless to one another but to make the countryside equally unknown. I probably spent my last hundred trips so glazed with familiarity that only a new shopping center or commercial development sprouting on farmland beside the highway could shock me into awareness of the terrain through which I sped.

Since 1990, I've driven I-10 west of Columbus only a few dozen times or so. I don't remember much about those trips—I'd seen it all before. Too often. But in the late '90s, that changed. Once again I left Houston and drove to San Antonio, but this time, the road looked different. No, not different, exactly. I was seeing past the old familiarity to a time when this highway was, for me, an entirely new experience. And there, visible beneath the recent development, were many of the older features I remembered so well, waiting only for recognition.

In particular, I noticed the old motor court. There it was, looking very much the same as when I first saw it thirty years before, abandoned and mysterious—and now, I realized, historic. Somebody ought to do an archaeological dig there. Surely beneath the loam lies a wealth of information about the culture of American travel before four-lanes made intercity trips so quick and so anonymous.

I was in a mood to dig up the past. After some detective work, I'd found Ditto. He was back in San Antonio, and I was on my to reunite with him after a separation of twenty-five years. I wondered what I would find. Would he be like the old motor court, a little more overgrown but still in character, or would he be like a patch of forest that had been cleared for development—recast and unrecognizable?

At last I pulled into Ditto's driveway. I got out of the car and peered toward the screened-in back porch. Someone stood within and stepped out. It was my friend. As we greeted and looked each other over, it seemed to me he'd not only grown a weed or two, but he bore traces of a few cleared forests, as well. Nothing is simple, especially after it has some history. But I recognized the terrain, and even if I hadn't seen it in a long time, it was still familiar. Right then, though, I wasn't thinking of any of that. I was just feeling the past, present, and future meld in my heart as we embraced and said hi.

Down the Bayou

OUTSIDE MY FRONT DOOR, THE future is calling. From the porch, I see the modern cars, satellite dishes, and electrical wires that will take my southeast Houston neighborhood into the twenty-first century. A mile across the nearby Gulf Freeway is Hobby Airport, from which jets whisk passengers to points near and far.

But outside my back door, the world is a different place. My yard is on the banks of Sims Bayou, and living here has shown me that the founders of modern Texas are but a moment gone, just as we are but a heartbeat from the future.

My stretch of Sims between the Gulf Freeway and the Houston Ship Channel isn't cemented or manicured. As I sit here, looking up and downstream, I see banks lush with riparian forest.

This is how Sims—like all Houston bayous—must have looked when the Mexican government granted this land in 1824 to John R. Harris as part of Stephen Austin's colony. Harris, for whom Harris County is named, founded the first town along Buffalo Bayou, between the confluences of Braes Bayou upstream and Sims downstream. At Harrisburg, he set up a trading post and built a steam sawmill, the first industry along the waterway that would become the Houston Ship Channel.

Harris died of yellow fever soon after founding Harrisburg, but his town survived, even though it was burned to the ground as Santa Anna's army pursued Sam Houston's army of irregulars toward San Jacinto and defeat. The years following Texas independence saw Harrisburg grow as a center of commerce. From the wharves on Buffalo Bayou, cotton and cattle were shipped to Galveston on shallow-draft side-wheel steamers. In 1852, Harrisburg became home to the Buffalo Bayou, Brazos, and Colorado Railroad—the first operating railroad in Texas. The line is still there, though the tracks are new, running down Griggs Road as they head off through south Houston to end at Stafford, then called Stafford's Point.

Eventually, though, the future caught up with Harrisburg, and that future had a name: Houston. In the years after 1836, when the Allen brothers founded the larger city just upstream on Buffalo Bayou, Harrisburg began its slide into obscurity.

Today, only a sharp eye can discern that this was once more than just another old neighborhood. Sandwiched between railroad tracks and a shipyard, there is a small but remarkable cemetery where monuments with names like Harris, Milby, and Allen honor early settlers. It's old as cemeteries go in Houston—the oldest, in fact—but a look at the dates shows that, in truth, our Texas heritage isn't really far in the past. And that past is alive on this side of town.

Ten minutes east by car lies a nondescript bridge that barely clears the dark waters of Vince Bayou. A weathered stone historical marker lurking in the weeds explains that a former bridge on this site played a pivotal role in Texas independence. Santa Anna's army marched across the old bridge on the last leg of its journey to San Jacinto. After the soldiers passed, a handful of Sam Houston's men circled back and burned the bridge, cutting off the Mexican army's only escape route.

It was a crucial move. A five-minute drive farther east leads to a small park on the banks of the Ship Channel, tucked into a nook between a petrochemical plant and a paper manufacturing company. The park's stone marker memorializes the capture of Santa Anna, who was found nearby the day after the battle of San Jacinto. He couldn't swim, and with the bridge over Vince Bayou burned, there was nowhere for him to go except into the arms of his enemies.

My stretch of Sims Bayou may look primordial, but the Ship Channel couldn't be more different now than it was on that day in 1836 when Santa Anna desperately sought escape. Could he have imagined the huge ships churning the water he could not cross? Could he have foreseen the petrochemical plants rearing twisted pipes into the sky or the city of Houston with its towers of steel and glass shining on the horizon beyond the small town he had just burned? Surely not, but his actions help set the stage for all that now is here.

As I sit on my own bank of quiet Sims Bayou, staring into the murky green water, I wonder if we are not all a little like Santa Anna, trapped by bridges burned, faced with uncrossable obstacles, and performing actions that will touch an unimaginable future in ways we can never comprehend.

Most likely so. But that doesn't matter much right now, because suddenly I hear the future calling me again. This time it's my teenage daughters. They want to go to the mall.

Guadalupe Thoughts

On the occasion of getting sick while camping in the Guadalupe Mountains, May 13, 2003

I WROTE LONG AGO THAT life was limitation. Certainly it is expansion as well, but the expansion is away from the material world. Within the material world, life is a constant process of limitation that science terms entropy. Nowhere is that more evident than in growing older and experiencing the onset of creeping decrepitude.

I'm out here in the Guadalupe Mountains with my friend Ditto. We'd planned to do a couple of overnight hikes through the mountains, but he needed to go home earlier than planned, so we drove separately. We also changed our itinerary to take in three one-day hikes: the first up McKittrick Canyon, the second into the lower reaches of the mountains, and the third up Guadalupe Peak, the highest point in Texas.

Let me say that I have done some hiking and backpacking in my life, but not much in the last few years. And right now, I'm fifty-two. But I'm in relatively good shape—I normally exercise four hours a week, and in anticipation of these hikes, I've been walking four days a week for the last seven weeks. The past couple of weeks, I've been doing three miles a stint at a pretty good clip—one hour. The last three stints, I carried a thirty-pound pack. Everything seemed okay, and I felt prepared.

McKittrick Canyon, the location of our first hike, is a lovely canyon that meanders into the northeastern Guadalupes. There is a streambed that is alive with water for parts of its stretch; a couple of miles into the canyon, there is a fine old stone lodge; and a little further along, a small but picturesque grotto is carved into the face of a small cliff. The grotto is as far as most day hikers go—about three miles into the canyon, but Ditto and I wanted to go a little farther. We thought we might go all the way to the upper point of the canyon, but we hadn't reached that at about four and a half miles into the canyon. With four and a half miles to return, we decided it was time to go back.

The trip back went well enough until the last couple of miles, when my left knee and hip started giving me a wrenching pain with every step. I might have expected my right—and weaker—leg to give out since I'd suffered from a degenerative bone disease in that hip as a child. But it was my left knee that was the culprit—maybe because I was favoring my right leg. By the time we got back to the camp and sat around for a couple of hours, my left leg had stiffened so much that it was excruciatingly painful to walk down even the slightest slope. It was still painful the next morning, so I encouraged Ditto to go ahead and do the second hike while I attempted to recuperate enough to hike to Guadalupe Peak the following day. I thought I'd go down to the ranger station and buy a staff to take along just in case.

So here I am, sitting out the hike into the lower reaches of the mountains, hoping my leg heals enough to hike up to Guadalupe Peak tomorrow. Actually, it's not the up that bothers my leg but the down. But damn—I want to go up there.

However, there is another problem. This morning after Ditto left, I went down to the outhouse to take a crap, and the passing was prolonged and accompanied by sharp abdominal pains and nausea. Since then, the nausea has vanished, but for the last couple of hours, the abdominal pains have become cramps that have been getting sharper and more frequent, settling in my lower left abdomen. It is a somewhat steady ache punctuated by sharper twinges that grow more knifelike as time progresses. Enough to make me flinch and groan. Moving doesn't seem to make them increase, but sitting still doesn't seem to make them abate, either.

Last week, I had an intestinal virus that started in my stomach and sent waves of cramps and gas through my intestines. Over the course of a couple of days, it worked its way down to my bowels and, I thought, out of my system entirely as I had not experienced any intestinal discomfort for several days after.

But since beginning our camping trip, Ditto and I have been eating a lot of trail food—a hard and harsh diet my system is not used to. The first night in the mountains, I had excessive and very smelly gas, and I passed more gas on the hike yesterday. And some more this morning following the sharp intestinal pains. Is this a reoccurrence of the intestinal virus?

So, even if my knee wasn't messed up, I couldn't have hiked today, anyway. The cramping has grown so intense that I could barely make it the half mile down to the ranger station to buy the staff. But I'd rather have a good knee and be on the trail with Ditto and most of the other people in camp. I'm left here virtually alone, and I feel like an invalid—a feeling I absolutely detest and a condition I don't do well with. It's not the being alone—I tolerate that pretty well. The bad things are the pain and the understanding that I have come all this way for a much-needed and anticipated vacation with my friend, and I'm going to have to cut it short. And I hate prolonged illness because it helps destroy my over-all health and vitality—conditions in short supply for folks who are growing older.

And that's the crux of the matter—growing older and having to give up things and activities and be forced to sit things out and watch from the sidelines. Being forced to give up more and more in an ever-increasing progression of loss. Lost flexibility, libido, strength, stamina, mental clarity. Memory.

If I sound like I'm whining, make no mistake—I know that each and every person who lives long enough must face the same decline, the same losses. For some, such as those who experience problems like injury or obesity in early or mid life, those losses are built into the psyche and are usual and normal and come as no shock. Those who remain active, however, must face a more precipitous decline—an avalanche, if you will, where one stone loosened eventually causes a cascade to come crashing down in a heap of rubble.

I'm not ready for the rubble heap, though is anyone? I admit I'm tired of many aspects of life, and most of what passes for culture and entertainment utterly bores me. Maybe that's why I like to go driving alone around the countryside—it's new territory and I don't have to deal with the people who inhabit it. But even the road wears thin and must, as with all things, eventually come to an end.

I recently called my dad on the phone to wish him happy birthday, though he's seventy-five, and at that age, birthdays are perhaps ugly reminders of how little time remains and how much more there is to give up before the final divesting of the body itself. I asked him about growing old, and he said that during the last few years, he has seen a definite physical change in himself. "I look in the mirror," he said, "and I've got old-man arms and old-man legs, and my flesh sags." Though he tries to take a Buddhist attitude of detachment, I thought I detected a wistful tone in his voice.

I'm more than twenty years younger, yet even without a mirror, I feel the changes creeping here, insinuating there. Stamina, sexuality, strength, all fading. Liver spots appearing like subtle hints of greater ugliness to come. And worst of all is a growing intellectual and emotional ennui, an increasing lack of giving a shit.

Both my parents say they don't mind aging—and I'm with them to a certain extent. I like having the wisdom of experience, but why must wisdom be purchased at the price of lost ability and drive to apply that wisdom to the world and one's own life? It's just one more of those eternal questions that do not seem to have answers. But surely the answer is not more life—or even eternal life—because I suspect there's too much life to live it all, even if one were to live an eternity.

We are who we are, we do what we do, and everything we are and do seems equally meaningless and meaningful. I suppose aging is really no different. Perhaps it is the opportunity—necessity!—to divest oneself of some of the meaningless dross. Maybe that's why we become wiser as we grow older—we've simply let go of some of the stupider characteristics within us. I hope so since I have plenty of stupid to spare. But I know that eventually I also must confront the loss of things that have been meaningful—or at least that seem to have some purpose no matter how transient. And I must accept those losses without regret or anger or frustration or longing, or they will simply drag me into bitterness as I vegetate toward whatever it is that death promises.

Perhaps I can begin with the pains in my leg and abdomen. Surely I can lose those and never look back with regret at their passing because here I am, looking with regret at the backside of Guadalupe Peak, knowing that attaining its summit on this journey is unlikely. I had hoped to return with a precious memory of that attainment, though I suppose, in the end, I will have to give up that non-memory along with everything else.

So, with my time growing shorter, I can only console myself that there is too much life for one life, and that for each of us there will be summits unattained. I can only attempt to continue divesting myself of the dross so that I can proceed, for as long as is given me, with pursuing the meaningful.

The 61st Minute

THE MAN FACING ME ACROSS the wide, grassy clearing held a paper grocery sack. He seemed innocent enough, but I knew that the sparse woods from which he emerged very likely held at least one of his friends. Probably with a .30-30 Winchester aimed right at me.

It was late spring in the late 1970s, and my friends— Charles and Michael—and I had been camping in Big Bend National Park for about a week. It had been a good trip during which, among other things, we'd driven the rugged River Road along the Rio Grande and camped in the badlands on the west side of the park where we'd seen a huge meteor light up the sky and heard it hit many miles out on the plains to the west. But now that the trip was about to wind up, we couldn't let go of the fact that we were right on the border with Mexico. We wanted to buy some weed to take home with us.

These days, buying marijuana in Mexico and transporting it across Texas is practically impossible. Roadblock inspection stations with drug sniffing dogs are on almost every road in the region as well as at the larger border crossings over the Rio Grande. And most of the smaller crossings over the river have been closed since the terrorist attacks of 9/11. These days, you can't visit any of the small villages across the river from the park. In those days, though, it was still possible to do a little smuggling, although the transportation would be problematic for hippie types such as us, who were favorite targets of law enforcement in this land west of the Pecos, where Judge Roy Bean once held sway.

Michael, whose Hispanic ancestry reached back to the Mexican land-grant days of Texas, spoke some Spanish, so he went across the river to the village of Santa Elena, now called Benito Juárez, to see if pot was available. Charles and I waited in the campground near the mouth of Santa Elena Canyon. Not long afterward, Michael came back with the news that he'd met somebody who said they had some weed to sell.

The guy invited us over to visit before the transaction. I think he and his compadres wanted to check us out before they did the deal. So the three of us went across the river in a small rowboat piloted by our contact. He moored the boat on the Mexico bank, and the four of us walked up the incline from the river to a dirt road baking beneath the midday sun. There, a battered red Chevy pickup waited. Our contact and Michael got into the cab, and Charles and I climbed into the bed, and we were off.

The roads in town were all dirt, rough, and heavily potholed, so it was a heck of a bumpy ride. Our contact drove faster than was comfortable, and Charles and I bounced and jounced around in the bed, hoping the ride wouldn't last too long. It didn't. Santa Elena was a pretty small town once you got past the handful of cantinas and taquerias that faced the river and catered to the few tourists brave enough to cross over. We reached the other side of town in under ten minutes, and our contact drove a little farther until there was just a scattering of dwellings dwindling into the desert. This was the poor side of town in a poor town. As the pickup stopped in front of an adobe house that must have been the last before the desert completely took over, the cloud of dust that had been chasing it through town engulfed us.

We got out, and our contact invited us inside. I don't know about Michael and Charles, but I was nervous. I was in a foreign land, and the fact that the United States was only about three miles away didn't make our surroundings any less dangerous. Except for the presence of motor vehicles, nothing much had changed around here for centuries, and we could have been in the middle of a real-life set for *The Wild Bunch*.

The house, though large by the standards of its neighbors, was unprepossessing. Its plain, mud-smoothed adobe walls were pierced by several rectangular windows. All were without panes of glass, but each had a pair of rude wooden shutters, all of which stood open. The roof was a sheath of river cane packed with dried mud. I suppose there was an outhouse in back of the house that I didn't see.

Inside, the temperature was considerably cooler than outside thanks to the open windows, which allowed a nice breeze to circulate. The floor was contiguous with the ground—hard-packed dirt—and the sparse furniture that sat on it was wooden, simple, rude, and mostly homemade. The house had four or five rooms, all with open doorways with no doors, and there was no electricity or running water. The only light was that which came in through the windows and doors.

There were two other guys in the front room, which seemed to serve as a kitchen. They'd been sitting at the simple plank table, drinking beer, but they got up when we came in. Three of us, three of them, all of us in our late twenties or early thirties. But the three of us were callow American city dwellers, and the three Mexican guys were tougher looking. One of them, in particular, was a little older than the others and was more hard-bitten. A .30-30 Winchester dangled casually from his hand. But all three seemed friendly enough, and the one with the rifle soon propped the weapon against a wall.

None of them spoke English, but through Michael, they offered us warm beers, and then we got down to business. We dickered about price and quantity, eventually settling on purchasing a kilo for a price that, if I remember correctly, was $120—reasonable enough that, among the three of us, we could come up with the cash. We arranged a time and a place to meet that we were familiar with—a large clearing in the mesquite forest on the American side of the river, near the Santa Elena campground and close to the river. With the business concluded and small talk impossible, we all shook hands and smiled, and our lead contact drove us back to the river crossing and rowed us to the American side.

We returned to our campsite to wait out the remainder of the day until the appointed hour, which was seven pm. At the appropriate time, the three of us got into Michael's pickup and drove to the clearing. Michael parked on the clearing's edge, and a few minutes later, we saw one of the Mexican guys emerge from the sparse trees on the other side of the clearing, maybe a hundred and fifty feet away. He was the hard-bitten one. The one who'd had the rifle. Only now he wasn't holding the gun but had a brown paper grocery sack, its rolled top gripped in one hand.

The guy glanced around the clearing then stared at us.

"Go on, Michael," I said. He had our money in his pocket, and he was the one who spoke Spanish.

But Michael didn't move.

"I don't want to," he said, and I realized that he was too nervous to go out into the clearing to finalize the deal.

I knew one of us had to act or the whole thing would go sour. The guy across the clearing didn't have the rifle, but very likely his two friends were in the woods somewhere behind him, and one of them surely had the gun.

"Give me the money," I said, and Michael handed it over.

I got out of the truck and walked around it so the guy across the clearing—and his friends—could see I wasn't obviously armed. Then I started walking toward the middle of the clearing, and the other guy did likewise. We met in the center, and he set the sack on the ground. I squatted and unrolled the top to look inside. A large brick of weed was in there, bound up in plastic wrap.

He said something in Spanish. I didn't really understand, but I caught the word *todo*—all—and understood him to be telling me that it was all there. It looked and felt like a kilo to me, or close enough.

I stood up and handed him the money. He counted it then looked at me, and his hard-bitten face broke in a smile that seemed genuine. Maybe he appreciated my courage. I smiled back, we shook hands, and I said, "Gracias."

With that, he turned on his heel and headed back the way he'd come. I picked up the sack and went back to Michael's pick-up, half expecting to feel a bullet that I'd never hear, but nothing happened. After all, why would these guys do something like that, which would surely ruin their setup? By the time I got into the truck, the guy had disappeared into the woods. Michael drove us back to the campground, and we returned happy campers.

The drive to San Antonio and, then, for Charles and me, to Houston, was uneventful, though we were paranoid the whole way. The smuggling incident faded as life went on, but it came back a few months later when I was visiting some friends one Sunday evening. [This was a Sylvie's Salon meeting with Steve and Lazaro.] We were watching *60 Minutes* on TV, and one of the segments—hosted by Mike Wallace—concerned drug smuggling on the Texas–Mexico border.

The segment was filmed at the Santa Elena crossing, and Wallace had gotten three local men to show him how people might do the smuggling. The three guys showed him how they'd load the pot into their rowboat and ferry it to the American side. The three guys were, of course, the same three that Charles, Mike, and I had actually bought pot from just a few months earlier, and when one of them leaned out of the boat to hand Wallace a prop grocery sack of "marijuana," I easily recognized the hard-bitten one. His face was cracked in mirth, but instead of the appreciative smile he'd given me when we'd exchanged goods and cash, this time he had a huge, shit-eating grin on his face. It was, after all, a great joke to be faking for the camera what he often did for real, and he was probably being paid as much or more for faking it as he'd make from an actual sale.

I couldn't help but laugh, but a couple of years later, when I returned to Santa Elena with other friends, I saw that it was no longer a laughing matter. A contingent of Federales who'd set up shop in a building overlooking the crossing gave us harsh glares as we trudged up from the river to go to one of the cantinas for a couple of shots of tequila and a beer. Of the three smugglers, there was no sign. I'm sure they were long gone to other occupations or for more fertile ground before the Federales arrived.

Vaya con Dios, amigos.

The End at Danbury High

THE DOORS PLAYED SOME FAMOUS concerts—think of the live recordings at the Whiskey A-Go-Go or the time Jim Morrison was arrested in Miami for allegedly exposing himself. And then there was the gig at Danbury High.

Okay, that one might not have gone down in the annals of rock history, but the events of that evening showed just how outrageous The Doors could be for their time.

I went to Danbury High School in Danbury, Connecticut. It was the late 1960s, and pop and rock music was in the midst of one of its greatest flowerings. The Beatles ruled the day, while other individuals and bands were creating seminal sounds that would create whole genres of pop and rock music: Bob Dylan originated folk rock, the Byrds were developing country rock, and Blue Cheer first split the heaven and earth alike with what would become heavy metal. Surf music and psychedelia were rampant on the West Coast, the Velvet Underground was ravaging New York with early punk, and a score of British bands like The Yardbirds were transforming rock through the motifs of American blues, spawning, in the process, the early super groups Cream and Led Zeppelin.

In a musical universe of such intense originality, it was difficult to stand out. But some bands managed it, and The Doors was one. Their eponymously named first album was immediately influential. Its unique, spooky sound, dark tone, and daring lyrics sung with heavy sensuality belied the bubble gum mentality of much of pop music and spoke in a way that went psychologically and psychically deeper than the counter-culture politics of Jefferson Airplane or the cultural criticisms that were the messages of so many other bands. It tapped directly into the Id. It said that sex was directly linked to raw creativity, to mysticism, to power, and to madness. And there, telling us all about it, was Jim Morrison—the perfect exemplar.

Living in Danbury, we often despaired of seeing our favorite groups live. Most bands were real to us only as sounds from speakers and pictures on album jackets, and to actually hear and see them live, we usually had to go either to New Haven or Hartford or down to New York City—not simple matters for teens without money or cars. So, we made do with local and regional bands and rare manna from rock heaven, such as the concert performed by Vanilla Fudge in a local dinner theatre. That concert took place in the midst of a blizzard, so only ticket holders within walking distance actually made it to the theatre. But the Fudge put on a good show even though there were only about thirty of us in the audience.

But much as we loved Vanilla Fudge, we revered The Doors, and so, when the news broke in mid-1967 that they were coming to town on their tour to promote their second album, *Strange Days*, we couldn't believe it. But it was true, and they were going to play, of all places, in our high school auditorium. I guess it made sense. The school was only a few years old, and it had a big auditorium with a wonderful, shiny, hardwood stage just begging for something to happen on it besides school assemblies.

We all bought tickets and, on the appointed night, dressed in our hippie best and went to school. I don't remember if there was an opening act. If there was, it was local. All I remember was the band I'd come to hear. Morrison was dressed in skin-tight black leather pants, a white, blousy shirt with ruffles down the front, and a sleek black leather jacket. We cheered, and the band played, starting off with several songs from their first album.

About twenty minutes into the concert, Morrison arched his back and gave a sensual shrug that slid him out of his jacket. As he tossed the jacket off to the side, electricity charged the air. He already had us in his power, and as the music went on, his every movement and vocal nuance produced a pronounced effect. The band was at the height of their skill and creative energies, and they didn't stint on the length of some of the longer songs, like "Light My Fire." There was even a primitive light show whose main feature was strobe lights.

Then they launched into new material from *Strange Days*, including an extended version of "When the Music's Over." At last, the band had played almost everything from both albums. Almost. Morrison, shirt now damp and hanging open and loose, torso glistening with sweat, approached the mike stand, leaned on it, and asked, "Have you had enough?"

The multitude of voices that answered were equally split between "No!" and "More!" and "The End!"

Morrison didn't even look at the rest of the band. They all knew. They'd been saving it for...well, the end. After all, that particular song—apocalyptic and final—really couldn't be played any other time.

Robby Krieger's slow, pensive opening guitar chord crept over the audience, Ray Manzarek's organ built like a rising wind beneath, and John Densmore's drums propelled the music forward as The Doors launched into a full-blown version of "The End." Mesmerized by the music and Morrison's commanding presence, we sat hushed and awed as the music and vocals washed over, around, and through us. Somewhere during the first half of the song, Morrison tore off his shirt. Then the song built to the climax where its protagonist enacts his terrible deeds, and the strobe lights went on, making the stage a flickering nightmare and Morrison's wild gyrations and gestures completely unworldly.

With the music swelling to its crescendo of swirling rage and madness, Morrison suddenly fell to his knees, gripping the microphone stand in his hands like an ax. His movements made as mechanical as they were maniacal by the flashing strobes, he began axing the microphone stand into the floor, bashing and battering, filled with his demons as much as he was exorcising them. People in the audience gasped and cried out and screamed, our voices becoming a chorus at one with the ferociously charged atmosphere.

Then, as the music began to shrink from its billowing madness, Morrison stopped bashing. He slumped forward across the bent mic stand, exhausted and drained. At last, he got to his feet. And as the final eerie refrain drained from the air, he lifted the microphone and intoned the song's verbal coda: "This is the end."

And it was. The stage lights went out, but there was no clamor for more. The Doors had given us all they had, and it was more than enough.

The Danbury daily newspaper carried an item the next day about how the deranged band had caused major damage to the high school stage, and the city eventually sued The Doors to make them pay to repair the hole Morrison had bashed in it. But we didn't care much about the stage. We simply cared that someone had understood that dark place we all have within us, that someone had courage enough to uncover it so that it would not remain a hidden, festering wound.

And I think that's why, even forty years later, The Doors remain vital. They spoke truth as few dare speak it, and from the darkness they shone a glimmer of hope.

The Plaquemine Ferry

YOU'D NEVER GUESS BY LOOKING, but this greasy, gravelly road of packed brown mud leading down the Mississippi River's eastern bank is a state highway. In the water, cabled to anchors embedded high up on the shore, sits a small, creaking, rusty barge, the only hopeful sign that something continues beyond the water's edge. But it *is* a state highway—Louisiana 75—and the metal ramp hinged up on the barge's foredeck proclaims that further travel on this route will have to wait for the Plaquemine Ferry.

It is just before eight am on a drab, overcast weekday morning in early spring, and I'm first in line. Or last, since I drive up just as the ferry's loading gate closes, and I watch a little wistfully as the boat churns across the Mississippi toward its landing a quarter of a mile or so upstream on the western bank. But being here by myself doesn't bother me a bit. That's why I'm here—to be alone. Ostensibly, I'm attending a conference in Baton Rouge, and one of the days, at least, my presence is required since I'm giving a presentation. But I'm not particularly equipped for social interaction on a large scale. It's not that I can't take crowds, but more that constant superficial social intercourse with strangers wears me down. I simply cannot seem to connect easily with others. And the social lubricants that make the wheels of such interactions roll smoothly—alcohol, sports talk, partying, and so forth—are not strongly present in my makeup.

So I'm out here alone. Perhaps I'm fleeing, perhaps merely seeking my own element, which certainly isn't back at the conference. If I can "network" at all, it is in some far more tenuous way and probably not directly related to professional concerns.

Besides, I've been to conferences, but I haven't experienced the Mississippi this close. Sure, I've crossed it many times and seen its waters, but always from some high bridge —through girders and in sporadic glimpses to keep from crashing into other speeding cars. I want a more intimate relationship with this greatest waterway of the continent— perhaps an intimacy, however brief, that will resonate more deeply than any I could ever find in a conference crowd.

I'm alone at the ferry landing for nearly thirty minutes, and in that time, I go down to the water's edge. There I squat and scoop a handful of the river then watch it trickle through my fingers and spill back into itself. I stand and look out across its broad sweep. The river is nearly a mile wide here, and at this early hour in early spring, a thick mist blankets its surface and clings to the trees that, on the far bank, are undifferentiated, dull-green masses. Up- and downstream, the water and haze soon merge into blank distance lit with watery gray light. The air is very quiet, the only sound the lap of small waves breaking on the greasy gravel.

The mist enhances the timelessness of this river they call the Big Muddy. The murky brown water definitely lives up to the name, being the color of America's topsoil as it washes south to make Louisiana grander if no less watery. And so does the river's size. As I drove along LA 75 to the ferry landing, I saw the levees that have been built to contain the water. The levees are reassuring and scary at the same time: reassuring because they help keep the river in check and scary because they're about twenty feet high. On one side, there's flat, rich delta farmland, soil the same color as the Mississippi, soil the river has been depositing for millennia from the continent's heartland. On the other side are billions of gallons of flowing water that occasionally and implacably remembers when there were no levees and it had free rein over this land. When those occasions arise, the river ignores the levees entirely and comes over anyway—as if a manmade pile of dirt could contain the continent's mightiest river when it doesn't want to be contained. I guess if the water comes over the levee, those flat fields where I drove could be twenty feet under.

That's the way it seems to be with humankind. All that we do to control nature is both reassuring and scary. It is reassuring because it is we who do it, and we take comfort in that fact and in our enterprise and efficacy when our efforts are successful. And it is scary because, on the one hand, anything we do seems inadequate in the face of nature, and on the other hand, our best intentions as a race often are lost amid our ignorance and worst inclinations and all too often go awry despite our greatest ambitions.

Rivers, especially big rivers like this, are an impediment to travel. They have a need to go in their own direction in their own time, and both often are at odds with the ways people want to go. The only passages across are bridges or ferries, and you might have to travel miles upstream or down to find one. Upstream from the Plaquemine Ferry, back in Baton Rouge, there is the I-10 bridge and maybe a smaller bridge. Downstream, about twenty miles, there's another bridge, and in between is another ferry, smaller and, so I hear from a local, more sporadically run than this one. Ferries are chancier and definitely take longer than bridges. You pay for your close-up view of the water in coin of time. I guess that's part of the price of slowing down. Everybody wants to speed up. I just want to slow down. And that, as much as getting close to the Mississippi, is why I'm here at this tiny ferry landing, watching the river drain the continent and waiting for the boat to return.

Driftwood logs bump and jostle along the shoreline just downstream from the landing. They are trees, uprooted and denuded of leaves and all but the heaviest stubs of branches and roots. A heavy metal creaking comes from the barge as it rocks in the current. What do they do with the ferry and the barge when the river floods? The barge is a tethered floater. With enough line they could just pay it out on the river's swollen bosom. But what if the power of the current grows too strong or if the water rises high enough to pour over the levee? The barge could find itself in a farm field. But no, not here. Here the levee is topped with trees that would let the water spill through but not carry the barge over. Barge jail.

Three small brown ducks emerge from the bank just downstream from the barge and swim out about forty feet to take off in low flight, skimming the water. They don't care about floods. They'd just rest in treetops until the water settled. Watching the birds fly out and disappear into the mists over the water gives lie to the notion that nature is mankind's preserve. The ducks survive in spite of us, not because we've done anything to help them.

Downstream, a long cargo barge pushes out of the void as if manifested—coalesced—from the water and mist and gray light. It comes upstream, barely seeming to make headway against the current. Walking up the Mississippi. Samuel Clemens has been dead for nearly a century, but this is still his river in some ways. He had Huck Finn talk about driftwood logs along the shores and about barges, but I don't think he could have envisioned diesel tugs pushing hundred-yard barge loads upstream where his character rode the currents downstream on a ten-foot log raft.

Three sparrows flutter in from over the water and land on the barge's mooring cables. Three sparrows to replace the three ducks. The spirits of the three ducks returned? What lies over there on the far shore across the misty river? I am reminded of that elder statesman of ferrymen—Charon—and understand that I am heading to the bank of the setting sun. But I'm no longer alone on my journey, for by now, several cars and trucks are parked behind me, their number growing slowly but steadily. Most of us are out, standing around or leaning on our vehicles, waiting for the ferry. It is staying an awfully long time over there on the western bank.

Waiting for a more complete load. Waiting to return souls to the morning shore in this ceaseless round we call life. It won't have to wait so long on this side. The way the cars and pickups are lining up, it seems we can't wait to get to the west.

About ten cars back, a sixty-something man and a boy of about fourteen emerge from an old white pickup whose bed is built in with a huge plywood box painted white, turning it into a homemade delivery truck. He and the boy climb the bank next to their truck, above the ferry landing, and I see, even from two hundred feet that he notices me—singles me out of all this gathering at the shore. He knows that I don't belong here and wonders who I am. I'm not sure, myself. I just know I'm not a choice but a state of being. And I understand suddenly and indisputably that he will come to me—must come to me—to find out what I'm about. And as I watch the misty river and wait for the ferry, he does, circumspectly but purposefully, like you might approach a skittish dog so it won't run before you can pet it.

Then he is here beside me, boy at his heels, to find out about this stranger. His questions are as discreet as his approach, but I won't give him the easy answers that mean nothing and can't give him the hard answers I don't really have. All I might truthfully say is that I am out of sync, but I don't. Instead, I tell him I'm attending a convention in Baton Rouge, but today I am out to see southern Louisiana. My reticence doesn't seem to bother him—maybe that's because he knows that answers are for the young and too often empty, or maybe it's because he realizes that the quiet acknowledgement we feel between us is all the answer there ever can be.

I ask him about the river, and he tells me the water is low. Eight feet. Weather's been dry. He's the patriarch of a crawfishing clan in Bayou Pigeon, and he's returning home after delivering a shipment to Baton Rouge. He sells crawfish all over Louisiana and as far west as Houston, and the presence of his grandson attests that the business might go on after he's made his final delivery. If the swamps survive. He's not

221

sure they will. Water levels have been inconsistent the last couple of years, and pollutants and pesticides coming down the river with the topsoil are not amenable to aquatic life. And there are more people.

He asks where I'm going, and I show him on the map. He says I'm welcome to visit him in Bayou Pigeon. He's serious about the invitation in a way that most people aren't these days—he remembers a time when it was only right to take in strangers and make them welcome. I say I might, and I don't say that I don't have time now or that I might never pass this way again. But he's old enough to know that if the southern Louisiana swamp proves ephemeral, how could human comings and goings be different?

The ferry arrives at last and debarks its load. The man from Bayou Pigeon and his grandson return to their truck. The ferry is certainly no big boat but designed for local traffic and can hold maybe twenty-five vehicles. The toll is a dollar for cars, two-bits for foot traffic—and there are half a dozen people afoot. Will the ferryman be an old bearded Greek in white robes? Should I put the Sacagawea dollar I'm carrying on my eyelid when I meet him?

But this is the New World. The ferryman isn't Greek or a man. She's a stocky, middle-aged black woman dressed in overalls. Her demeanor is gruff. She's seen too many passengers on this recapitulatory though not redundant boat, and her look says she can tell I'm an ignorant stranger. I think I'd better not mess with her, so I cross her palm with George Washington instead of Sacagawea and take my place on the ferry.

After I park, I get out and go to the side facing the east, back the way I've come, as if to get some sort of perspective. I'll be driving west soon enough. I stare up stream and down. The mists are dissipating under the brightening sun, and the water is beginning to look like a river instead of an endless current shrouded in timelessness.

The man from Bayou Pigeon and his grandson join me, and we lean over the rail and watch reflectively as the Mississippi's brown roil slides past. The ferry describes a wide arc upstream to buck the current as it chugs toward the opposite shore. We don't talk much during the short ride, but that is no matter. In our few moments together, we have become, if not friends, then less than strangers, less than uncomfortable with one another. Perhaps he can tell that, while I don't belong here, I don't belong there, either, and that lends me a certain alliance with those who are here, like him and his grandson, who also belong elsewhere. Between us has grown a small but definite sympathy of questions unanswered and, thus, mysteries that remain to give life meaning. If we meet again, we will have old times to talk about and unknown understandings to reach.

In interesting contrast to the stop-gap arrangement of the landing barge on the eastern shore, the landing on the west is a permanent, paved, and bulwarked installation. Though it may well become inundated at high water, a vagary of the bank—of angle and curve—protects it from the ravages of the current in flood. The man from Bayou Pigeon and I say goodbye. Even the kid, always silent though attentive, acknowledges our parting with a friendly nod.

Leaving the ferry behind, I drive two-lane blacktops that meander across the Delta and between swamps. On this cool early morning after the sunny warmth the day before, all the lakes, ponds, swamps, and waterways exude plumes of steam. Some of them, if they are large bodies of water like lakes, have very large clouds that hover and attenuate in the sluggish breeze.

Everywhere, ancient farm machinery lies rusting beneath vines, nearly as ubiquitous as the motorboats parked in yards on collapsing trailers. The old equipment would probably bring a few dollars from some antique hunter who could then sell it for thousands to upscale country gentry as just the thing to lend an air of authenticity to their rural fictions.

I'm not here to learn anything—I'm just looking at terrain I've never seen. But I live on a bayou myself, and the lure of johnboats sliding through green channels overarched with branches heavy with Spanish moss is unmistakable. Theoretically, I could board a boat in my backyard and eventually pilot it right up to the dock of the man from Bayou Pigeon. How nice to get lost somewhere, and this maze of waterway and hummock is as good a place for that as any desert, mountaintop, snowfield, or tiny foreign country.

So, no, I admit to myself. I'm not here to learn anything or, really, to look at the terrain. I'm here to get lost for a precious day in the only way our society now allows—to become an anonymous shadow in an anonymous car driving narrow back roads through towns easily forgotten. It's something I've done frequently, and there's always a peace on the empty back roads. And oddly, no matter where I've been—swamp, desert, forest, mountain—the terrain that I'm not really here to see forms an appropriate backdrop to my mood.

I suppose the questions are these: What gives one validity? Does it come from within or without? Is it real or manufactured? What kinds of activities do it for you? Most people seem to get it from outside themselves. We rely on the approbation of others—hence our desire for the accolades of others. Hence our slavishness to the almighty dollar. Money lends cachet and power, and everyone jumps for a buck. Everyone wants to be the one pulling the purse strings and issuing directives. Everyone wants to be the elite for whom money equates not only as worth but as worthiness. But few seem to be looking inside. Do they have nothing there to look for? Or are they afraid they will find only an empty yearning for fulfillment and the perpetual question of what can fill their emptiness? To this, I answer: How can it possibly be filled from without?

As I reflect on these questions, I meander over to Bayou Lafourche, and as I drive south along Louisiana 1, which parallels the bayou's length, I watch the channel widen and deepen from a sluggish, algae-scummed canal to a major waterway lined with huge fishing boats. The bayou is one long fishing community with an identity and culture all its own. Although its one-hundred-and-fifty-mile length is broken into protracted neighborhoods masquerading as towns, that doesn't detract from its homogeneity.

The towns—Thibodaux, Lafourche, Lockport, Golden Meadow, and others—are like pearls on a string. Each is separate, distinct, and precious, but all come from similar beds and are linked in a whole that compounds their special individual qualities. The huge boats often bear family names on their bows—entire dynasties have made their living taking these boats down the bayou and out into the Gulf of Mexico to supply America's tables with the harvest of the sea.

At last, I arrive at Grand Isle—the end of the bayou, the end of the road, and the end of the land. Before me lies the Gulf of Mexico, and the only place left to go is out into the water. But my vehicle is not made to float, so I simply stand there for a time at the edge of land, sea, and sky, feeling the blaze of the sun and thinking of the way I came to this place. What is the geography of alienation that precipitates the mud of the delta upon which ancient farm implements rust in humid sunlight? Who charts the Mississippi as it empties America's soul?

And then, as always happens when there is no place left to go, it is time to go back. By now it is late, and to be in Baton Rouge by dinnertime, I must travel the most direct and rapid route, which means the I-10 bridge. So I do not retrace my steps and do not again ride the Plaquemine Ferry. Perhaps it truly was for me like Charon's boat—an insubstantial vehicle to be ridden but once.

Yet I remain curious about the man from Bayou Pigeon—he who shared quiet understanding with a stranger and offered welcome. And as I ponder the circumstances of our meeting at an obscure passage over the main stream of America, I can't help but compare him with the faceless crowds at the conference that have blurred in my memory and become as featureless as the misty trees I saw across the Mississippi on that early morning.

But his face and my encounter with him remain vivid in my mind, and I have to wonder at the odd dichotomies of life, where I leave people so I can be alone yet cannot help but meet people who then become the most important parts of the journey.

Spring Break 1969

CRAZY GLEN WANTED ME TO hitchhike to California with him. We were eighteen and it was spring 1969, so it seemed like the thing to do.

Glen wasn't really my friend, but he was my roommate, and we did hang out together some. We lived in Taub Hall, one of the old dorms at the University of Houston. I'm not sure why most people called Glen crazy. He wasn't obviously nuts. There was no overtly irrational behavior, no wild-eyed rantings or brooding mutterings. He didn't even do drugs, which was pretty rare for a young longhair in early 1969. That and the fact that he was a loner made some of my friends suspect him of being an undercover narcotics agent. I don't think that was the case. I got to know him probably as well as anyone, and he seemed too screwed up and self-involved to be a government plant. Besides, illegal substances constantly flowed freely right under his nose, and no one was ever busted.

Glen did drink beer, and he insisted on doing it almost nightly in our dorm room, which often got him in trouble with the dorm authorities. Maybe that's partly why we thought he was off, but looking back, our actions couldn't have been any more rational since we were smoking pot and dropping acid in our rooms all the time. I don't know what dorm life is like these days, but a lot of things we were involved in were probably more dangerous in spring of 1969 than they are now, especially in Texas, where it wasn't unheard of for a black political activist—namely Lee Otis Johnson—to be sentenced to twenty years in prison for possession of two joints handed to him by an undercover agent.

Glen had a habit of flouting authority that went way back. He was from Pennsylvania, where his father had the unusual dual role of prominent minister and member of the state legislature. With that kind of paternity, Glen had a lot to rebel against, and apparently, he spent a lot of wild nights sneaking out and getting drunk—the usual teenage preoccupation before more interesting drugs became popular. One night, so he said, he passed out in a cold rain and wound up with a case of pneumonia from which he almost died. He told me he never fully recovered and had a hole the size of a quarter in one of his lungs that was sealed with some kind of medical plastic.

I don't know if it was true. I did come back to the room one night to find Glen stretched out on the floor, unconscious. At first I thought he was feigning, because that wouldn't have been out of character, but there was a slackness to his face and dead weight to his body that said he was really out and not just miming. I knew he wasn't passed out drunk, either, because there was no odor of alcohol. I called the campus cops, but before they arrived, I managed to rouse Glen out of his stupor. He was still half groggy when he learned I'd called the cops, and he quickly staggered out the door and vanished into the night, leaving me with a seemingly crazy story to explain to Officer Harris and the other cop with him.

But there was something different about Glen that went beyond his flouting of authority. Maybe he did live near death and that gave his actions a certain edge that the rest of us didn't have. Like I said, it didn't manifest in overt craziness, but fairly frequently he'd do something pretty off the wall, like arguing with a street gang that stuck him up while he was on his way back from the convenience store with a six-pack. They had fun roughing him up, and then one of them slashed him down the breastbone with a switchblade. He came back, eyes glazed, with blood all over his shirt, and the rest of the year he proudly bared his chest to display the two-and-a-half-inch red welt.

Maybe I wasn't much better off, though the scars were inside. I barely had any personality when I arrived at the University of Houston as a new freshman six months before, and I'd spent a good portion of that time zonked on pot and acid, habituating rock clubs, and generally destroying my academic prospects. But I was learning, or at least it seemed that way, even if the lessons had nothing to do with academics or degrees. So when Glen suggested we hitchhike to Los Angeles over spring break, I agreed. It would be an adventure.

Yes.

To prepare, we went out and each bought a small gym bag to carry our stuff. I'm talking about those half-moon-shaped, flat-bottomed vinyl bags with a zipper and loop handles on top. You don't see them anymore—backpacks and gym duffels have replaced them, but those didn't exist then except in Army surplus versions. At the time, the gym bags were ideal—cheap and easy to carry—and we were poor and traveling light. We also bought a black magic marker to letter signs. We figured we could find scrap cardboard along the way

That was the extent of our preparation. When we left Houston, I had about forty dollars, a light jacket, a change of clothes, and my toiletries.

A friend drove us out I-10, just west of Houston's city limits, and let us off. There we stood for a couple of hours with our thumbs stuck out and brandishing a cardboard sign with the words "San Antonio" scrawled on it in black magic marker. We weren't ambitious enough to write "Los Angeles," and anyway we figured that people who might give us a ride at least to San Antonio might not bother if we were advertising for a much longer journey. We'd settle for stages.

At last a car stopped, and we ran up. A young woman was behind the wheel. I reached the car first, hopped in the back seat, and shut the door, figuring Glen would sit in the front. Instead, he opened the other back door and slid onto the seat beside me. I couldn't believe he did that, but like I said, he was prone to unpredictable behavior.

The young woman asked us where in San Antonio we were going, and we told her we were actually going to Los Angeles. She said she'd get us as far as San Antonio, we said that was fine, and that was that—all our conversation was used up during the first minute of a nearly four-hour ride. I felt sorry for her, driving all that way with two possibly dangerous, but actually numbskull, freaks in the back seat. For my part, I wasn't a particularly good conversationalist, especially around women, so embarrassment kept my mouth shut. Maybe Glen felt the same, though he used to talk about having sex with his girlfriend back home. Or maybe I'd just been taken in by his brash front, which undoubtedly masked deep insecurity.

After the young woman let us out in San Antonio, we stood for another few hours until late sunset, when a clean-cut guy in his mid thirties picked us up. He was driving a brand-new and very expensive Pontiac Grand Prix with dealer plates, and he was headed to Midland. That was off the I-10 path, but it was a hell of a long way across a hell of a wide state, so we got in. This time, anticipating Glen, I went ahead and sat in the front seat—a tactic I used the remainder of the trip.

The driver was a salesman for a car dealership in Midland, and the Grand Prix wasn't his. It had been ordered by a rich oil man who lived in that West Texas pump-jack paradise. Our driver had gone to San Antonio to pick up the car and deliver it to the dealership. It was a fancy ride—plush and comfortable and fitted with all the amenities of its day. Since it wasn't the driver's car, he didn't care if he stressed it. "Fuck him," he said of the oil man. "If it breaks, he can buy another." To prove his point, the driver drove at a pretty good pace. Not that the car was ever in danger of breaking, at least from speed. It was a powerful machine, and the highways of West Texas, including the state highways, are just made for eighty-five miles an hour, even at night.

Around midnight, we finally came to a town named Eden, which was little more than a bump in the road. Despite its name, it was no paradise—at least not for hippies. Our driver pulled into a gas station, and while the attendant pumped the gas, we all got out to stretch, take a leak, and get a soda. Almost immediately, an older man hurried out of the office and over to our driver.

"Get those boys back in the car!" he said, voice not especially loud but full of urgency. "Get them back in the car!" he repeated when we just stood there like idiots, wondering what he meant. Then we looked around and saw.

Across the highway was the local cowboy bar. Parked out front in the dusty, unpaved lot were a dozen pickup trucks around which lounged fifteen or twenty cowboys. Or rather, they had been lounging until they spotted us. Now they were clustering near the highway shoulder, looking us over as we stood spotlit in the glow of the gas station lights. And they were muttering among themselves. I couldn't hear what they were saying, but they didn't look very friendly.

These days, even cowboys and rednecks have long hair, but in 1969, long hair was tantamount to waving the Russian flag, shouting anti-American slogans, and assaulting upstanding womenfolk in the street. The movie, *Easy Rider*, which came out just months later, amply demonstrates how those good old boys of the South and West felt about folks who dared to be different. Conservative America did not recognize hippies and freaks as being fully human. Like Blacks or Hispanics, we were social anathemas and fair game for violence, as most of us knew from personal experience. The antagonisms depicted in *Easy Rider* were all too real and still are.

Actually, though, until that moment, Glen and I hadn't thought too much about our long hair and hippie clothes. I guess we were just young, idealistic, and inexperienced in the ways of the real world. Most of our friends were like us, and no one at the university seemed to care, at least not enough to express their displeasure in gratuitous violence. Even the clean-cut Midland car salesman hadn't mentioned our hair or attire. But then we'd never been to West Texas, and the rapidly brewing belligerence of those redneck cowboys across the road was plain to see. By now, some were gesticulating, and their voices grew in pitch.

We got back in the car.

The attendant finished pumping the gas, our driver paid, and we pulled back out on the highway.

Six pickups, rear-window gun racks bristling with rifles and shotguns, pulled out of the kicker bar parking lot and began trailing us.

For the next mile or so, while we were still in town, we made a nice little parade—six "floats" depicting an extremist West Texas theme—including the fully laden gun racks—led by the grand marshal's car carrying the grand marshal—that was our driver—and the two special guests of honor—those were Glen and me.

It was all rather nice and peaceful until we hit the city limits. Then the six floats roared into life—or was it death?—behind us, and the grand marshal stomped on the gas. In about ten seconds, we were all traveling at eighty-plus miles per hour down the two-lane blacktop. Ahead was only pitch-black desert night.

"What are we going to do if they catch us?" Glen asked after several tense minutes during which the only sounds were the roar of the Grand Prix's engine and the rush of wind. What a stupid question, I thought. They're going to beat us until we die—or wish we had. That's what was going to happen. Maybe we'd be lucky, and they'd shoot us right off the bat.

But the grand marshal just uttered an easy laugh. He knew something we didn't. He was driving one of the most powerful and well-made American cars on the market, and not only was it brand new and built for speed and handling, it was full of gas and it wasn't his. He was the grand marshal in command of this parade, and he knew it.

"I'm only playing with them," he said. "Watch this."

Seconds later, we were going a hundred and ten.

The cowboys chasing us valiantly tried to keep up. Their pickups were powerful work machines, and they could travel at a good clip, but they weren't built for sustained high speed, and they certainly couldn't take the curves like the Pontiac. Plus, the cowboys didn't plan on driving hundreds of miles to Midland like our driver did. Gradually the pursuing headlights began to drift back in the darkness. At last, pair by pair, they were swallowed by the night until all were gone. It had been twenty minutes since we left town.

The grand marshal eased up on the gas, and the Pontiac slowed to eighty. He'd used American know-how and panache to whup American ignorance and bassackward thinking, and in the process, he'd saved a couple of innocent college kids from brutality and mayhem. He was a pretty damn good driver, too.

He turned to us, grinning.

"Nice car, huh?"

We grinned back. If I'd had the cash, I'd have bought a Grand Prix from him on the spot.

The rest of the ride passed in quiet darkness, the road hissing beneath the tires, the tiny towns and distant ranch house lights drifting by us like shadows of a dream.

"Look at that," the grand marshal said at last, pointing.

Up ahead we could see a large area of sky glowing in the profound West Texas night, though we couldn't see what caused the phenomenon. It was too early for *Close Encounters of the Third Kind* to have hit movie screens, or I might have suspected that the Mother Ship had arrived. But no, it wasn't the Mother Ship, though it was probably just as alien.

"That's Midland," the grand marshal said, then he pointed off to another, fainter, more distant glow. "And that's Odessa."

The air was so clear and dark that the cities' auras hovered in the dry atmosphere above them and could be seen thirty or more miles away, even though the towns themselves were still well below the horizon.

At about four am, on the near side of Midland, the grand marshal pulled over. It had been a good, long ride, and we were reluctant to leave the safe haven of the vehicle in which we had passed unscathed through certain travail. Who knew what rednecks waited for us on Midland's nighttime highways? But it was the end of the ride. We got out and waved good-bye as the grand marshal exited into Midland's radiance.

We may have entered the periphery of Midland's glow, but there wasn't much to see where we were except a dead-empty freeway interchange and the lights of a distant neighborhood. After about half an hour, a curious state trooper slowed, gave us the once-over, and drove on. Maybe he didn't harass us since he knew that oil-patch roughnecks would take care of us as soon as the refinery shifts changed.

Another hour passed, and an old Chevy pickup slowed and stopped long enough to let us in. A middle-aged Mexican man who spoke good English was driving, and maybe he saw us as potential fellow victims. We didn't care what his reasons for stopping were, just that he made the effort. Luckily for us, he was going all the way to El Paso.

We were in the truck for only a short time when a terrible stench began to permeate the air. To me it was suffocating, but the driver seemed not to notice.

"What the heck is that smell?" I asked.

"Oh, that. That's the oil refinery," he replied, gesturing off to the side. Sure enough, there it was, replete with aerial plumbing, huge tanks, and even a few pump jacks.

I've lived near the Houston Ship Channel for many years, now, and have become familiar with such odors, but back then, I had no idea that oil and petrochemical products could be so smelly. Not that proximity and long association have made the odors any less pungent.

234

At last we left the odor behind, and by dawn, we were entering El Paso. The red morning sunlight on the rugged, barren hills and mountains was absolutely gorgeous, making it seem as if the earth itself was aglow and golden. Our driver got us back to I-10 and dropped us off at his exit. The air was dry and dusty though not yet hot. Where we stood, the interstate cut through the foot of a low hill, and right beside us was a steep cement embankment about fifty feet high. Over the top of the embankment sat a low-rent motel, its back to the highway.

We hadn't been there more than fifteen minutes when we heard a voice calling.

"Hey!"

We looked around. A ride we'd missed?

"Hey!"

At the top of the embankment was a young blonde woman, about our age. We could tell she wasn't a natural blonde because all she wore was a half-buttoned man's shirt and a smile.

"We've got a room," she called. "Come on up."

I was callow enough to be intimidated by a mostly naked strange woman beckoning me to a strange motel atop a cement embankment in a strange city, but Glen got one look at the dark patch of hair showing beneath the shirt tails and started scrambling up the slope. I guess he *had* been having sex with his girlfriend. He didn't even look back to see if I was following.

What else could I do?

I'm sure Glen thought he was going to get laid, but when we got to the room, we found it was occupied by another mostly naked young woman and a scruffy half-naked man in his mid twenties. All three affected hippie-type attire, but I could tell immediately they were vagabonds and maybe criminals, not flower children, freaks, or students.

We passed a few amenities back and forth, then the motel trio got down to business. They'd been in the motel for three days and didn't have any money. So they said. Did we have any? If we did, they'd let us travel with them.

We'd be on a bus and not hitchhiking if we had any money, we told them. By now, Glen was beginning to realize he wasn't going to get laid, though he might get screwed, and that we didn't need to be here. After about half an hour, we extricated ourselves, left the motel room, and slid back down the embankment.

Our next ride, which came along about an hour later, was in a beat-up, light brown, ten-year-old Cadillac Eldorado driven by a man of indeterminate middle age looking about as shabby as his car. He wore a faded, light-colored plaid sports coat and equally faded slacks whose color might be defined as dingy, day-old Dijon mustard. He needed a shave and a toothbrush, but he gave a genuine-seeming smile when we got in the car. Next to him on the front seat was a tallish young woman in her early twenties who looked like she might be Indian mixed with Anglo. She wasn't pretty, but she was attractive and built like a brick house, nipples showing beneath her tight, plain white T-shirt. She had long, straight, glossy-black hair and was missing one of her upper front teeth. That didn't stop her from smiling, and her smile, too, seemed to be the real thing.

Glen and I had to crowd into the front seat with the driver and the young woman because the back of the Caddy was completely filled with clothes and other stuff and looked well lived in. This pair had been on the road a long time and probably were going to be on it a lot longer. They were friendly, though, and as we talked, it became apparent that they'd picked us up not from pity or to take advantage of us or out of the need for company but because it was the right thing to do for other people living on the road.

The ride was short, only to Las Cruces, New Mexico, but it got us out of Texas in time for our best ride yet. This was with a hippie couple in their late twenties. They were driving a ten-year-old Ford pickup and were going all the way to San Diego.

"Hop in the back," the guy said, and we did. About fifty miles farther on, they stopped again for two more hitchhiking freaks, and there were four of us in the pickup's bed. The cowboys back in West Texas would have had a field day with that truck.

We spent all day in the bed of the pickup, traveling across America's great southwestern deserts. Memory has compressed the transit to a few images and vignettes, but at the time, it was one great blur of sun-blasted sand and rock that seemed to go on and on forever. I'd never seen the West except in movies, and in one day I saw the whole thing in cross section with nothing between me and it but wind shear. We couldn't talk because the wind blew away our words. All we could do was sit and watch the desert change from morning to afternoon to evening.

A highlight was passing through Tucson, which we did toward the late afternoon. The experience was surreal. One minute we were driving across harsh brown desert, and the next we were in the middle of green lawns and trees. Because the terrain was so flat, we couldn't see the greenery except when the truck went up the overpasses over city streets. Every time we ascended, for a few seconds, we could see the suburbs, with their boxy houses, verdant lawns, and azure backyard pools, spread like a toy city across the otherwise barren landscape, then we'd come down to ground level and have it all disappear behind a facade of houses, buildings, and fences. Then, just as suddenly as it had all appeared, it was gone, and we were outside the city, where the desert remorselessly wiped away any hint that a green, leafy plant or blue swimming pool might reside within a thousand miles or a thousand lifetimes.

At last the sun went down, just about the time we approached the California border. The second pair of freaks had sleeping bags, and they crawled into them and went to sleep, but Glen and I, with our meager kits, could only sit in the cold desert night wind and shiver. And then the truck started to climb into the tail end of the Sierra Nevadas—

between the Little San Bernardino and Orocopia Mountains—and the air turned bitterly cold.

Thank goodness the hippies in the cab took pity on us, stopped, and let Glen and me climb into the cab with them. The heater blew toasty air on our feet, and the couple's friendliness warmed us in other ways. In two hours or so, we were in San Diego. The hippie couple dropped all four of us hitchers at a restaurant on Coastal Highway 101 then drove out of our lives.

The restaurant, part of a modest chain, was called Sambo's, and it specialized, of course, in pancakes. I couldn't believe that there was a restaurant called Sambo's. This was a time when the Step-n-Fetchit and Mammy stereotypes were beginning to fall, black power and the natural look of the Afro were in, and even Aunt Jemima was on her way to a face lift. And here was Sambo's, playing off a derogatory stereotype. Okay, yeah, Sambo was a smart young fellow who triumphed in the face of adversity and outrageous odds, but to name a breakfast restaurant after him? What a slap in the face to black people everywhere.

But it was late, we were hungry, and Sambo's was just what we needed after a long ride across the desert. The four of us went in and ate. Once inside, I had to revise my idea that Sambo's was a slap in the face to African Americans—it was a double slap because Sambo, as depicted in the menu and the illustrations on the walls, was white. I guess the owners of the chain figured that no black man could be as clever as Sambo, so Sambo must have been white. Or maybe, to give them the benefit of the doubt, they were trying to be politically correct twenty years ahead of the trend. Whatever the case, the plan, and the chain, utterly failed within a couple of years. Recently, I saw an old Sambo's that had turned into an independent restaurant. Apparently, the new owners were on a shoestring budget when they started, because they kept the original sign and replaced only a single letter to read, Simbo's.

After we ate, the other two freaks decided to remain for a time in San Diego. Glen and I got on the 101 going north and stuck out our thumbs. A couple of hippie chicks picked us up, though I can't understand why two good looking young women would pick up such a scruffy, grimy pair as Glen and me. My long hair was a tangled, mopish mass after being whipped for fourteen hours in the back of the pickup during the ride across the desert, and my face felt pretty sunburned. Glen didn't look much better than I felt, though he had a beard to help protect his face and his hair wasn't as long. The girls took us up the coast for twenty miles or so and let us out. By now it was after midnight—the witching hour when the crazies came out. And one of them came along and picked us up.

He was a couple of years older than us, driving a Volkswagen Beetle, and seriously tripping on acid. He'd also probably taken speed, because he kept up an incessant stream of ranting and raving that was so voluminous and continuous it threatened to turn into a solid. Despite its density—or perhaps because of it—most of what he said was completely unintelligible.

At one point, he took his foot off the accelerator, drifted the car to the side of the road, and stopped. Suddenly and uncharacteristically silent, he stared through the side window as if mesmerized. Glen and I looked, too. Out there in the pitch blackness of the midnight Pacific Ocean, ragged lines and sheets of glowing electric blue were washing towards us. I'd never seen anything like it, and for a second, I thought that somehow I had contact high from the driver and was tripping, too.

"What is it?" I asked.

"Red tide," the driver murmured. "Little creatures that glow when the surf stirs them up." It was the most comprehensible thing he'd said.

We stared at the beautiful sight for about ten minutes, then the driver brought himself out of his trance.

"Wow, man," he said as he accelerated back onto the highway. "I'm glowing, too." And that was the last thing I understood, though he immediately resumed his aimless rapping and talked all the way to LA.

But at least he didn't have a wreck, and he finally let us out, seemingly at random, on a madhouse morning rush-hour freeway. Houston's freeway traffic has gotten that bad—or worse—in the thirty years since, but LA was an innovator and still remains tops in bad traffic. We didn't get much attention from the busy traffic, so after a couple of hours, we found a pay phone, and Glen called his aunt, who lived alone in a distant suburb west of the city. She came and picked us up and took us home.

As soon as we arrived at her house, I went into the bathroom and looked at myself in the mirror. My nose felt funny, and I wanted to see what was wrong. It was all white and puffy looking—not like the flesh was swollen but as if there was something wrong with the skin. Bending close to the mirror, I touched my nose, and the skin fell off into the sink.

I was too shocked to do anything but stare at the raw red thing that was my nose. It didn't really hurt any more than a regular sunburn, but it sure looked weird. I wondered how I was going to explain to Glen and his aunt that my nose skin just fell off. I decided not to bother unless they asked. I flushed the skin and went back into the living room. They both looked at me a little strangely at first but quickly got used to my new appearance.

Glen's aunt was a pleasant woman of about forty, recently divorced, and we stayed with her for a couple of days. She was happy to see Glen, though he seemed embarrassed to be there. We ate well and slept in beds, and she took us to Disneyland.

Nowadays, Disneyland isn't any big deal. Today there are Disneyworlds all over the place, a lot of Six Flags, and many other large amusement parks of similar ilk, but back in the '60s, Disneyland was what set kids' imaginations afire. Sure, there was Coney Island if you lived in New York, or the Quassy Amusement Park if you lived in Connecticut, or Frontier City in Oklahoma City, or the amusement park at Myrtle Beach, South Carolina. And there were a handful of other lesser amusement parks scattered across the nation. But if you were like most American youth who grew up in the American hinterlands in the '50s and '60s, you got your kicks only in the fall, when the state fair came alive. Or maybe you had to settle for the smaller county fair if you couldn't make the state shindig.

Walt Disney had not only taken the concept of the fair's midway, enlarged on it, and turned it into a year-round event, he'd constantly bombarded virtually every kid in the nation with images of his super amusement park. Disneyland was on TV, at the movies, and in magazines. For kids at the time, Disneyland was a bit like the Promised Land, only better, since you could actually go there, have a great time and maybe even be on TV, and then go home afterwards and brag about how great it was to your friends and classmates.

Naturally, I was excited. Glen's aunt told us we'd arrived at just the right time. Until just a few weeks prior, Disneyland officials had barred hippies from enjoying the park. I guess they'd been worried that Disneyland might lose its homey image and family atmosphere with a bunch of stoned freaks running around, grooving on the rides and making fun of the straight people. But maybe the officials also had begun to worry about anti-discrimination laws, which those same hippies were doing their best to get enforced with regard to women and minorities. So the park finally had begun to allow hippies and freaks into its pleasures. It didn't last. A few months later, I read a newspaper article stating that a massive influx of stoned hippies grooving on the rides and making fun of the straight people prompted Disneyland officials to once again close the park to longhairs. So it was indeed fortunate that I was there during that narrow window of opportunity.

I had a great time. Rode the rides, saw the sights, smelled the smells. It was smaller and dingier than I'd expected, but I was old enough to appreciate the mechanical wonder of it all. I was particularly impressed by the Abe Lincoln automaton because it kept shifting its weight from foot to foot as it stood there, delivering the famed "Gettysburg Address."

That night, Glen told me he wanted to leave. Not LA, but his aunt's house. Maybe it felt too much like home to him, with parents watching over his every move and stifling his restless, loner spirit. Or perhaps it was just too safe.

Besides, we hadn't hitchhiked halfway across a continent just to spend our precious few days cooped up in a suburban house. So after breakfast the next morning, we bid his aunt adieu, hopped a city bus, and headed into downtown LA. We wandered around for a while and finally found our way to Sunset Strip. I knew the street from the television show of the same name, and supposedly there were good rock clubs along it where some of the great rock acts of the day—such as Love and The Doors—had gotten their starts. I'm not sure what I expected of this fabled drag, but I remember feeling faintly disappointed that it wasn't constantly hopping. It looked like any other sallow, seedy neon drag. We failed to locate the Whiskey a Go Go, and we couldn't find a single club that we wanted to go in.

We stayed in the Diggers' crash pad, which was a real experience. The Diggers were a hippie sect based on simplicity and communal living, and their crash pad, located in a decrepit one-story building a few blocks off Sunset Strip, was a haven where homeless hippies could find a safe place to sleep. It was pretty much a homeless shelter that catered to hippies. Maybe I should say stay instead of sleep, since I didn't get much of that in the two nights we were there. One guy snored constantly and loudly, and another, just a couple of sleeping spaces away from me, was suffering from heroin withdrawal. He was sick and moaning and groaning all night long and getting up every ten minutes to vomit in the toilet. But we were off the streets, and that was probably good. Not that we were in particular danger from other hippies. LA was a little like West Texas—it was the establishment that was dangerous.

My first inkling of that fact came soon after we arrived at the Diggers' crash pad. It was early evening, and we decided to go out and take a stroll on the Strip to see what was happening. We stashed our stuff with the Digger clerk and headed out the door. We turned onto a narrow side street that would take us the few blocks to the Strip, and a couple of blocks later, we came to an intersection where a second street met the street we were on. On our side of the street, the intersecting street devolved into a service alley that ran between the buildings. This intersection was protected by a traffic light, which showed red for traffic on our street and green for the intersecting street and alley.

It was eight pm, and though there was some traffic up on Sunset, a couple of blocks ahead of us, no cars were bothering with our street or the intersecting one—and certainly not the alley. So, without a pause and without a second thought, Glen and I walked on across the alley.

Not a single car had been in sight as we began to cross the alley, but by the time we'd reached the far side, twenty feet distant, three cars were plainly evident—mostly because they were screeching to a halt in a ring around us, roof-top lights blazing, headlights pinning us to the wall in their stark glare.

The cops.

LA cops.

There were two in each car, and to add to the excitement, a seventh on foot patrol was drawn like a moth to the lights.

Seems Glen and I had committed the heinous crime of jay-walking across the alley. We were searched and interrogated for nearly half an hour. Maybe I should say we were harassed for half an hour. I guess things were slow out on the Strip, and the cops needed something to do to work off their testosterone-fueled aggression. At last, we were each given a ticket for jaywalking—the fine was $10—and told to watch our asses.

In retrospect, considering the reputation the LAPD had built over the years with hippies and any sort of minority, we were extremely wise not to crack wise with them or they'd probably have cracked our skulls. And the political climate certainly was ripe for that at the time, as illustrated by a second incident that highlighted the dangers of LA culture.

It happened the next day, after Glen and I again hopped a city bus, this one headed for Santa Monica. We wanted to see the beach—the Pacific, man!—even if the water was too cold for swimming. So far, the only glimpse of the Pacific we'd had was driving up the coast highway with the tripped-out freak a few nights before, when we'd seen phosphorescent blue waves rolling in from dark infinity.

We were on the bus a long time—maybe an hour—and during the ride, the passengers were predominantly poor working folks and old women. The old women all wore cotton print dresses and sported "Re-elect Mayor Yorty" pins. Sam Yorty was LA's notoriously arch-conservative mayor. It wasn't an election year—the elections had happened the previous November, about five months earlier. I couldn't help but wonder why election pins were in evidence so late. Maybe the women kept wearing the pins in a show of post-election solidarity, sort of like a club corsage. Or maybe they'd just forgotten they had them on.

When Glen and I got on the bus, there were only three empty seats, all of them on those benches that face inward at the front of the bus. Glen sat right behind the driver, and I sat next to him, with the sole remaining empty seat to my right. At the next stop, two of Mayor Yorty's gerontological pep squad stumped up the steps and onto the bus. I got up and offered them my seat. They took it and the remaining vacant one, their lack of a thank you accompanied by suspicious glares.

I hung onto the overhead bar for a few more blocks, then the front seat immediately next to the stairwell came open, and I sat down. The bus jolted on for a few more blocks, when out of the corner of my left eye, I saw another Mayor Yorty acolyte shuffling up the bus aisle. This woman had to have been eighty or more, and she had absolutely no business being on her feet on a moving bus. The bus was closing in on the bus stop as she came between me and the driver, and suddenly the car in front of the bus stopped. Our driver hit his brakes, and the old lady toppled forward, taking a nosedive down the stairwell.

Instinctively, I grabbed her arm and managed to keep her from going down any but the first step. She didn't even hit her knees, though the effort nearly wrenched my shoulder out of its socket. I was a scrawny hundred and twenty-five pounds, and using only one arm to grapple and haul a nose-diving hundred -and-sixty-pound old woman wasn't part of my physical repertoire.

I got out of my seat to help her back on her feet, when a strident, cracking voice cut the air. It came from the old woman to whom I'd given my seat earlier. She was sitting ramrod straight, pointing at me like a prophet of doom, eyes aflame with righteous indignation.

"He tripped her!" she shrieked. "I saw it! He tripped her!"

Feeling helplessly railroaded into a guilty verdict though I was innocent of the charges and had in fact acted the hero and nearly dislocated my arm in the process, I looked up at the bus driver, who was right there and had seen everything. He looked back at me. He didn't say anything, but his lips drew into a thin line, and he rolled his eyes. I understood instantly that he had to deal with the Yorty pep squad daily—hourly—and that this incident rated only a footnote in his book.

I finished assisting the old woman off the bus and got back in my seat, all beneath the baleful glare of the woman who accepted my former seat then falsely accused me. She continued to poke hot visual holes in me until she and her friend debarked a few blocks later. As they stood and moved toward the door, I was sorely tempted to pretend that I was going to trip them, but I prudently refrained.

Santa Monica was a beach with lots of sand, cold water, and a slightly nippy wind. Even so, a fair number of people were out, enjoying the beautiful weather. We stayed for a couple hours, warming in the sun, then bussed back to the Diggers' crash pad. By then, thankfully, Mayor Yorty's pep squad were all safely ensconced within their homes, and the ride was uneventful.

After one more night in the Digger's crash pad, we left LA, beginning with a bus ride to the edge of the city. Our first real ride was with a guy about thirty. He wasn't going out I-10, but he was headed vaguely east—to Las Vegas—so we got in. He played a lot of '50s rock-n-roll on an 8-track tape player—his only concession to more up-to-date music was Velvet Underground's first album. When he learned that I liked the band, he played the song "Heroin" for us several times. I couldn't appreciate the song too much, though, since I hadn't had enough sleep the last couple of nights because of the guy on heroin withdrawal at the Diggers' pad.

Our driver actually drove us completely through Las Vegas, explaining that he was going to take us east of the city before he let us out. It seemed that Las Vegas cops didn't like hippie hitchhikers any more than the LA cops or West Texas cowboys did. He took us right past all the big hotels and casinos, so I got a good look at Las Vegas. I know several people who love Vegas and go there whenever they can. I think I'd get bored—I don't gamble, drink, or whore, and those strike me as Las Vegas's primary attractions. Oh, yeah, I guess now there are magic shows, Cirque du Soleil, overblown cabaret acts, and other fare, but I rode through before Vegas became "family oriented." Back then, it was "crime family oriented." This was about the time in which the middle scenes of Martin Scorsese's *Casino* are set.

True to his word, our driver drove us out east of Las Vegas and over Hoover Dam before he let us out. You can't do that anymore. Not since 9/11. He returned to town, leaving us faced with having to work our way back to I-10 down the scant ribbon of US 93. Three local boys in a late-model Chevy Bel Air gave us a start.

They were whoopin' and hollerin' and wavin' and drinkin' beer. They'd been drinking beer for some time, by all appearances. That was fine by Glen, who joined in with them, but I didn't drink and was worried about the way the driver couldn't seem to keep in his own lane. Not that it mattered, since traffic was virtually nonexistent on this two-lane desert blacktop, and in the desert valleys, you could see anything coming for at least five miles. But just because the driver could see something coming from five miles away didn't mean he wouldn't hit it when he got to it, and he was driving at an erratic seventy-five miles per hour—fast enough to cream us all even if he chose a telephone pole to pile into instead of an on-coming vehicle.

Then a Pontiac Grand Ville convertible roared passed us, and if I thought the drunken whooping and hollering had been loud before, it reached pure crescendo when our local boys spotted the two women in the front seat. They were young, blonde, and beautiful in the way of Vegas showgirls, and they were coming from that direction. And they were topless, catching some desert rays to encourage that all-tan look. The driver clutched a T-shirt across her breasts long enough to pass us, but the passenger simply bent forward until we were behind them.

Our drunken driver developed a foot that was heavy in direct inverse proportion to the lightness of his head, and in seconds, we were careening after the topless women at eighty-five. Then ninety, then a hundred. Unfortunately for our drunken chums, a Grand Ville had far greater power than the overloaded Bell Air, and though our driver kept his foot to the floor, the girls were soon the requisite five miles ahead and lost to sight. Our driver had been too drunk to hit what he'd aimed at.

It made a nice bookend to the chase through West Texas, though. Each had involved inferior vehicles chasing Pontiacs, but in West Texas, we'd been the pursued, and now we were among the pursuers. And both chases had proved fruitless, thwarted by the pure V-8 horsepower beneath the hoods of big, expensive American cars.

The drunk kids let us out soon after, and we caught a ride with a thankfully sane and sober businessman heading into Phoenix. Our driver let us out on the eastern outskirts of the city at about 10 pm. At least we were back on I-10, and it was a straight shot back to Houston.

Or so we thought.

We stood on an entrance ramp until one am, when a somewhat dilapidated dark blue Ford sedan stopped about fifty feet beyond us. The back door opened invitingly, and Glen and I ran up and jumped in. The car took off and was on the highway before we could look at each other and think that maybe we had made a mistake in getting into this car. We didn't know it, but our straight shot back to Houston was about to take an instructive and unsettling detour.

Our driver, still accelerating onto the highway, turned and growled, "Are you flower children?"

It sounded like a threat, and the driver looked threatening. He was a rough-looking man in his late forties or early fifties, wearing a grimy plaid shirt and a beat-up black leather jacket. Coarsely cut dark hair stuck out from beneath the beret on his head, and gold loop earrings festooned his earlobes. He had tattoos on his cheeks, which hadn't seen a razor in several days. The guy riding shotgun couldn't have been a greater contrast, though no less strange. He was nearly gaunt and wearing fancy and immaculate dude cowboy clothes. Black dude cowboy clothes. All black. His hat was black, his shirt was black, his pants were black, his boots were black, his hair was black, his string tie was black, and his upper lip sported a thin little black mustache. Perched on his long, sharp nose were a pair of black wrap-around sunglasses. I wondered if his underwear was black, too.

Remember, it's the middle of the night in the middle of the desert. If there hadn't been the illumination from the dashboard lights, this guy would have been invisible. I wondered just how much he could see through his blackened lenses. Unlike his companion, his cheeks were neat and crisp.

"Uh, no," Glen stammered. "We're students."

"Ah," the man with the tattooed cheeks nodded sagely. "Scholars. What school you go to?"

Glen told him, and the guy introduced himself and his friend. He was Gypsy and the black-garbed cowboy was the Kid.

The Kid nodded a greeting.

"And this is Maisy," Gypsy said, gesturing to the seat between him and the Kid.

We peered over, and lying there was a smallish, three-legged female mutt nursing a fresh litter of pups.

Gypsy and the Kid were truck drivers. They'd just dropped off a truck in Phoenix and were on their way home. These pleasantries over, Gypsy abruptly swerved onto the next exit ramp.

"We'll get out here," Glen and I said in unison as the car left I-10, but Gypsy didn't bother slowing to barely sane ramp speed. In five seconds, we were on a two-lane blacktop, the lights of Phoenix fading into the darkness behind us as we headed north, into the desert.

"Naw," Gypsy said. "Trust us. We're truckers and this is a trucker route. You'll get lots of rides up this way."

Yeah, right. In the hitchhiking I'd done up to then and all I did after, I've only been picked up once by an eighteen-wheeler. But there wasn't much we could do except jump out, and by now the car was going sixty-five. We'd just have to sit out the ride with Gypsy, the Kid, and three-legged Maisy.

Gypsy liked to talk, and he kept up a steady stream of it, mostly about trucking life, until about the time we drove through Superior. That was when he began telling us about his and the Kid's involvement in the local KKK. He told us, among other things, how they and a bunch of their buddies "took this nigger out into the desert and strung him up." What fun it was.

There was no way to know if he was telling the truth or just trying to freak us out. He certainly did the latter. But just as easily as he'd started the KKK diatribe, he segued into something else, though I couldn't pay much attention. All I could think of was their purported victim's fear and anguish because I was feeling the fear myself and expecting the anguish. After all, people who would commit heinous crimes against others because of racial differences wouldn't hesitate to do similar things to "commie hippie scum"—especially if we were "scholars," which also meant "intellectual commie bastard scum," to a redneck America that then was preaching "Love it, or leave it."

A few miles before we reached Globe, Gypsy abruptly and without a word twisted the wheel, and the car spun off the road and lurched into the pitch-black desert. In an instant, fear filled me completely. I looked at Glen, who was staring back at me with bottomless pits of eyes that said he was feeling like I was—that we were about to experience the final moments of our lives in the middle of the desert at the hands of two insane truck drivers who would later joke with their buddies about the two commie hippies they strung up. What fun it was.

The car jolted on for another couple of minutes, and I was beginning to grope for the door handle, thinking about jumping out and trying to escape into the darkness, when suddenly Gypsy hit the brakes and the car ground to a stop in a clatter of gravel. This is it, I thought as dust billowed around the car and across the headlight beams. Where's the rope?

Then the dust began to drift and settle, revealing a trailer home, half-obscured by weeds and cactus, sitting just in front of the car. The Kid gave Maisy a pet, nodded good-bye to us, got out, and sauntered to the trailer.

The fear that had ballooned inside me collapsed, leaving a stunned void. We were just dropping off the Kid at home.

Then into the void rushed a blessed breeze of relief that buoyed my spirit. It wasn't my time to die quite yet. And fluttering on that breeze was an amusing note: During the hour and a half we'd been in the car, the Kid hadn't said one single word.

Gypsy stayed just long enough to light the Kid's way to the door, then he turned around and, in a few moments, steered the car back onto the highway.

"Now, where was I?" he said. "Oh, yeah. This truck stop up here. I'm going to drop you off there. I know the wait-ress, and I'll tell her to take care of you. You'll do fine. A truck'll pick you up in no time."

Yeah, right.

A little way past Globe, Gypsy pulled into the scant parking lot of a ramshackle truck stop that was open despite the fact that it was around two in the morning, the parking lot was empty, and we hadn't seen a single truck since leaving I-10. It wasn't really a truck stop but a diner in dire need of paint with a couple of diesel and gas pumps out front. Gypsy took us inside and introduced us to the waitress, who gave us a desultory nod. As soon as we went back outside, she forgot all about us. Then Gypsy parted company with us, vanishing like an enigma into the desert night.

We stood out on the pavement about a hundred feet beyond the diner for more than an hour, and not a single truck came down the road from either direction. Nor were there any cars. I wondered what kept the diner open all night. Then a truck pulled up. The driver got out and went inside. He came out half an hour later and ignored us as he pulled out of the parking lot and drove off.

A little while later, another truck came and went. And another. Okay, there were trucks, but they sure weren't picking us up.

At last, a car pulled into the parking lot and a big Jewish kid about our age got out. We knew he was Jewish because of the black yarmulke he wore. He barely had the door shut before we were next to him.

"Hey," Glen said. "Would you give us a ride out of here?"

The kid, who looked pretty straight, wasn't too excited about having a couple of raggedy freaks hit him up for a ride in the middle of nowhere in the middle of the night.

"I'm only going about twenty miles up this road before I turn off," he said, hoping to dissuade us, but hell, that was twenty miles farther on.

"That's good," I said. "We've been stuck here for hours. We're just trying to get back to school." I added this last to let him know we weren't a threat to him, since he was probably a student himself going home for spring break.

"Okay," he said. "Get in. I have to use the rest room. I'll be out in a few minutes. Be careful of the strawberry plants. They're for my mom."

We got in the car, and sure enough, half the floor in the back was covered with little plastic planters sprouting tiny seedlings. The driver came out a couple of minutes later, and we left the truck stop behind. About twenty miles farther on, he stopped at a nondescript side road.

"This is where I turn," he said, obviously glad to get rid of us.

We got out, and he turned onto the side road and was gone. I didn't know it then, but there's nothing up that way for more than a hundred miles but Indian reservation—kind of a strange place for a Jewish kid to grow up.

Dawn was beginning to light the sky, and a scattered handful of cars and pickup trucks were drifting up and down the road, but none of the ones going our direction stopped. Then, just after the sun peeped over the desert landscape, a pickup truck, its bed filled with roped-down mattresses, pulled up beside us.

"Hop in, boys," said the fiftyish, friendly faced man behind the wheel, and we did.

"Where you boys headed?"

"Back to Houston," I said.

"Well, I'm just going to Safford, but I'll take you that far."

Our driver turned out to be a really nice and generous fellow. He got the basic outline of our journey, and said he admired us for being so adventurous. He didn't live in Safford—Arizona, that is—but he owned a motel there, and he was taking the load of mattresses to the motel. The motel was on the leading edge of town, and about an hour later, he pulled into the parking lot. We got out, thanked him, and turned to walk up to the highway, when he stopped us.

"You boys must be hungry. Come on in. I'll stake you to a meal."

He took us inside, told the waitress to give us anything we wanted on the house, then left to unload the mattresses.

We ate. And ate some more. We hadn't had a real meal since dinner at Glen's aunt's house four days earlier. Toward the end of the meal, the motel owner came in, sat down with us, and had some coffee.

"If you boys are still in town tonight, come on back here, and I'll give you a room for the night free of charge."

We thanked him but said we'd probably be back in Texas, at least, by nightfall.

Maybe he knew something we didn't.

At about eight o'clock, we left the motel, walked about a hundred yards down the highway, and stuck out our thumbs.

By eleven, every yahoo in town had driven by us at least twice, gawking, and many three or four times. Some of them shouted insults and obscenities, some threw beer cans at us, and a few swerved dangerously close. The winners were three teenage girls in a pickup. They came by us four times, and each time, they'd slow down like they were going to pick us up, then they'd peel out, laughing wildly at their clever joke and waving gaily out of the windows. Their fourth time around, they threw a Coke can at us. I guess they were too young to drink beer.

By one pm, we were thoroughly tired of being the main attraction in town, and we certainly weren't having any luck catching a ride. Figuring it was because we were on the highway leading into town, we decided to go to the outbound side of town where we might have better luck—anybody going our way would be leaving this unfriendly place.

It took us thirty or forty minutes to walk from one side of Safford to the other. Along the way, we could see the stark, grim walls of a federal prison looming over the landscape. It was one of the biggest employers in town. I later learned that David Harris was incarcerated there not long after Glen and I passed through. Harris, who was then married to the folk singer Joan Baez, was the counterculture's most famous antiwar protester, having gone to prison rather than fight unjustly in Vietnam. I wish I'd known at the time that he'd soon be in that prison. It would have set just the right mood to appreciate Safford. As if the girls in the pickup and the rest of the yahoos hadn't done that already.

The other side of Safford was a lot quieter. Here, the highway wound out of the city instead of arrowing straight in, and there were some trees. We stopped just up the road from a little burger shack that was set up near a small train yard where half a dozen boxcars sat on a siding. We were there for several hours, and although no one gave us a ride, no one came by to harass or throw beer cans at us, either.

At about five, a VW Beetle stopped. Inside were three hippieish kids about our age—a boy, who was driving, and two girls.

"You trying to get out of town?" the guy asked. There was something about the way he said it that relayed hidden information. Maybe it wasn't a question.

"Yeah," we replied in a tone that indicated understanding.

"We live here, so we can't take you far," the boy said. "But there's a rest stop about twenty miles out. Maybe you'll have better luck out there."

"Anything's better than this," we said, squeezing into the back.

The driver, like us, was a college freshman, and he'd come home for spring break. He was friends with the two girls, who were sisters, one a high school senior and the other a junior. The girls' parents had come to Safford a couple of years earlier to teach Spanish in the high school, but their jobs had been terminated because they were too liberal. The family was moving at the end of the school year. They all hated Safford, and Glen and I readily sympathized.

They dropped us off at the rest stop, wished us good luck, and headed back to town.

We'd thought that anything would be better than Safford, but now that we were here, we weren't so sure. The rest stop consisted of a wide place on the shoulder and a rusted, gut-shot, fifty-five-gallon drum containing about sixty-five gallons of rotting garbage. More was strewn on the ground beneath it. All around us stretched flat desert, with distant mountains humping the horizons on either side of the road. If it had been midday, it would have been a frying pan. Now, with the sun going down and a cold wind sweeping across the plain, it was turning into an icebox.

In the couple of hours we stood there, the cars and pickups that passed were all obviously locals. Maybe they were checking up on us. It didn't look like anybody going any distance was leaving Safford tonight.

Glen and I discussed our options. We could stand here and freeze our asses off waiting all night for a ride, or we could, somehow, get back to Safford to the burger stand. We could eat a burger and then spend the night in a boxcar. We even toyed with the idea of trying to hop a freight going east. The latter was Glen's idea, but the colder it got, the more I took him seriously. By seven, we'd moved to the other side of the highway, heading back into Safford.

Astrophysicists have, during the last few decades, discovered that black holes—places that suck up everything, including light, space, and time—are scattered throughout the universe. It's absolutely true, and there is such a place right here on Earth called Safford, Arizona. We'd struggled like hell to get out of this singular burg with its maximum security prison holding those who couldn't escape the system, and literally hundreds of cars and trucks had passed us as we tried to free ourselves from its warping gravitation. Yet we were there on the other side of the road for less than five minutes when the first vehicle that came by stopped. Safford was easy to fall into, but getting out of it would require a major alteration of the laws of physics.

We ran up to the vehicle and got on.

I say on, not in. It was a dune buggy with only two bucket seats, and those were occupied by the man driving and his woman passenger. They were coming back to town after a day of fun in the sun, tearing up desert dunes. Glen and I perched on the back of the frame, whipped by the freezing wind, clinging to the cold metal with one hand and our gym bags with the other, trying to keep our flapping clothes from getting caught in the engine's whirling pulley or fan blades, and watching the road whiz about two feet beneath us at sixty or seventy miles per hour.

The dune buggy people let us off at the burger shack, which, to our consternation, was now closed. So much for dinner. And the boxcars were all locked up. We briefly considered going back to the motel, but there was no way we were going to run the Safford gauntlet to get there, so without enthusiasm, we resumed our position beside the road at the very spot where the young freaks in the VW had picked us up three hours earlier.

About twenty minutes later, the same VW with the same three occupants pulled up beside us.

"What happened?" the driver asked.

We told them we'd been cold, hungry, and thirsty and had come back to eat, but the burger shack was closed.

"Get in," said the older girl. "We'll take you home with us."

"Won't your parents get mad?" I asked.

"Naw. We told them about you, and they were concerned. They sent us out to check on you. That's why we're here. It'll be all right."

And it was. Their parents hated Safford, too. They welcomed us, fixed us dinner, dragged out sleeping bags so we could spend the night, and generally made us feel right at home. After we ate, the boy, the two girls, Glen, and I squeezed back into the VW and drove out into the country. The boy stopped near an irrigated field of short, green grass that must have covered a couple of thousand acres. I guess it was part of a turf farm.

We walked out into the middle, lay on the downy turf, and watched the incredibly spangled sky. Everyone knows how clear and beautiful the desert night sky is. Everyone, that is, except the population of Safford. Too bad they never look up to consider the wonder of existence instead of harassing innocent people who were different and running their federal penitentiary where they locked up those same different people. The only time they stopped to wonder was when they wondered what those damned stinking hippies were doing in their town.

But the night sky was gorgeously mysterious and our newfound friends companionable, and the grim realities of Safford seemed light years away.

The next morning, the girls' mom fixed us a hearty breakfast, shoved big sack lunches into our hands, and sent us off with her daughters and the boy, back out to the rest stop.

"We'll check on you," she promised. "If you're still there tonight, we'll bring you back here."

Our friends let us off and chugged back to town. I don't remember the names of the boy or the younger girl, but the older girl's name was Molly. She and I wrote to each other a few times during the next year or so, but we eventually lost touch.

Glen and I were set for another long wait at the rest stop, but only half an hour went by before a car stopped to give us a ride. I hopped into the front seat, Glen into the back, and Safford soon disappeared into the past. Our friends may not have altered the laws of physics, but at least they'd broken Safford's black-hole gravitation and helped set us free.

The guy driving was about thirty-five. He said he worked at a small airport, and he gestured vaguely to the desert north of the highway. We hadn't been in the car ten minutes before his right hand crabbed across the seat and started trying to grope my thigh. I wasn't interested and shoved it off. It came back, and I shoved it off and put my gym bag in my lap. He stopped the car.

"This is where I turn," he said, though there wasn't an intersection in sight.

I didn't care, and we got out, though Glen was puzzled by it all until I told him what had happened. Luckily, we didn't have to wait long for our next ride, and it was a good one—a young married couple going all the way to El Paso. They were nice enough to take us completely through the city before dropping us off on I-10.

Back on I-10, back in Texas, with a straight shot home.

Yep, we'd had similar thoughts before.

A couple of hours later, just after dusk, a big, new American station wagon with two guys inside stopped to give us a ride. The man behind the wheel couldn't have been more incongruous for the archetypal family machine he drove. He was a big guy—large and beefy without being fat —and about thirty. His coarse black hair was edging over his ears, and it was raggedy, as if it was growing out from a crew cut. His coarse beard hadn't seen a razor in several days. He wore old Marine fatigues. The shirt's sleeves and insignia were cut off, and it was unbuttoned. Around his neck on a thick gold chain hung a heavy and incredibly ostentatious ersatz gold peace symbol about five inches in diameter. It lay on his hairy chest like some kind of talisman. Military and arcane tattoos colored his arms, and scuffed black military boots completed a spectacle that was altogether imposing and intimidating.

But he smiled when we got in, and said loudly, "How's it going? How far you wanna ride? I'm goin' all the way."

The passenger was another freak hitchhiker like Glen and me. The driver had picked him up just west of El Paso, and he was headed for somewhere on the East Coast.

The driver had been in the U.S. Marines until a few weeks earlier, when he'd mustered out. He said he'd done three tours in Vietnam, and though there was nothing to prove this true, we didn't doubt him. He was wild and a bit crazy, like a beast kept caged too long and bursting with energy to be free. Or a beast totally unused to cages who now saw one at the end of the trail.

The car wasn't his—it belonged to some upper-middle-class family that had moved from LA to Atlanta, and he'd contracted to drive it to Atlanta for them. He'd left LA only that morning, which meant he was really pushing it to have made El Paso by dusk. And the car wasn't the only thing that was speeding. He had a bottle of amphetamines to keep him alert, energetic, and driven.

And talkative. He drove and rapped about how cruddy the military was and how terrible and craven officers were, and how being in Vietnam had been good and bad and scary and satisfying, all at the same time. He talked about the weirdness of being immersed in such a totally different culture and how the Vietnamese people were as sophisticated as they were barbaric, as sly as they were courageous. And he told us, but didn't dwell on, some of the terrible things he'd seen and done. He spoke with great rapidity, in great detail, and with total conviction, and the three of us sat and listened and tried to remain as calm as possible.

Remaining calm in a car pushing a hundred and twenty at night isn't easy, particularly when the driver has been through hell and has accumulated a certain contempt for human life, especially his own, and is steadily popping speed. The fact that large sections of I-10 were under construction and he had to veer off onto treacherous dirt-road detours didn't phase him a bit. Or slow him down. At one of these detours, the pavement dipped abruptly to the dirt road, and for a moment, the heavy station wagon was airborne before it crunched onto the detour, lurching and swaying dangerously.

"Guess I'd better take it easy," the driver commented with a mordant chuckle. He let off the gas, but we were going so fast that the station wagon decelerated for several seconds before the speedometer needle separated itself from the peg at one-twenty and descended to one-ten. He deemed that speed sufficiently reduced to make it safely through the rest of the detour.

Not too far west of San Antonio, the driver caught sight of a sign that pointed the way to a nearby town, and he whipped the station wagon, squealing, onto the exit ramp. The town was Johnson City. He said he just had to see the town of the great president who'd made him go to war.

Personally, I wasn't anxious to leave I-10. Too many potentially ugly things had happened during the last ten days, and most of them had occurred off the interstate. Nor was I interested in meeting face-to-face the sort of redneck cowboys who had chased us across northwest Texas. But I didn't suggest to Glen that we ask the driver to let us out. I suppose by this time I was ready to accept whatever fate had in store. Maybe we'd met a certain degree of mortal danger on this trip, but the fact was it had passed us by, leaving us unscathed though more aware. Also, the driver promised to take us all the way home—if we survived the ride.

And truthfully, I was fascinated by the driver. He was an extremely dangerous individual—tough, experienced in life-and-death situations, and seething with obvious if suppressed violence. Clearly he had killed people—maybe a lot of people. Yet none of his violence and aggression were ever, even for an instant, directed toward his three passengers. I think we, as hippies, represented to him the real thing he'd been fighting for—not mom and apple pie and the military-industrial complex, but people who saw a better world in which individual freedom and lack of violence were the norm. He desperately wanted to identify with that world—that's why he wore the peace symbol and had torn the sleeves and insignia off his fatigues. But he knew he'd seen too much of the wrong kind of life to ever be a hippie or even espouse the hippie philosophy. He was kind of like Billy Jack, seeing the idealistic truth in peaceful coexistence but too aware that violence is the real way of the world and too prone to violence himself to turn the other cheek.

In Johnson City, he stopped for gas at a redneck truck stop. I think he intentionally picked the worst one he could find. Glen and I weren't too happy since the midnight chase across West Texas was sharp in our memories. Not that anyone would be able to catch up with this driver if he didn't want them to—no sane person would drive like he did. But the problem was that he probably would let them catch up just to get into a ruckus. And now the rednecks who might cause us problems weren't across the road or in pursuing vehicles—they were right there in the truck stop, and we were about to enter the lion's den. Even the other freak was hesitant.

Maybe our driver sensed our reluctance. As he got out, he said jovially, "Come on in, guys. I'm buying."

What else could we do? We were all hungry, thirsty, and needed the rest room, so we followed the driver through the door.

The tension inside was thick enough that movement was almost like swimming. Then one of the rednecks sitting on a stool at the counter turned and made a loud and somewhat threatening comment about it being time "to kick some dirty hippie ass."

With an almost instantaneous predatory movement, our driver stepped uncomfortably close to the redneck—so close that the man couldn't turn farther on his stool without bumping into him.

"You want to kick some ass?" the driver asked in a voice gone flat and totally devoid of emotion as he stared straight into the redneck's eyes. There was no anger, no fear, no tension—only the question.

But it wasn't his voice that I really noticed. Like I said, he was a big guy and pretty imposing, but where he'd shown us only joviality and camaraderie, he now literally radiated lethal menace. It was almost like standing in front of a heat lamp. I'd never felt such a thing before and never since, but I knew in that instant and without a shadow of a doubt that our friendly driver really had killed men who were trying to kill him. Maybe a lot of them. He'd looked them in the eyes and taken their lives, and he didn't care if he did it again. He'd been trained well and steeped in the mysteries of dealing death, and all he needed to ply his trade was the flimsiest excuse from some idiot in Johnson City. I knew that if the guy on the stool and the other rednecks in the place tried to brace him, he'd walk away, but they wouldn't.

Apparently, they realized it, too, for the one who'd spoken shut up and sullenly turned back to his beer, and the others followed suit. The tension in the room didn't lighten, but suddenly it felt like we were in a protective bubble floating through it. The thing was, our driver was the nightmare of America's war against the Commies come home and shoved in its face. He was the soldier these men could never be and would always fear. They didn't like him or the situation one damn bit, but there was nothing they could do because, unlike his passengers, he wasn't a young and inexperienced guy. He was a maiming and killing guy.

We used the restroom, got our supplies, and the driver unhurriedly paid for them and the gas. As soon as we were back in the car, the driver's demeanor shifted back to his jovial mode just as quickly as it had flared into the dangerous. He laughed as he pulled off, asking, "Did you see that stupid asshole's face?"

We laughed, too, because we had, though I think we were all a bit more wary of our driver now that we'd seen his scarier side. But that side never surfaced again, and when, just after daybreak, we arrived in Houston, he took Glen and me straight to the dorms. We told him he and the other freak were welcome to spend the night and get some sleep, but he just pulled out his bottle of speed, popped a couple of more pills, and said, naw, he was anxious to get to Atlanta. Then the station wagon squealed out of the parking lot and disappeared up the street.

Glen and I turned, and there before us, lit by the morning sun, was our dorm. It looked no different than it had when we'd left nine days earlier, but somehow it didn't seem entirely real. Something had changed. We picked up our bags, went inside, and trudged up to our room.

Notes

Human Bounty: Blade Runner and the Essence of Humanity

1 The version of *Blade Runner* referred to in this article is the 2007 release, subtitlted, *The Final Cut.*

Private Snafu's Hidden War: A Historical Outline and Analytical Perspective

1 Jerry Beck and Will Friedwald, *Looney Tunes and Merrie Melodies: A Complete Guide to the Warner Bros. Cartoons* (New York: Holt, 1989) 379.
2 Beck and Friedwald 379.
3 Beck and Friedwald 379.
4 Steve M. Barkin, "Fighting the Cartoon War: Information Strategies in World War II," *Journal of American Culture*, Spring/Summer 1984: 114.
5 Barkin 114.
6 Barkin 115.
7 Barkin 117.
8 David Culbert, "'Why We Fight': Social Engineering for a Democratic Society at War," *Film and Radio Propaganda in World War II*, ed. K.R.M. Short (Knoxville: U of Tennessee P, 1983) 173.
9 Culbert 175.

10 Culbert 177.

11 Culbert 175.

12 Shamus Culhane, *Talking Animals and Other People* (New York: St. Martins, 1986) 267.

13 Culbert 181.

14 Culbert 182.

15 Culhane 269.

16 Steve Schneider, *That's All Folks!: The Art of Warner Bros. Animation* (New York: Holt, 1988) 88.

17 Leonard Maltin, *Of Mice and Magic* (New York: Plume Books, 1980) 254.

18 Clayton R. Koppes and Gregory D. Black, *Hollywood Goes to War* (New York: Free Press, 1987) 28.

19 Koppes and Black 28.

20 Koppes and Black 43.

21 Beck and Friedwald 379.

22 Culhane 270.

23 Danny Peary and Gerald Peary, *The American Animated Cartoon* (New York: Dutton, 1980) 165.

24 Schneider 87-88.

25 Barkin 115.

26 Culhane 268.

27 Peary and Peary 165.

28 Maltin 254.

Primary Source

Private Snafu: Complete and Uncensored. Compiled by Dave Butler. (Cudahy, WI: Bosko Video. Contains fourteen Private Snafu cartoons produced by Warner Bros.):

Secondary Sources

Barkin, Steve M. "Fighting the Cartoon War: Information Strategies in World War II." *Journal of American Culture* Spring/Summer 1984: 113-117.

Beck, Jerry and Will Friedwald. *Looney Tunes and Merrie Melodies: A complete Guide to the Warner Bros. Cartoons* New York: Holt, 1989.

Culbert, David. "'Why We Fight': Social Engineering for a Democratic Society at War." *Film and Radio Propaganda in World War II.* Ed. K.R.M. Short. Knoxville: U of Tennessee P, 1983. 173-191.

Culhane, Shamus. *Talking Animals and Other People.* New York: St. Martins, 1986.

Koppes, Clayton R. and Gregory D. Black. *Hollywood Goes to War.* New York: Free Press, 1987.

Maltin, Leonard. *Of Mice and Magic.* New York: Plume Books, 1980.

Peary, Danny and Gerald Peary. *The American Animated Cartoon.* New York: Dutton, 1980.

Schneider, Steve. *That's All Folks!: The Art of Warner Bros. Animation.* New York: Holt, 1988.

The Private Snafu Series

Produced by Leon Schlesinger
Music by: Carl W. Stalling
Voice characterizations: Mel Blanc
Narration: Robert C. Bruce
Writers: Theodore Geisel, Phil Eastman, and W. Munro Leaf

Title (Date, Director)
"Coming Snafu" (June 1943, Chuck Jones)
"Gripes" (July 1943, Friz Freleng)
"Spies" (August 1943, Chuck Jones)
"The Goldbrick" (September 1943, Frank Tashlin)
"The Infantry Blues" (September 1943, Chuck Jones)
"Fighting Tools" (October 1943, Bob Clampett)
"The Home Front" (November 1943, Frank Tashlin)
"Rumors" (December 1943, Friz Freleng)
"Booby Traps" (January 1944) Bob Clampett)
"Snafuperman" (March 1944, Friz Freleng)

"Private Snafu vs. Malaria Mike" (March 1944, Chuck Jones)
"A Lecture on Camouflage" (April 1944, Chuck Jones)
"Gas" (May 1944, Chuck Jones)
"The Chow Hound" (1944, Frank Tashlin)
"Censored" (1944, Frank Tashlin)
"Outpost" (1944, Chuck Jones)
"Pay Day" (1944, Friz Freleng)
"Target Snafu" (1944, Friz Freleng)
"The Three Brothers" (1944, Friz Freleng)
"In the Aleutians" (1945, Chuck Jones)
"It's Murder She Says" (1945, Chuck Jones)
"Hot Spot" (1945, Friz Freleng)
"Operation Snafu" (1945, Friz Freleng)
"No Buddy Atoll" (1945, Chuck Jones)
"Coming Home" (unreleased, Chuck Jones)
"Secrets of the Caribbean" (unreleased, Chuck Jones)

John Donne's Metaphoric Voyage

1   Milton Allan Rugoff, *Donne's Imagery: A Study in Creative Sources* (New York: Russell & Russell, 1962) 137.
2   A. C. Partridge, *John Donne: Language and Style* (London: Andre Deutsch, 1978) 151.
3   Rugoff, 129.
4   Sir Leslie Stephen and Sir Sidney Lee, eds., *The Dictionary of National Biography—Vol. V* (London: Oxford UP, 1937-1938) 1129.
5   Stephen and Sidney, 1130.
6   George Parfitt, *John Donne: A Literary Life* (London: Macmillan, 1989) 13.
7   John Donne, *Juvenilia: Or Paradoxes and Problems* "Why Does the Pox So Much Affect to Undermine the Nose?", *The Literature of Renaissance England*, eds. John Hollander and Frank Kermode (London: Oxford UP, 1973) 519.

8 Donne, *Juvenilia*, 519.

9 Richard Hakluyt, *The Principal Navigations, Voyages, Traffiques and Discoveries of the English Nation* (London: Penguin, 1972). See: "1558—Voyage of Anthony Jenkins from Moscow to Bokhara."

10 Hakluyt. See: "1553—Discovery of the Kingdom of Muscovy," "1555—Second Voyage to Muscovy," and "1556—Navigation and Discovery Towards the River OB."

11 John Hollander and Frank Kermode, eds., *The Literature of Renaissance England* (London: Oxford UP, 1973) 520.

12 John Donne, "Elegy XVIII: Love's Progress," *The Literature of Renaissance England*, eds. John Hollander and Frank Kermode (London: Oxford UP, 1973) 520-522, lines 1-3.

13 Donne, "Love's Progress," lines 91-92.

14 Rugoff, 130.

15 Donne, "Love's Progress," lines 43-44.

16 Donne, "Love's Progress," lines 47-50.

17 Donne, "Love's Progress," line 53.

18 Donne, "Love's Progress," lines 60-61.

19 Donne, "Love's Progress," lines 63-64.

20 Donne, "Love's Progress," line 65.

21 Rugoff, 140.

22 Donne, "Love's Progress," lines 41-42.

23 Rugoff, 141.

24 John Donne, "Elegy XIX: To His Fair Mistress Going to Bed," *The Literature of Renaissance England*, eds. John Hollander and Frank Kermode (London: Oxford UP, 1973) 523-524, line 6.

25 Donne, "To His Fair Mistress Going to Bed," lines 27-30.

26 John Donne, "The Sun Rising," *The Literature of Renaissance England*, eds. John Hollander and Frank Kermode (London: Oxford UP, 1973) 525-526, line 17.

27 Hakluyt. See: "1583—Voyage of Ralph Fitch to Goa and Siam."

28 Donne, "The Sun Rising," line 30.

29 Hakluyt. See: "1577—Voyage of Francis Drake About the Whole Globe," and "Voyage of Thomas Cavendish Round the Whole Earth."

30 John Donne, "The Canonization," *The Literature of Renaissance England*, eds. John Hollander and Frank Kermode (London: Oxford UP, 1973) 526-527, line 11.

31 John Donne, "A Valediction: Of Weeping," *The Literature of Renaissance England*, eds. John Hollander and Frank Kermode (London: Oxford UP, 1973) 533, lines 10-16.

32 John Donne, "The Good Morrow," *The Literature of Renaissance England*, eds. John Hollander and Frank Kermode (London: Oxford UP, 1973) 524-525, lines 12-14.

33 Clay Hunt, *Donne's Poetry: Essays in Literary Analysis* (New Haven: Yale UP, 1954) 59.

34 John Donne, "Valediction: Forbidding Mourning," *The Literature of Renaissance England*, eds. John Hollander and Frank Kermode (London: Oxford UP, 1973) 538-539, lines 25-28.

35 David Novarr, *The Disinterred Muse: Donne's Texts and Contexts* (Ithaca: Cornell UP, 1980) 56.

36 Rugoff, 134.

37 John Donne, "Hymn to God My God, in My Sickness," *The Literature of Renaissance England*, eds. John Hollander and Frank Kermode (London: Oxford UP, 1973) 554-555, lines 7-21.

38 Rugoff, 141.

39 Hunt, 100-101.

40 John Donne, "A Sermon Preached at St. Paul's for Easter-Day, 1628," *The Literature of Renaissance England*, eds. John Hollander and Frank Kermode (London: Oxford UP, 1973) 561.

41 Donne, "A Sermon Preached at St. Paul's for Easter-Day, 1628," 562.

42 Donne, "A Sermon Preached at St. Paul's for Easter-Day, 1628," 563.

43 Donne, "A Sermon Preached at St. Paul's for Easter-Day, 1628," 563.
44 Donne, "A Sermon Preached at St. Paul's for Easter-Day, 1628," 563.
45 Hunt, 83.

Works Cited

Donne, John. "The Canonization." *The Literature of Renaissance England.* Eds. John Hollander and Frank Kermode. London: Oxford UP, 1973. 526-527.

Donne, John. "Elegy XVIII: Love's Progress." *The Literature of Renaissance England.* Eds. John Hollander and Frank Kermode. London: Oxford UP, 1973. 520-522.

Donne, John. "Elegy XIX: To His Fair Mistress Going to Bed." *The Literature of Renaissance England.* Eds. John Hollander and Frank Kermode. London: Oxford UP, 1973. 523-524.

Donne, John. "The Good Morrow." *The Literature of Renaissance England.* Eds. John Hollander and Frank Kermode. London: Oxford UP, 1973. 524-525.

Donne, John. "Hymn to God My god, in My Sickness." *The Literature of Renaissance England.* Eds. John Hollander and Frank Kermode. London: Oxford UP, 1973. 554-555.

Donne, John. *Juvenilia: Or Paradoxes and Problems* "Why Does the Pox So Much Affect to Undermine the Nose?" *The Literature of Renaissance England.* Eds. John Hollander and Frank Kermode. London: Oxford UP, 1973. 519-520.

Donne, John. "A Sermon Preached at St. Paul's for Easter-Day, 1628." *The Literature of Renaissance England.* Eds. John Hollander and Frank Kermode. London: Oxford UP, 1973. 558-564.

Donne, John. "The Sun Rising." *The Literature of Renaissance England.* Eds. John Hollander and Frank Kermode. London: Oxford UP, 1973. 525-526.

Donne, John. "A Valediction: Forbidding Mourning." *The Literature of Renaissance England*. Eds. John Hollander and Frank Kermode. London: Oxford UP, 1973. 538-539.

Donne, John. "A Valediction: Of Weeping." *The Literature of Renaissance England*. Eds. John Hollander and Frank Kermode. London: Oxford UP, 1973. 533.

Hakluyt, Richard. *The Principal Navigations, Voyages, Traffiques and Discoveries of the English Nation*. London: Pengin, 1972.

Hollander, John, and Frank Kermode, eds. *The Literature of Renaissance England*. London: Oxford UP, 1973.

Hunt, Clay. *Donne's Poetry: Essays in Literary Analysis*. New Haven: Yale UP, 1954.

Novarr, David. *The Disinterred Muse: Donne's Texts and Contexts*. Ithaca: Cornell UP, 1980.

Parfitt, George. *John Donne: A Literary Life*. London: Macmillan, 1989.

Partridge, A. C. *John Donne: Language and Style*. London: Andre Deutsch, 1978.

Rugoff, Milton Allan. *Donne's Imagery: A Study in Creative Sources*. New York: Russell & Russell, 1962.

Stephen, Sir Leslie, and Sir Sidney Lee, eds. *The Dictionary of National Biography—Vol. V*. London: Oxford UP, 1937-1938.

Discrimination's Double-Edged Sword: Exclusion and cultural demise in Douglas Turner Ward's *Day of Absence*

1 John MacNicholas, ed., *The Dictionary of Literary Biography: Twentieth-Century American Dramatists: Part 2: K-Z* (Detroit: Bruccoli Clark, 1981) 302.

2 Douglas Turner Ward, *Day of Absence, Contemporary Black Drama: From A Raisin in the Sun to No Place to Be Somebody*, ed. Clinton F. Oliver and Stephanie Sills (New York: Scribners, 1971) 356.

3 Ward 354.

4 Ward 356

5 Ward 356

6 Ward 357

7 Douglas Turner Ward, "American Theater: For Whites Only?" *Modern Drama and Social Change*, ed. Robert A. Raines (Englewood Cliffs: Prentice–Hall, 1972) 334.

8 Ward 349.

9 Ward 351.

10 Ward 350.

11 Genevieve E. Fabre, "Drama: Introduction," *Afro-American Poetry and Drama, 1760-1975*, William P. French, Michel J. Fabre, Amritjit Singh, and Genevieve E. Fabre (Detroit: Gale Research, 1979) 260.

12 Ward 350.

13 Paul Carter Harrison, *The Drama of Nommo* (New York: Grove Press, 1972) 7.

14 Ward 344.

15 Ward 347.

16 Ward 347.

17 C. W. E. Bigsby, "Three Black Playwrights: Loften Mitchell, Ossie Davis, and Douglas Turner Ward," *The Black American Writer*, ed. C. W. E. Bigsby (Deland, Fla.: Everett/Edwards, 1969) 150.

18 Harrison 3-4.

19 Ward 350.

20 Adam David Miller, "It's a Long Way to St. Louis: Notes on the Audience for Black Drama," *Drama Review* (Summer 1968) 150.

21 Ward 348

22 Ward 354.

Primary Source

Ward, Douglas Turner. *Day of Absence. Contemporary Black Drama: From A Raisin in the Sun to No Place to Be Somebody.*

Ed. Clinton F. Oliver and Stephanie Sills. New York: Scribners, 1971.

Works Consulted & Cited

Abramson, Doris E. *Negro Playwrights in the American Theater, 1925-1959*. New York and London: Columbia U. P., 1967.

Bigsby, C. W. E. "Three Black Playwrights: Loften Mitchell, Ossie Davis, and Douglas Turner Ward." *The Black American Writer*. Ed. C. W. E. Bigsby. Deland, Fla." Everett/Edwards, 1969.

Fabre, Genevieve E. "Drama: Introduction." *Afro-American Poetry and Drama, 1760-1975*. Eds. William P. French, Michel J. Fabre, Amritjit Singh, and Genevieve E. Fabre. Detroit: Gale Research, 1979.

Harrison, Paul Carter. *The Drama of Nommo*. New York: Grove Press, 1972.

MacNicholas, John, ed. *The Dictionary of Literary Biography: Twentieth-Century American Dramatists: Part 2: K-Z*. Detroit: Bruccoli Clark, 1981.

Michener, Charles. "Setting the Stage Everywhere *Newsweek*, December 24, 1973: 80-82.

Miller, Adam David. "It's a Long Way to St. Louis: Notes on the Audience for Black Drama." *Drama Review*, Summer 1968.

Patterson, James E., interviewer. "The Negro Ensemble Company." *Players*, June-July 1972: 224-229 and 256-257.

Taubman, Howard. "Douglas Turner Ward's Plays at the St. Marks." *The New York Times*, November 15, 1965: 56:1.

Ward, Douglas Turner. "American Theater: For Whites Only?" *Modern Drama and Social Change*. Ed. Robert A. Raines. Englewood Cliffs: Prentice–Hall, 1972.

(Ward), Douglas Turner. "Needed: A Theater for Black Themes." *Negro Digest*, December 1967: 34-39.

Let Me Talk with This Philosopher: Edgar's role in Shakespeare's *King Lear*

1 Shakespeare, William. *King Lear.* Ed. G. K. Hunter. London: Penguin, 1972.

An Equestrian Tragedy: The image of the horse and the fall of Troy in Chaucer's *Troilus and Criseyde*

1 Chaucer, Geoffrey, Troilus and Criseyde, R. A. Shoaf, ed., Colleagues Press, 1989.

T. S. Eliot Consults the Oracle: The Sibyl and "The Waste Land"

1 T. S. Eliot, "Ulysses, Order, and Myth," *The Dial* (November 1923).
2 Translation from: Donald McQuade, Robert Atwan, Martha Banta, Justin Kaplan, David Minter, Cecelia Tichi, and Helen Vendler, *The Harper American Literature.* (New York: Harper & Row, 1987) 1884.

Primary Sources

Eliot, T. S. "Ulysses, Order, and Myth." *The Dial* (November 1923).
Eliot, T. S. "The Waste Land." *The Waste Land and Other Poems.* San Diego: HBJ, 1934. 27-54.

Secondary Sources

McQuade, Donald, Robert Atwan, Martha Banta, Justin Kaplan, David Minter, Cecelia Tichi, and Helen Vendler. *The Harper American Literature*. New York: Harper & Row, 1987.

Works Consulted

1. Graves, Robert. *Greek Myths*. New York: Doubleday, 1981.

Charting Terra Incognita: Maps, Guidebooks, and Guides in Joseph Conrad's *Heart of Darkness*

1 Conrad, Joseph. Heart of Darkness. New York: Bantam Books, 1981.

Good Science, Bad Science, and Nons(ci)ence: Jonathan Swift's Satiric Backfire

1 Joseph Addison, *The Spectator*, No. 420 (1712).
2 Jonathan Swift, *Gulliver's Travels*, ed. Robert A. Greenberg, 2nd ed. (New York: Norton, 1970) 18.
3 Christophil Philochrone, "Style and Year to be Regulated by the Sun," *The Gentleman's Magazine*, XXI, April (1751) 167.
4 Mr. Whifton, "Date of Christ's Birth Uncertain," *The Gentleman's Magazine*, XXI, April (1751) 168 and content page.
5 Swift 238-239.
6 Convexo, "Discoveries by the Microscope," *The Gentleman's Magazine*, XXI, Jan. (1751) 7.
7 Convexo, "A Microscopic Discovery—Bodies Exist Without the Mind," *The Gentleman's Magazine*, XXI, Feb. (1751) 59.

8 S. Dunn, "Mr. Urban, Credition, March 19, 1751," *The Gentleman's Magazine*, XXI, March (1751) 125.

9 Swift 147.

10 Allan Bloom, "An Outline of Gulliver's Travels," *Gulliver's Travels*, ed. Robert A. Greenberg, 2nd ed. (New York: Norton, 1970) 305.

11 Swift 100.

12 Swift 199.

13 Swift 205.

14 Swift 223.

15 Swift 236-237.

16 Swift 219.

17 Louis A. Landa, "Jonathan Swift," *Gulliver's Travels*, ed. Robert A. Greenberg, 2nd ed. (New York: Norton, 1970) 287.

18 Geoffrey Tillotson, Paul Fussell, Jr., and Marshall Waingrow, eds., *Eighteenth Century English Literature* (New York: Harcourt, 1969) 354.

19 Swift 135.

20 Bloom 305.

21 Swift 138.

22 James Gunn, ed. *The Road to Science Fiction: From Gilgamesh to Wells* (New York: Mentor-NAL, 1977) 115.

23 Swift 151.

24 Robert P. Fitzgerald, "Science and Politics in Swift's Voyage to Laputa," *Journal of English and Germanic Philology*, 87 (1988) 213.

25 Swift 149-150.

26 Swift 137.

27 Frederik N. Smith, "Science, Imagination, and Swift's Brobdingnagians," *Eighteenth Century Life*, 14.1 (1990) 100.

28 Graham Greene, "The Destructors," *Collected Stories* (New York: Viking, 1973) 327–346.

29 Swift 102.

30 Swift 169.

31 A. D. Nuttall, "Gulliver Among the Horses," *The Year-book of English Studies*, ed. C. J. Rawson (London: Modern Humanities Research, 1988) 53.

32 Swift 63–64.

33 Swift 93.

34 Swift 96.

35 Robert Scholes, *Structural Fabulation: An Essay on Fiction of the Future* (Notre Dame, U. of Notre Dame P, 1975) 30.

36 Bloom 305.

37 Swift 143.

38 Stanley P. Wyatt, *Principles of Astronomy* (Boston: Allyn and Bacon, 1971) 227.

39 Wyatt 241.

40 Swift 109–111.

41 Swift 145.

42 Bonamy Dobree, "Swift and Science, and the Placing of Book III," *Gulliver's Travels*, ed. Robert A. Greenberg, 2nd ed. (New York: Norton, 1970) 387.

43 Dobree 387.

44 Swift 153.

45 Swift 154.

46 Swift 156.

47 Swift 156.

48 Swift 113–114.

49 Swift 244.

50 Swift 220–221.

Works Cited

Addison, Joseph. *The Spectator*, No. 420, 1712.

Bloom, Allan. "An Outline of Gulliver's Travels." *Gulliver's Travels*. Ed. Robert A. Greenberg. 2nd. ed. New York: Norton, 1970. 297–311.

Convexo. "Discoveries by the Microscope." *The Gentleman's Magazine*, XXI, Jan. (1751). 7.

Convexo. "A Microscopic Discovery—Bodies Exist Without the Mind." *The Gentleman's Magazine*, XXI, Feb. (1751). 59.

Dobree, Bonamy. "Swift and Science, and the Placing of Book III." *Gulliver's Travels*. Ed. Robert A. Greenberg. 2nd. ed. New York: Norton, 1970. 386–389.

Dunn, S. "Mr. Urban, Credition, March 19, 1751." *The Gentleman's Magazine*, XXI, March (1751). 125.

Fitzgerald, Robert P. "Science and Politics in Swift's Voyage to Laputa." *Journal of English and Germanic Philology*, 87 (1988). 213–229.

Greene, Graham. "The Destructors." *Collected Stories*. New York: Viking, 1973. 327–346.

Gunn, James, ed. *The Road to Science Fiction: From Gilgamesh to Wells*. New York: Mentor-NAL, 1977.

Landa, Louis A. "Jonathan Swift." *Gulliver's Travels*. Ed. Robert A. Greenberg. 2nd ed. New York: Norton, 1970. 287–296.

Nuttall, A. D. "Gulliver Among the Horses." *The Yearbook of English Studies*. Ed. C. J. Rawson. London: Modern Humanities Research, 1988. 51–67.

Philochrone, Christophil. "Style and Year to be Regulated by the Sun." *The Gentleman's Magazine*, XXI April (1751). 167.

Sholes, Robert. *Structural Fabulation: An Essay on Fiction of the Future*. Notre Dame: U of Notre Dame P, 1975.

Smith, Frederik N. "Science, Imagination, and Swift's Brobdingnagians." *Eighteenth Century Life*, 14.1 (1990) 100–114.

Swift, Jonathan. *Gulliver's Travels*. Ed. Robert A. Greenberg. New York: Norton, 1970.

Tillotson, Geoffrey, Paul Fussell, Jr., and Marshall Waingrow, eds. *Eighteenth Century English Literature*. New York: Harcourt, 1969.

Whifton, Mr. "Date of Christ's Birth Uncertain." *The Gentleman's Magazine*, XXI, April (1751). 168.

Wyatt, Stanley P. *Principles of Astronomy*. Boston: Allyn and Bacon, 1971.

Journey to Freedom: *The Adventures of Huckleberry Finn* and the American Civil War

Work Cited

Twain, Mark. *The Adventures of Huckleberry Finn*. Centennial Facsimile Edition (Harper & Row Publishers, 1987).

Throwing Down the Gauntlet

1 Cirlot, J. E., *A Dictionary of Symbols* (Jack Sage, trans., Philosophical Library, 1962, p. 114.)

Phosphene Publishing Company publishes books and DVDs related to literature, drama, history, Texana, film, the paranormal, spirituality, and the martial arts.

For other great titles, visit
phosphenepublishing.com